CONFESSIONS

OF A

HOLLYWOOD COLUMNIST

Also by Sheilah Graham

BELOVED INFIDEL (with Gerold Frank)

REST OF THE STORY

COLLEGE OF ONE

Confessions of
a Hollywood
Columnist

by Sheilah Graham

WILLIAM MORROW & COMPANY, INC.

NEW YORK : 1969

Film stars, as is well known, are changeable. What
is true today can be wrong tomorrow. I ask indulgence
for new marriages, new divorces, or anything that changes
between the time of finishing this book and publication.

S. G.

Contents

CONFESSIONS

OF A

HOLLYWOOD COLUMNIST

1)

The Beginning and The End

Barbra Streisand and I were dancing together on stage. A sort of mod minuet. It was Barbra's show, and I had no idea how or why I was dancing with her. I could not see the audience, but it was out there in the vast darkness. The steps were quite intricate and I was vaguely worried. But surprisingly, without any previous instruction, I was keeping up with Barbra as she weaved and feinted, now elaborately slow, now fantastically fast. I tried not to hold too tightly to her hand. And then my attention was riveted on her hand. It was large and flat and as smooth as an old pebble. "Why do you write such bitchy things about me?" Barbra demanded, and tried to jerk away her hand, which abruptly turned into a sandwich. "Don't worry," I said with strained gaiety, "I'm not going to eat it." I awakened, the dream and its implications vivid in my conscious mind.

I have been biting the hand of Hollywood for thirty-two years. And now, when all except its sun is set, it is time for a change; but before the last red and gold and black-veined dawn rises over Beverly Hills, I, the last of the unholy trio— Louella, Hedda, Sheilah—will tell the final story of a spoiled unique society that can never happen again. Perhaps it never really existed. Perhaps it was only a dream in the feverish mind of a press agent. And a gullible columnist. And the need of people to believe in magic. Whatever it was, it isn't there today. It is a different Hollywood, a duller Hollywood.

When I started my column in January 1936, Hollywood was the mecca for all the beautiful, talented personalities of the world. They were nourished and spoiled and pampered to the most extraordinary degree. "I was like a kept woman during my twenty-one years at M-G-M," Walter Pidgeon told me recently in Rome, where he was starring in a modest film. "Hollywood was like an expensive, beautifully run club. You didn't need to carry money. Your face was your credit card—all over the world." Hollywood today is like a cheap jungle. It is a tired town, mostly manufacturing mediocre television films that could not qualify as "B" pictures before Hollywood surrendered its supremacy, a town haunted by its splendid ghosts on the late, late show.

I have straddled four decades of its history. The Sick Sixties with its new breed of stars. The Frightened Fifties. The Fabulous Forties. And the Thirties, Hollywood's Golden Age, when giants filled the screen. I have known them all: the beautiful, and the damned, old stars, new stars, the good guys, the bad guys, the weak, the brave, the boastful, the frightened, the fearless, the winners, and the losers.

In the past ten years it has become harder to be part of the dying dream. I have used the excuse that more films are made abroad as the reason for staying away from what used to be an extravagant, reckless, surprisingly exciting city, but is now merely a convenient name for all the film kingdoms—London, Hollywood, Paris, Rome, Madrid, Athens, Nice, New York—owing allegiance to nothing but American dollars. The stars must go where the work beckons and I have followed the stars. But it was still a repetition, more of the same egos in different clothing. New actors, new actresses, all quite efficient, and some are talented, and some are not. But the glamor evaporated with the abolition of the star system. The tycoons are dead or abdicated: Louis B. Mayer, Harry Cohn, Cecil B. de Mille, Irving Thalberg, Darryl Zanuck, who has rarely set foot in the place since he left his wife in the mid-fifties to make pictures in Europe. The last tycoon, Jack Warner, recently sold out for $32 million. Big Business has moved in and the sons and lovers have taken over.

I have listened to them all, from the eccentric Garbo the Great to the mixed-up Grant; Brando, whose acting in the past ten years should have embarrassed him; Beatty, who has finally made it as a star, but cannot leave a nonstop treadmill of sex; those desperate sisters of horror films, Davis and Crawford; the unconventional Christie; the ungrateful Connery; Caine, who plays the antihero on and sometimes off the screen; and all the Robin Redgraves; and the frightened Humphrey Bogart. And John Wayne, the last of the giants. And Elizabeth Taylor, once fragile as a flower, and now? And Richard Burton, of the magical voice, waving a glass while orating sweatily in bars. Orson Welles, a slim, handsome young man, now wide as the universe. And Frank Sinatra, who thought he was God until a pretty girl and a one-two punch knocked out his mystique and his two front teeth. The suspiciousness of Steve McQueen; Rod Steiger's problem; the fears of Gregory Peck; Julie Andrews, the woman nobody knows. The arrogance of the Beatles. Rita Hayworth, who went up then down and still doesn't know what hit her. And Ava Gardner, who drowned her anguish in fast living. And Marilyn Monroe, soft, foolish, uncertain Marilyn is dry dust on my tongue. Peter Sellers, with his superstitions and spoilt-child behavior; George Hamilton, who wouldn't or couldn't marry the daughter of the President of the United States; soft Rock Hudson; foul-mouthed Burt Lancaster; Ronald Reagan, who did not get my vote for Governor of California. The amazing saga of Katharine Hepburn and Spencer Tracy. And self-centered, suspicious Barbra Streisand, who will have her enemies as long as there is a Hollywood where the bongo drums of gossip will still be beating when the little town is silent and not a columnist to tell why thou art desolate can e'er return.

I have seen and heard them all and now, perhaps for the

first time, I will try to understand them—it won't be easy, because most of them don't understand themselves. What causes the erratic behavior, the Proustian changes of character, the reaction to success and failure, a cat looking at the kings and queens dozing through a twilight of unreality some still with adoring subjects all over the world, and kowtowing corrupt lackeys at court, where hungry jackals flourish on the insecurities of men of talent. And when the *danse macabre* is over, what do any of them have?

2)

Barbra

The main industry of Hollywood has never been the making of films, or even television. It is gossip. The circuits are busy all day and far into the night spitting up choice tidbits into straining ears about the plastic-plated darlings who live in transparent palaces where everything can be seen and heard. The main sport, destroying reputations. Nearly everyone is vulnerable. Nearly everyone is eaten alive. So when an egotistical woman like Barbra Streisand stumbles into the snake pit, she is lucky to get out alive. And I'm not sure she did.

The childhood years of poverty and frustration had stripped her of the protective covering that might have concealed her shortcomings as a human being. She came to Hollywood in the raw, and the hounds of gossipville exposed every idiosyncracy, every tactless remark, every indiscretion, every sample of selfishness. And there were enough to feed the whole pack. She was barbecued on the revolving Hollywood spit and consumed with enjoyment. And she is still wondering how it all happened. Didn't they know she was little Barbra, the poverty-shriven ugly duckling who made it by sheer guts all the way from a Brooklyn tenement to the cathedral-like shrine that Garbo built in that far-flung outpost of culture, Beverly Hills, for which she paid $3,250 per month?

Why should she waste her time pretending to be interested in anyone but herself? Who was interested in her before she made it as a star? Who had cared whether she made it as a star? Okay, so I'm a star now and by God you will know it. You will bend the knee and bite the dust. This is not an unusual behavior pattern for young stars who succeed quickly when they come to Hollywood. But with Barbra, it was more so than with anyone I have seen in all the time I have lived there. And I have seen all the temperamental shrews who operate under the name of talent. So if Barbra is still bleeding from the stomping and the chomping, she and you might like to know how and why it happened.

Hollywood is the most sensitive place in the world. If you forget to say "good morning" to each and everyone when you arrive on the set, and "good night" to everyone when you leave, you are called high-hat and you are hated. Why do you think every Oscar winner goes through an interminable list of thank-yous? Miss one and you have made a mortal enemy. If your eyes are weak and you don't recognize people immediately, you are called a snob. This happened to me when I first came. I'm blind as a bat (although I can hear a gossip item a mile away), and I was amazed to read nasty little bits about me in the local trade papers, and hear remarks repeated that I might have said jokingly or not at all.

Barbra—crude, unpolished—has many areas of ignorance when she is not actually performing. When you are fearful and trampled by life as a child, you become either very considerate or very despotic when you grow up and are in a position to do as you please. Barbra was not considerate. She was the small girl who must strike you before you can strike her. She came out of her battle with Hollywood with a bloody nose and a bloodied psyche that by Hollywood's own peculiar standards were entirely justified. I doubt whether she was much worse than anyone else. She just showed it more. And perhaps because there was a paucity of people making pictures at the time in Hollywood, Barbra's behavior was scrutinized more minutely and megaphoned to a world that enjoys seeing its idols shot out of a cannon, and Barbra provided plenty of ammunition.

She is either a monster or a perfectionist, depending which side of Streisand you are on. She has her champions and there are people who dislike her. Strangely, for a woman who is not beautiful, the men seem to like her more than the women. But apart from a very small circle who really know her, Barbra does not relate to people and she won't let them get close. All she is concerned with is "my work, my work, my work." Her regard for you is measured by the yardstick of her career. She strives for perfection, and this can be trying. It isn't that she is difficult per se, but her insatiable curiosity, her insistence on poking her nose into everything that concerns her work, has raised the Hollywood hackles. She is suspicious. You are guilty until proved innocent. She's the wolf who walks alone. If you zoom in for a landing, she will turn her back on you, as I watched her doing at a Cocoanut Grove function in Hollywood. When acquaintances came up to say hello, she turned away from them and gave them the back of her hand—literally. I think she sometimes tries to be interested in people and things outside of herself, but she can't be.

I met Barbra before she came to Hollywood, during the stage run of *Funny Girl,* while she was still somewhat dazed by her instant success. She was easier to reach and talk to then. I had seen her on the opening night of *I Can Get It for You Wholesale* in 1962. She had stopped the show with her "Miss Marmelstein" number, but she had bored me. I had much preferred the easygoing performance of the young masculine lead, Elliott Gould, the tall, shaggy-haired, brown-eyed young man she married on September 13, 1963. I was surprised to read the raves for her performance by the New York critics, at times the most easily persuaded (for better or worse) group in the world. I didn't expect Miss Streisand to go too far. She was too homely with her nondescript mousy hair, her glittering blue-green lizard's eyes, Nefertiti nose, and angular figure. There is the story that when she considered trimming her nose, David Merrick advised, "Don't. You'll be like everyone else."

I was surprised when she was chosen to star on Broadway in *Funny Girl*. Billy Rose, one seat away at the opening night, assured me he had picked Miss Streisand personally to play the part of his first wife, Fanny Brice, who was no beauty winner either.

I became interested in Barbra after reading the cover story about her in *Time* magazine amid the avalanche of praise and attention that followed the premiere of *Funny Girl*. Showing me around her duplex penthouse apartment at Ninety-second Street and Central Park West, she was like an excited Alice in Wonderland, not sure that her unexpected affluence wouldn't vanish in the next sentence. Talk about the Mad Hatter's tea party! Barbra was fortified with a two-pound can of Iranian caviar—"$42 a pound. Have some." She offered me a spoon and I took a long swallow before it could disappear. She tried to sound casual about her kitchen with its red patent-leather walls, and the antique—in age, not beauty—bargains she had picked up all over the Village and at Salvation Army sales. She was especially proud of a couple of dentist's cabinets and an old captain's desk, and dozens of buckled shoes and hats by the score. She whooped with pride of ownership over the raised, canopied four-poster in the bedroom upstairs, surrounded by a bleak terrace overlooking Central Park—she had just moved in. Some carpets were in, but not the drapes, about which she asked my advice from the corduroy samples. A Brooklyn beggar on horseback. I enjoyed her excitement and delight.

A few stories of kookiness and Barbra being difficult had seeped through the protective phalanx of press agents, but like a long-stockinged pixie darting from each disconnected sentence, she put the stories down to jealousy of her success. "If they only knew," she moaned dramatically, "how I hate being a star. How I hate to sing. How I dread going on stage every night." I clucked sympathetically.

Soon after, I wondered whether Barbra had taken me for

a ride. It was the custom for the National Design Center in New York to put on an annual Ten Best-Dressed Rooms display, and to have top interior decorators create dream rooms to match the personality of ten important persons, the rooms to be named for the stars. There was a small condition. The opening day of the exhibition was for charity, at $10 a ticket. The other days were free. The chosen ten must agree to appear for at least fifteen minutes. Barbra, with the other stars— Sean Connery, Joan Crawford among them—readily agreed to be present. There was a great prepublicity in the newspaper and on television for the rooms and the stars, with Barbra garnering more space even than Connery, who was then at the height of his James Bond fame. On opening day one star was missing. Barbra. A week later I happened to be at the Design Center near closing time, and who did I see sneaking in for a peek at her room? The star of *Funny Girl*. She was somewhat embarrassed and pretended not to see me.

My next confrontation with Barbra was in the week prior to her London stage opening in *Funny Girl*. "Hey, you're a writer," she greeted me with mixed respect and disbelief. She had read or been told about *Beloved Infidel*. The magnificently furnished house in Belgravia was owned, she told me, by "some aristocrat. I'm paying $1,000 a week, and there isn't a goddamned shower in the place." She brightened when the butler silently entered and inquired, "What will my lady have for tea?" His enchanted mistress could barely refrain from laughing in his face. "I'll have those cute cucumber sandwiches," she replied in a mincing high-life British accent. "Oh, yes, and crumpets and tea, you know, the whole schmear." Her laughter exploded with his retreating back.

"Shh," I warned, "he'll hear you."

She dried her eyes. "All my life I wanted cucumber sandwiches and little cakes and tea, with a butler and a London flat, and now," triumphantly, "I've got it." The satisfaction turned wistful as she added, "I'd really rather have a Coke," and then shouting, "Have you any idea how much a Coke costs in London?" Her friends were sending or bringing them

over to her from New York along with other delicacies—
salami, hot dogs from Nathan's—they were cheaper or better
there than London.

She was wearing a woolen dress that ended an inch above
her knee—this was at the beginning of the mini-skirt craze—
"It was a long dress I had. I cut it myself." She showed me
where she had turned it up. I had heard of Barbra's thriftiness, and in New York she had assured me she would never
shop on Fifth Avenue as long as there were little places in the
Village where she could get things "for nothing." Later, she
became dress-conscious and landed on some best-dressed lists.
"Cary Grant had this before me," complacently scanning the
gleaming mahogany antiques, "and guess what?" falling over
herself. "He would send his chauffeur in his Rolls-Royce to
the East End on Sundays to buy him fish and chips in a newspaper." I could see she was planning or had already done the
same moneysaving thing.

Funny Girl opened in London to acclaim and stories of
backstage temperament. Barbra had walked into her dressing
room at the Prince of Wales Theatre with her entourage and
walked right out. No word of explanation until her manager
telephoned to say his client would not return until she had a
suite worthy of her talent. A few walls were knocked down,
some fancy furniture hastily collected, and The Star returned. The back staircase was reserved for her exclusive use,
and no one was allowed to dress on the same floor. Her un-
derstudy, who succeeded her when she left the show, has only
bitter memories. "In the fourteen weeks she was here, she
never said one word to me." She seemed unaware of anyone
else in the show, except when they got in the way. Her desire
for perfection was driving them all crazy. Even after her last
performance, she was still sending notes to the musical director advising how the show could be improved. She complained about the acoustics. She complained about people
casting shadows, blocking her light. She was always complaining, period. All in the name of a better show. Her leading
man, Michael Craig, still cannot speak coherently about her.

The management was equally irritated. Saturday night in the theater everywhere is the big night, but as soon as Barbra discovered she was pregnant, she refused to do the Saturday night show, only the matinee. With the star absent on Saturday nights, the theater was always half empty. Actually when Barbra had discovered the miracle of impending motherhood, a few weeks after the play opened, her doctor had advised her to quit the strenuous role. There was a meeting with her agent, manager, husband, lawyer, and the doctor. They decided they had legal grounds to get her out. Barbra said no, even though she felt ill and wanted very badly to return home to hatch her precious egg in the penthouse in New York. It was agreed that she would not do both the matinee and the evening show on Wednesday and Saturday. She would cut the Wednesday matinee and the evening show on Saturday, giving her a long rest to the Monday night performance. She finished her scheduled fourteen weeks, then gave a party complete with orchestra for the cast and crew at a pub, The Cockney Pride, with hot dogs and other kosher delicacies flown in from New York. It cost her about $4,000. And yet the uncomplimentary stories continued.

Barbra had not wanted to do the play in London. She had played *Funny Girl* on stage and was sick of the nightly grind and exhaustion. She was more or less forced into the London production by her producer, Ray Stark, who cautioned, "No London, no film," and Barbra was ready to give her soul to breach the Hollywood barricade. The date of her arrival in Europe coincided with the wedding day of the press agent who was commissioned to "handle" her. He sent a car to meet her at the airport with a message explaining why he regretfully could not be there in person. Arriving late in the evening at her hotel suite, Barbra telephoned the new groom (who had retired for the night with his bride) and told him to come on over at once. His wedding was his affair, but he was working for her. The hapless lad was kept for several hours in Miss Streisand's sitting room going over the publicity campaign, while his young bride cried into her pillow and wondered whether her husband really loved her and if he did, why wasn't he with her on their wedding night? I believe Barbra had not intended to be cruel. All she was concerned with was the play and how it would be presented to the public, and she had to know *now*. The same press agent is one of her boosters. He explained, "You have to admire someone who is so dedicated to her work."

When Barbra came to Hollywood to star in the screen version of *Funny Girl,* Ray Stark gave a party for her in the expensive house he bought from Lauren Bacall after she left Hollywood soon after the death of Humphrey Bogart. Barbra was almost an hour late, but they tell me her continual lateness at functions is due to nervousness, not the desire to make a flashy entrance. At the Stark party Barbra floored her hosts with her first remark, "The lights aren't right for me." She is conscious of her lack of beauty and has made the most of a bad job, and good lighting is a homely star's best friend. She lingered uncertainly in the entrance hall, then plunged. She was nervous. There had been so much written about her talent and her temperament and you could not blame her. The place was packed with stars who don't ordinarily go to a party to publicize a new celebrity. But they came to pay homage to Miss Streisand: John Wayne, Marlon Brando, the Gregory Pecks, the Jimmy Stewarts, Merle Oberon, Robert Mitchum, Claire Trevor, and Barbra's director, William Wyler. For all she talked to anyone, they might have been in Timbuktu. After a strained five minutes with Brando—a gasped "What are you doing here?"—in the main living room, where she sat tensely upright gripping the sides of a small table with Marlon leaning over her so she could hear him, she disappeared into another room with her husband. And no amount of coaxing (not that Mr. Stark would have dared) could have brought her back to the party. "It wasn't her fault," Barbra's stanchest friend, a young female publicist on *Funny Girl,* assured me. "She was the guest of honor and why should she go to them? She expected Ray Stark to bring the people to her."

It was the same when Barbra attended Rock Hudson's party, engineered by his press agents to boost his career, which at that time had sagged a bit. She came, she saw, and she hastily retreated. Photographers pursued her for a rare candid picture, but she covered her face with a huge handbag. (The lights were wrong again.) "She thought it would be an intimate gathering, like a party at home in New York," the same loyal henchwoman told me. "She was upset when she saw the photographers and the press." She must be naïve, as her husband assured me later. Surely she must have heard that it is rare for a Hollywood star to give a party except for publicity. And the more famous the guest list, the greater the publicity.

Some of the stories of Barbra's temperament on the set might have been exaggerated. Johnny Flynn, head of Columbia publicity, assured me the party for the cast and crew at the conclusion of *Funny Girl* was friendly, although in the City of Fear you never know whether a press agent is telling you the truth. She gave her albums to everyone, and to each a gold charm with the upside down *Funny Girl* insignia, engraved "From Barbra with gratitude and deep affection." To the phlegmatic Mr. Wyler, a silver megaphone.

Anne Francis, who had a good role in *Funny Girl* that was snipped to nothing during the five months of filming, has a different version of the party. "I stayed for twenty minutes," she told me. "It was embarrassing. Barbra didn't speak to me or anyone else. She just stood there in a corner." Rightly or wrongly, Anne believes that her role was emasculated by Miss Streisand. We will never really know. These operations are performed in the privacy of the producer's office and Mr. Stark, who would be a fool to hurt his film, has gone on record that the cuts were because the film was overlong. An associate of Anne's is just as positive that her film footage was thrown out because she looked too pretty in her Irene Sharaff gowns. To be fair to everyone, it is not unusual for the star of a film to protect his or her status by insisting on the elimination of scenes that might threaten it.

"Barbra was difficult in the areas where she should be difficult," said Mr. Wyler bravely when it was all over. Barbra was striving for 100 per cent perfection in her first film. "This is for posterity," she said optimistically. "Everything I do will be on film forever." The girl who had never made a movie before told the cameraman, Harry Stradling, how to photograph her and he obviously bears her no ill will because she would have no one but Harry as the cameraman for *Hello, Dolly.* Stradling is famous for making women beautiful. He refused to turn Elizabeth Taylor into a homely, middle-aged virago for her role in *Who's Afraid of Virginia Woolf?* and left the production rather than be known as the man who had destroyed the looks of the most beautiful woman in the world. Barbra antagonized the make-up people by insisting that she knew her face better than they did, and at the end they agreed that perhaps she did. She told the lighting man how to do his job and he had to admit that she knew how.

For a girl making her first picture, she knew more about how to make it—or thought she did—than any previous newcomer to Hollywood. Mr. Wyler, who won Oscars for his direction of *Mrs. Miniver* and *The Best Years of Our Lives,* had to prove to her satisfaction that he knew his job. It could have been a battle between dinosaurs, except Willie walks off a set when the fighting gets rough. In an interview with a local reporter, Barbra stated, "Willie learned to trust my instinct." "Don't be too hard on her," a friend advised Wyler, "it's the first picture she's ever directed." His parting present to her was a director's chair. Mostly, Willie turned his deaf ear to her tantrums, and when she was convinced beyond all doubt that he really did know his job, they got on fine, sometimes doing it her way, but mostly his. She had not wanted Wyler to direct her. "Who's he? I've never heard of him," she said flatly. Then one morning she called Ray Stark and said, "You know that director you mentioned? I saw a picture he did on the late show last night and I think he's pretty good." The picture was *Wuthering Heights!*

This bewildered girl from Brooklyn had not wanted Omar

Sharif as her man in *Funny Girl.* "Gregory Peck or Marlon Brando, but not Sharif," she said. But they made excuses. To get Omar they had to build up his role. His first remark about Barbra was that she was not beautiful, but a woman is a woman is a woman and he was soon saying, "This woman is beautiful, I lust after her." The news of the real or pseudo romance was all over Hollywood before the second kiss was consummated. Also the times he spent in her dressing room on the set. It was a delicious story for the gossips—a Jewish girl and an Arab, so soon after the six-day Arab-Israeli war had become a nine-day wonder. Jim Bacon, then the *Hollywood Reporter*'s gossip columnist, even printed the name and the year of the champagne Barbra and Omar were quaffing at the Beverly Wilshire Hotel. "We were going over the script," she assured her loyal husband, who had been angry with her over the gossip about Omar. After she had paired with her leading man at the Courrèges fashion show at The Factory, he called Barbra and told her off. "I'm furious with her," Elliott admitted to me during lunch at the Voisin Restaurant in New York. "I called her and said, 'What the fuck are you doing with Omar Sharif? Don't you know that Hollywood is not New York and that the press out there hate you?' Guess what she replied?" He laughed abruptly. " 'The tickets were $250 each and he had two and I wanted to see the show, but I didn't want to spend $250 of my own money.' That's also why she was seen in some restaurants with him—to save money. You know something, she's still a naïve little girl from Brooklyn trying to save a buck." This about a woman who was offered $1 million for ten concerts and was paid $200,-000 for the film version of *Funny Girl,* and who will receive $350,000 for starring in the screen version of *On a Clear Day You Can See Forever* and $750,000 with a percentage of the profits for *Hello, Dolly.* Elliott, more calmly, "But I love her and I trust her all the way." I said that was nice. He gave me the impression that no matter what the rumors and gossip about his wife today or tomorrow, he will prefer to remain her husband even though, as he told me, he is sometimes re-ferred to as "Mr. Streisand," and nothing can shake his confidence in her marital integrity.

However, he said he was glad that she was continuing her psychiatric sessions in New York. (Her analyst had made some trips to Hollywood during the filming of *Funny Girl*.) Some important people had believed the gossip—Marlene Dietrich was among those who believed that Barbra and Omar were madly in love and were each getting a divorce and would marry. Omar was confiding that Barbra was the only woman he had ever really fallen for in Hollywood, but I was skeptical because Omar is not the re-marrying kind. In Egypt, as well as other Moslem countries, when you initiate the divorce, you have to release to your wife the money you put in escrow at the beginning of the marriage as protection against the disaster of divorce. Omar is generous, as his *Funny Girl* chauffeur will testify—$50 a week in tips and a parting gift of $100. But I would swear—and he has assured me—he will remain married though separated from his Egyptian actress-wife: "It's such good protection."

It is easy to like Omar. He has the sexiest eyes, soft brown velvet drapes that he raises and lowers with devastating effect on the nearest female object. I know. I was nervous and upset in Madrid where he was making *Dr. Zhivago* and I went back to work too soon after an operation and the traffic terrified me—the louder I shouted to the driver to go slow, the faster he went—and I had burst into tears and wondered with red eyes whether to keep my dinner interview appointment with Omar at Horchers and he came out and brought me in and was kind and gentle and he raised and lowered the brown curtains and I had a definite reaction.

But I did not take the "romance" with Barbra too seriously, because I honestly believe that Omar would make love to any woman regardless of her looks. For Barbra, the "naïve" once "schleppy" little girl from Brooklyn who falls in love with Omar in their movie, it was a lovely experience. An executive on the film doubts whether Barbra really fell for Omar. "She is such a perfectionist, she would do almost anything to make their love scenes realistic." In *Hello, Dolly,* Walter Matthau was another kettle of fish, and the columns were filled with their feuds. But love or hate, it does not matter much, although a leading lady tries hard to convince herself that she is in love with her leading man. So if Barbra resisted Omar, she is an extremely strong-minded woman. And in all respects, she is. You cannot be a star unless you are intelligent and half of you is made of steel. Even Marilyn Monroe, who was so vulnerable, was tough in certain areas. But Barbra isn't even pretty, so the tensile strength and the determination have to be there in double dose. There must be respect for a girl, still in her twenties, who was jeered at when she practiced her dancing in the hallway of a dingy tenement and who vowed that one day she would be a star in all the mediums of entertainment, who is now one of the biggest attractions in show business. She performed the miracle entirely on her own, with utter dedication to the impossible goal she had set for herself, with no time for the usual diplomatic pleasantries and to hell with what people say. Small wonder she puts you through the wringer of mistrust before she accepts you completely. As long as we have a Streisand around, Hollywood will still be breathing.

3)

Cary

The shrill call of the telephone caught me at the door of my New York apartment. I was rushing. My lunch date was for one o'clock. I barely had twenty minutes to make it.

"Who is it?" I asked somewhat testily.

"Cary—Cary Grant," said the nasal voice I recognized.

"Oh." I was not surprised. He knew I was lunching with his now divorced wife, Dyan Cannon. I had mentioned this to Cary's friend, Bob Taplinger, the public-relations man with whom he was staying. (Cary had become enamored of Dyan, an ambitious actress from Chicago, when he spotted her on a television show. He immediately wanted to test her for a film. She was in Europe and refused to return for the test when she found that Cary would not pay for her ticket. Later, when she was ready to come home, she called on Cary to make the test, but decided to make Cary instead.)

"You can help me," said Cary, coming to the point. There was none of the usual gay bantering about my weight, about my happiness, whether I was living right, loving myself. The voice, still with its tinge of cockney, was pleading, almost tearful. "I want my wife back, I want my daughter back. You can help me." It was a cry from an anguished heart.

"I'll do anything she wants," he continued.

"She wants to resume her career and to live in New York," I replied.

"I know," said Cary. "Poor baby. If she'll come back to me, I'll buy her the finest house in Manhattan. I'll costar with her. With me, she can be the greatest star in the business. But now, poor baby, it's hit or miss."

Dyan's play on Broadway had received bad reviews. When the marriage had started to crack soon after the premature arrival of their daughter Jennifer, Cary had tried to save it by making Dyan his leading lady in an original script, *The Old Man and Me,* by Isobel Lennart, one of the top film writers in Hollywood. He would do it, he said, on one condition: "That you sign Dyan, without a screen test. You must take my word for it that she'll be good." They couldn't do that, not even for Mr. Grant, and the project fell through.

Cary had not wanted his wife to work, especially with him, but she had prodded him with "Rex Harrison is making a picture with Rachel Roberts, and Mia with Frank" (when she was still scheduled for *The Detective*), and Cary hoped that a costarring role with him might still save their marriage.

"I realize I've made mistakes with Dyan," continued the man every woman over twenty-five has dreamed of loving. "Poor baby," and now his voice was soft and commiserating, "I'll give her all the odds. I won't fight. She can have everything she wants."

"Everything" did not include what her lawyer considered a fair property settlement, and Cary had his own ideas of what constituted a right and proper trust fund for the baby. "I'll leave everything to the judge," Cary told me, and his confidence was justified. Dyan's settlement was much less than Cary's first offer. "She's a strange girl, Dyan," said Cary, speaking sort of man to man. "She believes I only understand rejection. She told me, 'You're only attracted to me when I reject you.' She has an attraction-rejection problem. I don't know why, but she has built up this kind of anger against me."

I said that from all I had heard, Dyan was a tough babe.

"No, not tough," he corrected me. "The tougher they seem to be, the weaker they are. Dyan is strong. That's why I married her. I chose her for her strength, but instead of joining her strength with mine, she has used it against me. Emotionally she's a child. I can understand it because I used to be like her." He still is—a combination of tremendous sophistication and five minutes later a confused man asking advice, not knowing whom to trust, talking of love and sex. "A man usually marries because he wants to 'cure' his mother." He didn't explain what he meant by "cure," but I could guess.

"I'd like to help you," I said, looking at my watch, calculating how fast a taxi could get me to the Four Seasons. I was going to be late. "How can I?"

"Tell Dyan she's making a big mistake. But don't say I'm unhappy," he said unhappily, "it adds to her power. Perhaps you shouldn't say *I* said it, it will only make her reject me more. Say it was Bob." He went into hurried instructions of how I was talking to Bob and Bob said, etc. "Poor baby," he repeated, "I'm really sorry for her." But he sounded sorrier for himself.

In relaying some of Cary's conversation to Dyan, I said I'd heard it from Taplinger, but this is a clever girl and I could see from the way she smiled and raised her eyebrows that she knew I had talked to Cary. Afterward I called Cary to say I didn't think I had changed her mind about the divorce, and he said, "I didn't really think you could. When I telephoned to know when I could see the baby again she was hysterical and shouted, 'You'll never see her again if I can help it!'" There had been photographs of Jennifer and Cary splashed all over the front pages. "I don't want crooks to see what my daughter looks like!"

Cary almost wept, assuring me, "I'll never go there. It's the worst thing I could do." He explained the cause of the new fight. "Usually I take the baby for a drive in the country. But Saturday, Dyan said I could have her for two hours only and I thought the child would like to drive around Chinatown and the Bowery. She likes a cup of tea so I took her to this small restaurant in Greenwich Village." The press agent knew he had a scoop that would put the restaurant on the front pages. He telephoned the New York *Daily News* and they sent a reporter and a photographer. "I do everything to prevent publicity of this kind," Cary continued. "When I'd call for Jennifer at the hotel, I'd stop the car half a block away. I'd make the chauffeur take off his cap and he'd bring Jennifer out. You can imagine the furor if I'd gone to the hotel and walked out with my daughter. There would have been reporters and press all over the place. I'm going to have more children," he promised me defiantly. "If not with Dyan, I'll marry another young woman and have as many children and grandchildren as I can."

As with the money, Cary did better on the visitation rights than he had dared hope for—60 days a year and the right to keep her with him overnight.

Cary's concern for Jennifer is an obsession. When Dyan left Hollywood for play rehearsals in New York, he turned up unexpectedly at the airport with a seat on the same plane. "Just to make sure the baby is all right." His extremely annoyed wife was too controlled to make a scene in public.

Wherever she went in New York—El Morocco, charity banquets, the theater—Cary just happened to be there and he managed to get in some kisses on her cool cheek while the cameras clicked.

"That isn't the way to get her back," I advised him. "Go away. Leave her alone. Make her think you don't care and she'll come running back on the double."

"I know," he replied miserably, "but I can't help myself." A bright thought: "She'd be worried if she thought I was interested in another woman. She'd believe I'd rejected her. Perhaps," diffidently, "you could put something like that in your column, me and another woman?"

"How about linking you with me? I'm safe." I covered my effrontery with a horrible giggle. I have always found Cary most attractive and I like it when he kisses me hello or good-by.

Cary is still regarded as a sex symbol except perhaps by the very young. He is still the most exciting star on the screen today. He is the unattainable dream, who falls apart at all his beautiful seams when he is left by a woman he wants, and he usually wants her more when she leaves him.

"He's a man who doesn't know his mind," Dyan is sure. "Some men cannot be married, and Cary is one of them." She could be right. "When I am married, I want to be single, and when I am single, I want to be married," Cary confessed to me during an analytical ratiocination of himself, his friends, and his enemies (very few of these), his films, his account books, and what he really wants from life. But with all his attempts at clarification, he is the most mixed-up man I have ever met.

The straw that toppled his marriage with Dyan, who knew him intimately for four years before the marriage in Las Vegas in 1965, was his refusal to buy a house for her. He prefers, for some reason he won't divulge, to rent them. During the brief marriage with Dyan he rented the San Fernando Valley home of Gordon and Sheila MacRae, who had separated.

Cary has an almost pathological fear of poverty. His conservation of his fortune is a Hollywood legend. They tell the story of Cary dining with a friend, and the pair, among the richest men in Hollywood, sat there until three in the morning waiting for the other to pick up the check. It could be an exaggeration.

When an old friend, down on his luck, first came to Hollywood, he bumped into Cary, whom he had known in New York, on a studio lot. He was delighted when Cary said, "Let's have lunch at Romanoff's." When the check came, Cary made no attempt to pay, and the other dug into his pocket and paid. "This is fun," said Cary, "let's do it again next week." They did, and it was the same thing. "Why don't we lunch every week?" said Cary. After the fifth week Cary took the bill, now automatically presented to his hard-up friend, looked at it reflectively, and said, "Didn't you pay last week?" "Yes," eagerly. "So you did," said Cary. "I tell you what. Why don't we go Dutch?"

Another tale told me by the wife of one of the stars during the Chicago location of Cary's *North by Northwest* film for Alfred Hitchcock: All members of a production are paid what is called a "per diem"—an amount of dollars every day on location—to pay for food and incidental expenses. The bigger the star, the bigger the per diem. It is the custom with stars on location to congregate for dinner together in the dining room of the hotel where they stay. The *North by Northwest* company stayed, at studio expense except for food, at the Ambassador East Hotel, and ate dinner in the elegant but costly Pump Room. "Cary would eat a hamburger at the nearest inexpensive restaurant, then join one of the groups in the Pump Room for coffee," my informant revealed.

But the printed stories that Cary in all his thirty-eight years in Hollywood has never paid for a house aren't true. He bought a place in Palm Springs many years ago, but he has never furnished it—just a bed and a couple of chairs. He also owns a small house in Beverly Hills where he lived part of the time he was married to Betsy Drake. Finding marriage too confining, he asked her to move into a rented house and they met periodically at his place or hers. He is still friendly with Betsy, who took on his problems during the marriage. When he couldn't sleep, she sat by his bedside and hypnotized him into slumber. He had agreed to do the remake of *A Star Is Born* with Judy Garland. He was rehearsing at Judy's house with the director, George Cukor. Soon after Cary went home, Betsy, in white shorts, dashed through the French windows, startling George and Judy and shouting, "You've got to let him go. You've got to give him his freedom. Leave him alone, you're driving him out of his mind." Cary disappeared. James Mason was persuaded to take the role. When last heard from, Betsy was taking a course in speed reading.

Cary adores his second wife, heiress Barbara Hutton. "We're great friends. I'm the only husband who didn't take a dime from her." A few days after the marriage to Barbara, I was on the RKO lot and he was beaming. He stopped to talk to a friend and I heard him say, "This marriage is really going to work. I've never had such a wonderful night in my life!"

I was in London when Cary brought Dyan to meet his mother in Bristol after their marriage. They stayed at a hotel where they were besieged by the press. (Previously he had advertised in the personal column of the London *Times* for a house in or near Bristol and had given his name in the advertisement. When I saw it I thought that if the renting home owner knew Cary Grant would be the tenant, he would not be charged as much. He decided it would be better if they stayed in a hotel.) The press was everywhere, and Cary called the Columbia studio press director in London for help. "You've got to get me out of here."

"Why don't you give a mass interview and let them take photos and then they'll leave you alone."

"I won't do that," snapped Cary. "I heard one of the sons of bitches say that if he could take a picture of us together he'd make enough out of it to get a car. If anyone gets a car out of it," his voice rising, "it'll be me."

At about 1:00 A.M., after two nights in the hotel, and after Dyan had met his mother, who is in her late eighties and very feeble, Cary telephoned a rich friend who lives in the country near London with his family and asked for sanctuary. He and Dyan arrived at five in the morning.

"To get out of the hotel unseen by the reporters," Dyan told me later, "we had to climb through a back window." They stayed two weeks with the friends who, with their teen-age daughters, were enchanted to have them, kept their whereabouts a secret from the press, and did everything to make them comfortable; but this was not Dyan's idea of a honeymoon.

After they broke up and Dyan stayed at Malibu with the baby, the frantic Cary begged her to be more accessible to him and live in town where he could see Jennifer. She acceded to his request although he grumbled about the rent, and refused to pay for a full-time nurse, not because of stinginess. Cary believed a baby, *his* baby, should have the love and care that only a mother can give. Of course it *was* cheaper.

Cary had been proud of Dyan during the four, interminable to Dyan, years of their courtship. There was great pleasure in his voice when he would tell me, "I'm taking Dyan to the ball game," or, "Dyan and I were at the Danny Kayes' last night." But once she was Mrs. Grant, he found fault with her. He nagged her constantly, and it made no difference when people were there. He didn't like her mini-skirts and he detested her boots. "Don't you know I hate boots?" he severely reprimanded her when she met him at the airport during the height of the boot fashion. And like most elderly husbands after they have swept a young bride into matrimony —although God knows Dyan didn't need any sweeping—he preferred mostly to stay home in the evenings. He loved having dinner in bed at eight o'clock and watching television. Dyan did not. I never heard of them giving a dinner party, and the few times they accepted invitations they went early and left early.

After the breakup, whether it was thriftiness or because he was lonely, Cary went to live with his friend Johnny Maschio, an agent, and his wife, actress Connie Moore, in their Westwood apartment. In New York he first took up residence at the Croydon Hotel, where Dyan was staying in a suite with the baby and the nurse. But the exasperated Mrs. Grant, who wanted to be quite separated from Cary, asked him to live somewhere else. Cary moved into the town house of Bob Taplinger and stayed and stayed. He did not have to pay for his keep, of course, but it was a sort of two-way thing. It was nice for Bob, who gives parties for the richest men and the prettiest girls in the East, to have a stellar attraction like Cary. When Bob entertained a group of fashion writers in the course of his business, Cary appeared unexpectedly on cue and charmed them all. He bought Bob a color television set for Christmas, and one for Bob's mother, plus 100 coat hangers for his host, which was still considerably cheaper than staying in a hotel for two months.

Although he has never been a spender—"I never quite know how much to tip"—he enjoys giving presents. The seven press agents who handled the announcement of his marriage to Miss Hutton each received an identical gold watch. For the Betsy Drake proclamation, gold cuff links. The presents lasted longer than the nuptials. Except for giving generously to charities, Cary mostly confines his nondeductible gifts to uplifting books—I have received several—the theme of them all: "How to make the most of your life." And he once bought a round-trip ticket to London for a favorite fan-magazine writer. Cary was over there and the woman tried to reach him without success.

In 1940, when his native England was at war, Cary gave two checks, $125,000 and $62,500, to American and British Red Cross. Another $25,000 in 1942. Recently he donated $25,000 to the Los Angeles Music Center, and similar sums to the United Jewish Relief. He is not as penurious as people suppose. His carefulness with a buck is fright of future poverty and a fear of being cheated. He screens every bill minutely, also the grosses from his picture percentages which have made him a millionaire. The negatives of all his films for Universal since *Operation Petticoat* in 1959 have reverted to him after seven years. He also owns the negative of *Penny Serenade,* his long-ago film with Irene Dunne. He'll make new millions when he re-releases them or sells them to TV.

Cary owes the growth of his fortune—most of the millions go into blue-chip stocks—to Stanley Fox, his long-time agent-lawyer and close friend. They met when Mr. Fox was a minor executive on *Penny Serenade,* which earned a billion pennies for his client. Cary never makes a business move without him.

He has never needed advice about pleasing people with small and large courtesies. The day before Ingrid Bergman was due in London to costar with Cary in *Indiscreet,* she had indiscreetly, in Rome, announced her separation from Roberto Rossellini. Every reporter and photographer in Europe was hot on her trail. She managed to dodge them in Paris, but they were lined up—150 of them—at the London airport. Realizing the ordeal awaiting her, Cary, who has adored Ingrid since their film *Notorious* for Alfred Hitchcock in 1946, insisted on accompanying the press agent to the airport. He sent word through to Ingrid that he was waiting for her. "I'm so relieved," she exclaimed thankfully, and was able to smile radiantly for the press while her devoted friend fielded all the questions. Cary, who will not appear on television for all the gold in the Treasury, made his one (unpaid) appearance accepting the absent Ingrid's Oscar for *Anastasia.*

But in spite of all the comforting help and advice he rushes to give his friends in trouble, Cary is at a loss on how to help himself. He is always pursuing will-o'-the-wisp clues for the answer of himself in relation to the universe. He was the first person I heard discuss lysergic acid, as LSD was called a decade ago. He was taking it under medical supervision, and it was then legal. "It's the only way to find the real truth," he glowed to me. "You get a new and wonderful conception of nature. You see everything so clearly. It's a marvelous experience." It sounded so glorious I was envious and wondered whether I should try it. "Let me know when you want to," he told me, "and I'll arrange it with my doctor." But I'm more cautious than Cary. I didn't like the idea of being controlled by a drug.

Later, he gave an interview on the joys of lysergic acid to a London reporter. It was picked up by a Hollywood writer, Joe Hyams. Cary repudiated the story and threatened to sue Joe, who was able to produce the recorded tapes of the original interview. He brought suit against Cary for a million dollars. It was settled by allowing Joe to write Cary's life story for a top magazine for which the happy Hyams received $75,000. "After my story was accepted by the magazine," Joe told me, "Cary appeared at their office and said, 'My grammar isn't good and my punctuation is terrible, but you don't mind if I change a bit here and there.'" By the time he finished his changes, he had rewritten the entire three-part story. "It was all his," said Joe. "It was brilliant." As you know, Dyan used Cary's LSD sessions in her divorce testimony. Another man might have paid to hush it up, but right means more to Cary than an exposure of this sort.

I, too, have had my fights with Mr. Grant. In my early years in Hollywood, when I was more slashing than I am now, I needled Cary in print every time I heard a new story of his parsimony. It reached a point during *Gunga Din* in 1939 that Cary called me and told me off for five minutes without pausing for breath. My boss, John Wheeler, was coming out from New York and he wanted to visit the *Gunga Din* set. Not wishing to tell him of my strained relations with Cary and Douglas Fairbanks, Jr., who was also in the film and whom I had also put down, but for different reasons (I thought he was a pompous bore), I decided to take a chance and visit the set. Fortunately Perry Lieber, then head of publicity at RKO, told me this was impossible as the director, George Stevens, had closed the set. Later Perry confessed that the two stars were planning to let me have it in front of my employer. "I couldn't let that happen to you," he said. I'm glad. I have always found it better to give than to receive.

A story I did not print about Cary during the making of *Gunga Din*—because I knew all hell would break loose—can now be laughed at in the retrospect of twenty-nine years. It reveals another facet of Cary's character—his determination to get to the top. He wouldn't do it in the same way now, I am sure, as I wouldn't do certain things now. There was a scene on a roof where the junior Fairbanks, at the sound of a shot, had to grab an Arab and hurl him horizontally into the street below. It was the best scene in the picture and Cary coveted it. He told Doug, "You really shouldn't do this. You might kill him. It wouldn't help your image. And you know your father would never have done such a thing on the screen." Cary was convincing and the troubled Fairbanks said to the director, "I don't think I should do it." As soon as it was agreed, Cary jumped out from where he had been waiting and said, "George, I'll do it." It *was* the best scene in the otherwise mediocre picture.

In the days when Cary was making sophisticated screen love to Katharine Hepburn, Rosalind Russell, and Ingrid (Can you ever forget the meal he made of her ear in *Notorious*? The whole publicity campaign for the picture was built on the scene.), he was difficult about the Lincolnesque mole near his mouth. His face always had to be photographed so it wouldn't show. I haven't seen it in real life for ages. He was also difficult with his adoring fans and would not sign his autograph except for children. He said any adult who wanted his name on a piece of paper was an idiot. He changed somewhat after a visit to Russia where no one knew him from the next stranger. He confessed he had not enjoyed the anonymity. But he has always had a fetish about his right to privacy in his personal life.

He was angry when Lew Wasserman, who came to Universal as president when it was taken over by MCA, devised a new method of adding to the studio revenue: Tours of the lot for out-of-town visitors or anyone who cared to pay $3, which included lunch in the commissary. "It's very unfair," stormed Cary, who has a bungalow with a self-contained suite of rooms at the studio—free. "I can hear the bus drivers say, 'This is Cary Grant's car,' 'This is where Cary Grant sunbathes.' You have taken away my privacy." He didn't go so far as to give up the bungalow, but he informed Lew he would never eat in the commissary again. "I don't like being stared at like an animal in the zoo." Instead, Cary, who eats carefully and meagerly, took his lunch and walked into the hills above the studio. He curtailed this healthy exercise when one of the touring busses followed him up the hill and knocked him down—accidentally, of course. Some time later, when he was injured in a car accident on the way to the airport, he thought he had played his final scene. He found it hard to breathe and he was sure he was dying. I was not surprised when I heard he was sharing a hospital room with the injured chauffeur.

It is easy to say, "Here is a man who has everything—money, health, enormous fame, and he is still very attractive. Why can't he be happy?" Even his best friends will tell you he is not. As with Miss Streisand, the answer perhaps is to be found in his early life when he was desperately poor. As Archibald Alexander Leach, the circus stilts walker who became Cary Grant, he sometimes starved. He thought he was rich when Jean Dalrymple, the long-time director of City Center in New York—"I was in my teens," she assured me—gave Cary, who was in his early twenties, a job at $75 a week in her vaudeville skit, "The Woman Pays." "The agent sent me Valentino types who were all wrong. And then Mr. Leach came in. He rolled when he walked—they called him 'Rubber Legs,' he told me shyly. He said he came from Australia [which I have never heard before]. He had a marvelous smile and a charmingly disparaging attitude toward himself that I liked."

I met him in Hollywood soon after he played Mae West's lover in *She Done Him Wrong.* It was a break for Cary because Mae was enormously popular all over the world after her stage hit in *Diamond Lil.* Cary was outgoing and sociable and there were always pretty girls in his pool at the beach house in Malibu. He became even more handsome as he grew older, and the marriage to Miss Hutton boosted his glamour. The smart comedies with the top women of the screen made him a top star, and by World War II he was receiving $300,000 for each picture, the equivalent of a million dollars today. Most of the Britishers—David Niven, Laurence Olivier, and Richard Greene—went back to England to fight the war. Cary, also British, was troubled. He didn't have as many complexes then as now—these came with success. But he wanted to do the right thing. His first wife, Virginia Cherrill, was now the Countess of Jersey, and the beautiful blonde was godmother to a Polish Flight Squadron. (She introduced me to all of them in her Hampton Court home near London during the war when I was covering the British war effort for my syndicate.) Cary might have applied to go back to

England—I don't know—but he was thirty-five years old, a little beyond fighting age, and he did the next best thing. He gave money.

Hollywood has been proud of Cary, particularly in the last decade. He has been a fine ambassador for the film industry. Whenever a banquet is given for a visiting king or queen or Prince Philip, Cary is at the head table, at the ready with his athletic looseness, tanned and smiling at the world in general. Except for his distress over Dyan, I have never seen him really discomposed. He is always projecting his personality on a seemingly confident level. "He is always 'on,'" says a man who has known Cary even longer than I have. "What is he like when he isn't 'on'?" I asked. "He's depressed," was the surprising answer. I would have found this hard to visualize—except for my own experience of his misery over Dyan. He is always so charming, so likable. Basically he is a kind man, in spite of his emotional ups and downs and his fixation that he must save his money for the future.

He has been more gregarious since the disaster with Dyan, and more extravagant. After they parted he bought her a sable fur coat although she didn't get an engagement ring from him. ("Are you kidding?" she said when I asked to see it.) In the final accounting Dyan holds the ace card—their child, who will inherit everything. At the rate Cary is not spending his millions, Miss Jennifer Grant will be the richest girl in the world, richer than Barbara Hutton, even if Daddy retired tomorrow, which I hope not, although he has insisted ever since he saw the aging Gary Cooper making love to the young Audrey Hepburn in *Love in the Afternoon* that he is too old even to flirt with the young charmers of the screen. This apparently did apply to his private life—Dyan is thirty years his junior.

Cary sometimes pretends to be naïve and sometimes he is. A friend took him to dinner at a country house of some people Cary had never met, soon after his lullaby record to his daughter came out. Without saying hello or how are you, Cary demanded of the owner of the house, "Do you have a record player?" He sat entranced for more than half an hour playing his record over and over. But he is not naïve in business transactions, although he would like you to think so. He is as sharp as the thinnest blade.

Cary says he has finally learned to live with the fame and the adulation, and he is always attractively embarrassed when I tell him every woman I know swoons for him. In spite of his friendliness, he remains aloof. He may confide in you one day, but the next day, when you expect more of the same, he will be cool and on the friendly-adviser plateau again, and you'd better not bring up the confidences of yesterday. And you know he is still an unsure man, even when he is advising you so sincerely on how to live your life. Recently he hunted up an old co-worker in the circus. Cary had heard he was in the United States and advertised for him to get in touch with him. Cary paid his expenses to Hollywood. When the man, who looked twice the age of Cary, came to see him, he took him for a ride in his limousine "to show him how well I was doing." You can see he still has to convince himself. But when you look at Cary Grant, you realize there is nobody like him or ever likely to be. And may he live to be a grandfather, even if he is a confused grandfather.

4)

The Greatest Love Story
Never Told

"Can I do it?" Spencer Tracy asked Katharine Hepburn anxiously. The woman on whom he relied for everything thought carefully before replying. How many years did he have left? One, at the most. To act would make him happy, remove the restlessness. The satisfaction of working might even prolong his life. Katharine regarded the much-lived-in face, with its unruly thatch of completely white hair. She was the one person who would know for sure whether Spencer Tracy, whom Sir Laurence Olivier called the greatest actor of our time, was capable of making one more film, Stanley Kramer's production of *Guess Who's Coming to Dinner*.

In the last decade, the early times of carousing in bars and raising hell had taken a terrible toll on the once iron constitution of the drinking Irishman. He had undergone several operations—kidney stones, bladder (during the latter he almost died on the operating table)—and he had a bad heart. Overnight he had gone from middle to old age.

In *It's a Mad, Mad, Mad, Mad World,* his previous picture for Kramer, he was sixty but he looked eighty. Mr. Kramer believed he would never work again. Spencer's last film with Katharine had been *Desk Set* in 1957, and she had not made a film since Eugene O'Neill's *Long Day's Journey Into Night,* a failure, in 1962. It seemed they had both given up, and now had come this story by William Rose which fitted them superbly, but was Tracy well enough to do it?

He had been grouchy and depressed since the most recent of several heart attacks. It had happened in the summer when he was moving into a house at the beach. Katharine had packed a basket of food. It was a lovely day and as soon as she had settled him in, they would picnic in the Malibu hills. Spencer stepped out of the car and slumped unconscious on the driveway. He was rushed by ambulance to the hospital. When he returned home, better in health, he had complained he was dying of boredom in the small house he had rented for seventeen years from their good friend, George Cukor, who had made Katharine a star in *A Bill of Divorcement* in 1932, when great roles were written for women.

In the Kramer film Spencer would play a rugged newspaper owner, Katharine his intelligent, liberal, good-family wife. And there was a nice part for her niece and namesake, Katharine Houghton, who in the film fell in love with an educated Negro, Sidney Poitier. But none of this was important beside the one overwhelming question: Could Spencer's damaged heart beat strongly enough to carry him through the twelve weeks required to make the film? The responsibility for the decision would have been too much for any other woman, but this brusque, often rude actress has great courage. "Yes, you can do it," she assured the man she loved. "You can do it."

The twenty-six-year-old saga of Spencer Tracy and Katharine Hepburn is the great love story of our time. Someone will fictionalize it one day. And it will be hard to believe that such love and devotion could exist in a cynical modern world. Especially in Hollywood.

Miss Hepburn, an extremely attractive woman still, could have had any man in Hollywood, but she chose to give her love to Spencer Tracy, whom she met in 1942 when they co-starred in *Woman of the Year*. Spencer was separated from his wife but still married to her when he died in June 1967.

No one would have had the nerve to ask him during his lifetime whether he had ever asked for a divorce from Louise, who had borne him two children, one of them, John, a deaf-mute. And I will not raise the question here except to say that Spencer was a devout practicing Catholic who went to Mass every Sunday. Louise is a Protestant. I believe she would have given him a divorce if he had asked for it. But divorce was contrary to Spencer's religious beliefs, although most people in Hollywood are still under the impression that Louise had blocked her husband's efforts to be free to marry Katharine. This was not true, as so many stories in Hollywood are not true.

There is the often-told anecdote that when they first met at M-G-M to discuss their first film, Kate, who is a tall 5' 7½" in her flat comfortable shoes, studied Spencer from top to toe and said, "Aren't you too short for me?" to which he supposedly replied, "Don't worry, I'll soon cut you down to size." He could be rude, but not that rude. It was the director, Joe Mankiewicz, with razor-edged wit, who made the remark.

Proust has written that love is never equal, one always loves more than the other, with the balance changing, sometimes one way, sometimes the other. Throughout the period of the Tracy-Hepburn relationship, the balance favored Spencer. And that was how Katharine wanted it. From the early years when she would be in the M-G-M patrol car, searching in the bars for the man she called her "dipsomaniac," to the time she flew to Havana to get the carousing Tracy in shape for the dry-docked production of Hemingway's *Old Man and the Sea*, to his dying days in his last film, she gave the man she loved her full measure of devotion.

When he died she wanted to attend his funeral, to pay her last respects to the man she had supported with her faith and strength. This would have been understood by his widow and family. Katharine discussed it with her close friends. Garson Kanin thought she should go, that it would ease her grief. Chester Erskine, the playwright who had written *The Last Mile*, which had brought Spencer to Hollywood in 1930, thought it would be wrong for Miss Hepburn to be at the funeral—the press and the photographers would have to take note of her presence and it would be painful for her. She decided to stay in the seclusion of his home. After the funeral their friends came to the house to be with her.

For several weeks Katharine was thoughtful and quiet. Even though she had known of Spencer's precarious hold on life, it had been a great shock when she had gone there early in the morning to find his heart had stopped beating during the night. She had run distractedly to the house next door. Then she had telephoned Mr. Cukor, who lived on the ridge above, and Mr. Erskine at the beach, and they had rushed to help her. She did not weep. There was the same self-abnegation and concern for Spencer in death as in life. In their twenty-six years she never once appeared with him in public. She had encouraged his visits to his wife and family several times a week. He adored his children and his grandchildren and respected Louise. Katharine had never demanded anything from him that he could not give. And she smiled as though she were with him on a faraway journey when his friends told the stories that are always remembered of the loved one who is gone. Bereft, she held her head high and behaved as she had always done, with dignity, and concerned only to do honor to the dead man.

And yet it was not easy to love Spencer Tracy. He was a difficult, sometimes irascible man. He always was, from the beginning of my knowing him. In the days of his early drinking, he was impossible. I remember a fight he had with John Wayne. A studio employee had been assigned the job of keeping an eye on Spencer at all times when he was working. Spencer and the Waynes—John was married to Esperanza then—had been a threesome, but when Spencer got out of control, Wayne sent his wife home and took Tracy to a nearby hotel room to sober him up. The M-G-M employee suddenly burst into the room. "You dirty double-crosser," Spencer yelled at the innocent Mr. Wayne, and hurled a haymaker at him. "Don't hit him back, he has to work tomorrow!"

screamed Spencer's terrified guardian. It was too late. The two men eased him onto the bed and went out and got drunk themselves.

When I was on his sets at M-G-M beginning in 1936, when he was starring in *Libeled Lady,* he would do his best to smile at me, but I knew he wanted me to ask my questions and be gone. Spencer rarely talked to reporters and he was always bawling people out, but he could be nice to those who worked with him. When Hy Averbach had a bit part in a Tracy film, he was twenty minutes late reporting to the set—his alarm had failed to go off. He was worried and showed it. "It's all right, Hy," Spencer comforted him as he stuttered his explanation. "It's all right. It happens to everyone." During *Judgment at Nuremburg,* when Montgomery Clift was drinking and had the shakes and could not remember his dialogue, Spencer helped him out. "Don't worry about the lines, just look at me and tell it to me." It was enormously effective.

Miss Hepburn was even more difficult than Spencer with the press. The first thing she does when starting a new film is to call over the nervous unit man and say, "If you want to get along with me at all, you'll keep the goddamned press off the set. Otherwise I'll make your life absolute hell." Sometimes (rarely) she will say yes to an interview after saying "It's impossible" (often for as long as four years), and then she will be cooperative to an unbelievable extent, directing the questions and the photographs. In a recent cover story for *Life* magazine she surprised the delighted photographer by standing on her head.

This woman has a biting tongue and yet, considering her abnormally antagonistic attitude toward the press, she has been treated quite well by the reporters she disdains, except for the played-up newspaper story in the late '30s when Katharine, with Joan Crawford, was listed among the ten stars who were poison at the box office. She pretended to be amused, but it was some time before she recovered from what she described as "a severe case of shell shock." The press is somewhat intimidated by her. With that peaked workman's cap she wears all the time, and the airman's jacket, and the dungarees that look better on her than any other woman I know, you feel she wouldn't be above giving you one on the snoot or chewing you out in loud, strong language. But with Mr. Tracy the masculine-looking actress was feminine. She was meek and motherly, and you knew she lived only to please the man she treated as lord and master. He knew the extent of her devotion and played on it to the end. He seemed to delight in bawling her out—no one knew how it was in private.

Once she stopped to tie her shoelace and he shouted, "What's the matter, Kate?"

"Well, I—"

"Hurry up, goddammit."

She left the lace untied and ran. If he was telling a story and she dared to interrupt, he would say brusquely, "Shut up, I'm talking." And this woman, who could tell others off in fierce language, would shut up and say, "Yes, of course, Spenc*er*," with the "er" an "ah" in her Bryn Mawr accent. At the beach home of their friends he would sprawl in an armchair like Professor Higgins with Eliza Doolittle and command, "Put another log on the fire, Kate." And she would jump to attention and say, "Yes*sir*," like a junior officer to the captain, and get the wood while he watched. And more coffee when he growled, "My coffee's cold, goddammit."

"It was a put-on," a friend told me. "They loved to make people think they were having a fight." If so, it was Academy Award acting, of which they were both capable. He won two Oscars, for *Boys Town* and *Captains Courageous,* and she has two for *Morning Glory* and *Guess Who's Coming to Dinner.*

She would take anything from Spencer because she admired him so much. She was his slave and he used his power over her. But he also knew he needed her. He couldn't function without her, especially in the last years. He worried about everything, especially about his son John, born a deaf-mute years before he had met Kate. Some good came of the tragedy. Mrs. Tracy founded a clinic to help her son and others afflicted like him. There are now seventy-five John Tracy Clinics around the world, and the greatest contributor was Spencer. He gave them all the money he did not need for his living expenses. There wasn't much to leave anyone, but what there was went to his family, and Katharine knew this before he died. If he had left her any money, she would have given it to his family. She has never wanted much for herself, just as long as she can hike and swim and play tennis. Tennis is her one extravagance. For years she paid a weekly salary to Harvey Snodgrass, the professional at the Beverly Hills Hotel, to be on call when she wanted him. She played several hours each day.

Spencer was sometimes like a helpless child, and no one could have been, or pretended to be, more difficult. He would not make the smallest move without consulting Katharine—was this right for him, should he do this or that, salt on his food, sugar in his coffee. They could not have children because they could not marry, and for Katharine it didn't really matter. She had married and divorced in her twenties. She had said she never wanted children. Whether this is true or making the best of a situation, I don't know. She came from a large family and adored her brothers and sisters. They were her children, and Spencer became the child or the brother who needed her most. When he died she was shattered as a mother, a sister, or a wife would be when she loses the person she loves most.

But there was no mourning when Spencer died. Katharine picked up the pieces of her life and went on as before with the compensation that she could now accept the offers she had previously refused. "You'd try to get Hepburn for a picture," a director told me, "and she'd say, 'I don't think so.' She was the first to be offered the Vivien Leigh role in *Ship of Fools*. Tracy was ill and the answer was no." Soon after his death she said, "I don't want to think at all for two years. I'm going to work hard. When I can think again, I'll retire."

I hope she will change her mind. Miss Hepburn is unique. She has become a legend in her lifetime, right up there with

Garbo. Perhaps more so, because the span of her career has been longer, and while she has hated to grow old, she has joked about it, which I can't imagine Garbo ever doing. "This carcass," she will say, referring to her lithe body, and, "Who enjoys looking in the mirror and seeing the wrinkles on your face or neck?"

There would have been fewer wrinkles but for her dedication to Tracy. The sun is harmful to her freckled complexion, but she remained in California, and she will not desert it entirely. But now she will be in the open. During her time with Spencer she lived willingly in his shadow. Now we will see her at more events. Not parties, but perhaps premieres of the films of her friends. One film she says she will never see—Spencer's last movie with her. She has seen all the others in private projection rooms and perhaps one day, when the pain is more bearable, she will slip into a theater to see what all the shouting was about for *Guess Who's Coming to Dinner*.

When Spencer, to please a producer, would attend one of his films, Katharine might see him off in the car but she would not go with him. When Mr. Kramer premiered *Judgment at Nuremberg* in Germany, he asked Spencer to appear with the picture. He didn't want to go. After he gave up drinking following his first serious illness, he had rarely been seen in public, and Katharine thought it would be good for him to get out, to learn how much he was loved. He grudgingly consented to go if she came with him. She said she would if her presence could be kept absolutely secret. Driving into Nuremberg, she got out of the car two blocks from the hotel and walked the rest of the way, entering by the back door and taking the freight elevator to her suite. Spencer attended the premiere while Katharine remained at the hotel. There were rumors of her presence and the German press hunted for her, but no one could find her. They knew of the Tracy-Hepburn saga, but very few allusions were made in print.

But the story is too remarkable to remain untold. And perhaps Spencer would be the first to want it written. He adored gossip. It was one of the real pleasures of his life. When his cronies came to see him, he would pump them for the latest goings-on in Hollywood and abroad. He would say, "Guess which twosome was at The Daisy last night?" or "Guess what I got in the mail from England about so-and-so?" or "Guess who was at Les Ambassadeurs in London?" His craggy face would be full of mischief, but there was nothing tricky about him, nothing cruel or mean.

He made some of the great films in Hollywood: *Captains Courageous, Inherit the Wind, Boys Town, State of the Union, Judgment at Nuremberg,* and a few bad ones, but he never was bad in them. He might say, years later, "What a stinker that was," but nobody listened. He knew his craft and Katharine learned from him. She usually knew what was right for her. When she came to Hollywood in 1932 for *A Bill of Divorcement,* the head of the RKO publicity department was nonplused by her appearance. He felt something must be done to glamorize the gawky, badly dressed girl. In those days you popped newcomers into a swim suit, sent them to the beach, and had them splashing around as the cameras clicked. Even Garbo served her term in the ocean. It was before the film was released, and when he asked Katharine to pose in a bathing suit, she did it under protest. After the photographs were taken she told him, "You're wrong. The part I play in the film is dramatic and serious. If you want this sort of thing, you should get a sexy starlet with a figure to match."

I followed Kate to Hollywood by four years, but I knew a great deal about her before I arrived. My first friends in this country were Judge Samuel Smith, his wife, and their two sons, who lived on Philadelphia's Main Line. I had met the younger son, Sam, in England, with a friend who had been to Oxford with him and he had said, "If ever you come to America, let me know and you must stay with us." He had cabled me on the boat that he would meet me and take me to his home. Sam was unmarried. Ogden Ludlow, the elder son, had a wife—an actress, they told me—Katharine Hepburn, then appearing on the New York stage. They lived in New York, and the Smiths promised me they would ask Ludlow and Katharine for the weekend the next time I came. I returned to England and the next time I visited the Smiths, the marriage was over and Katharine had become a famous Hollywood star. Mrs. Smith told me of the dreadful time they had during the divorce with the reporters and photographers hiding in the trees.

Soon after I came to Hollywood I asked for an interview with Miss Hepburn. She was making *Mary of Scotland*. Her director was John Ford, who liked to refer to me as "Miss Poison Pen." The producer, Pan Berman, was easier to approach, and I asked his help in reaching the unapproachable actress. He had an idea. "We all lunch together every day in the commissary. Come as my guest and I guarantee you'll get a great story. Don't say anything. Just listen." I listened while Katharine joked with everyone there. Pan mumbled my married name in the introduction. I was his guest and she was polite to me, including me with her glance in the conversation. I was doing fine remembering what she was saying until Mr. Ford leaned close to her and whispered something in her ear. She gave me a piercing look and demanded, "What is your name?"

My mind blanked out and all I could think of was the surname of my employer. "Sheilah Wheeler," I muttered, blushing, not knowing where to look.

"Who do you work for?" she continued relentlessly.

"John Wheeler," I replied, wishing an earthquake would blot out the café.

"That's funny," said Miss Hepburn. "Your name is Sheilah Wheeler and you work for John Wheeler."

"That's right." I felt sick.

She dropped the cross-examination. I felt bad for Pan, who had wanted to help me. We decided we must tell her my real name and that I was a reporter, which in any case she already knew from Mr. Ford. Pan told me later that Katharine had roared with laughter and said, "I know her. She's a friend of my in-laws." If I had just sent in my working name I might have gotten one of her rare interviews.

Over the years I have tried to interview Miss Hepburn, but she has always said no. I had several chats with Spencer at M-G-M, but I was always careful to see what mood he was in. If he smiled, I moved in. When he scowled, I moved out. But my feelings as a reporter toward Spencer and Katharine have always been submerged in my respect for them as honest human beings, and admiration for their acting ability. They don't make them like that any more.

There was great satisfaction for Katharine that Spencer had completed his last film and had given such a splendid performance. It had been touch and go whether he could finish it. "One day near the end of the picture," Stanley Kramer told me, "Spence said to me, in a matter-of-fact voice, 'I was thinking of all the scenes we have done in the picture, and even if I died today, you would have enough to finish it.' At first, in spite of the willingness of Kate and Spencer, we didn't think we'd be able to make the film. We couldn't get insurance because of his health. And that made him mad. 'Put in my salary,' he said—$300,000, but it wasn't enough. The studio was hesitant about putting up the rest. 'Take my salary,' said Katharine. The $200,000 she was getting for the film went into the pot. In effect, they were both working for nothing. We all knew he was a dying man and held our breath that he would get through each day. I had promised Katharine we would take care of him. He didn't start work until ten in the morning and he left before lunch. The front office would have been nervous had they known. It was the best-kept secret in Hollywood."

What Mr. Kramer did not know was that every morning at four or five o'clock, Katharine would be with Spencer going over his dialogue, rehearsing with him until he was word perfect and had absorbed his scenes, so that they were part of the man when he faced the cameras. It was harder in the last two weeks when he was failing visibly. Tracy had always learned his roles by concentrating and absorbing the character. It is this that gave his portrayals such sincerity and honesty. He pondered and thought and labored, and he worried about his talent. "I don't have it," he cried. "I can't bring it up. It isn't there." But when the time came, when the cameras turned, he performed as he always had, although the effort was agonizing, while Katharine hovered close, her heart in her eyes, willing him to do it. In the afternoons while he rested at home, Katharine, Sidney Poitier, and the rest played their scenes with him to a blank space and no one complained.

"He was pleased with the progress of the picture, but always wondered whether he could finish it," Stanley said. The final day for Spencer was a process shot in a San Francisco drive-in (they could not tire him by actually going there). When it was done, Spencer shouted jubilantly, "I've finished!" And crowing to Mr. Kramer, "Now you'll have to pay me!" He called Cukor and Kanin and told them, "I finished it, goddammit, I finished it!" Then he put his arms around Mr. Kramer and wept. Even the controlled Katharine broke down as she hugged her costar. Two weeks later he was dead. Like the pro he had always been, he had waited to die when he knew there would be no retakes. The tears in Miss Hepburn's eyes in so many of the scenes were real. Some of his speeches in the film—especially the last when he looks straight at her with all his esteem for her showing, when he tells her how much she has meant to him, that he's old, burnt out, but the spark between them could never die if he lived to be a hundred and ten—had everyone on the set choking, while Kate, through the mist of her tears, smiled with pride and gratitude, as millions have seen up there on the screen.

5)

Frankie

"Frank Sinatra is the kind of guy, when he dies, he's going up to heaven and give God a bad time for making him bald," said Marlon Brando, when the two actors were costarring in *Guys and Dolls*.

Sinatra is a different man to different people. You are either violently for him or vehemently against him. To some, he is kind, shy, and gentle. To others, a cruel egomaniac. To Brad Dexter, the actor who saved him from drowning in Hawaii, Frank is an ungrateful son of a bitch. To Rosalind Russell, a life member of the Sinatra inner circle, he is a "compassionate, forgiving, sentimental slob." He is fantastically generous to his friends, family, and associates. Furs, cars, jewelry, private rides in his two jet planes. He gives large sums of money publicly to charity and small amounts in private to people he does not know. From the flamboyant gesture of chartering a Boeing 707 jet to bring Claudette Colbert and her ailing husband, Dr. Joel Pressman, from Barbados to Los Angeles at a cost of $26,000, to the anonymous 50 pounds to a poor couple in England whose home, he read, had been vandalized. He will take 60 people to Las Vegas for an all-night winging to celebrate the twenty-fifth wedding anniversary of Miss Russell and her husband Freddie Brisson.

And he will walk away from the chauffeur of a studio limousine without giving him a tip because he did not drive fast enough. He is compassionate one day, unforgiving the next. He is an angry man.

And a kind man. He knows hundreds of people. And he is the loneliest man in the world. His friends swear by him. The others dislike him. When his son, Frankie, Jr., was kidnaped and the ransom was $250,000 in cash, he called his friend, Al Hart, late at night and Al, President of the City National Bank, went to the vault and took out all the available notes. It wasn't enough and he awakened his banker friends and they made up the rest, which he personally guaranteed. Sinatra will tip a waitress or a bell boy $100—"I never carry a note less than $100"—and when he turned in $7,075 worth of chips in Las Vegas, he looked at the $75 as though it were foreign currency and gave it to the man nearest him. I doubt whether he is rich; he spends the money as fast as he makes it—his two jets standing by all the time with a pilot on full pay, homes in London, Palm Springs, New York, Mexico, and Hollywood. He'll pay anything for what he wants. It cost him $6,000 to fly one of his musical arrangers from Hollywood to New York to assist at a two-and-a-half-minute recording.

I must admit to some pleasure when the mighty Sinatra mystique was shattered by a skinny girl, weighing ninety-nine pounds, from the right side of the tracks in Beverly Hills. In Mia Farrow, who had once thought of being a nun, Frank Sinatra amazingly met his match. It was a Pyrrhic victory for Mia, because in the end she lost him. Mia put him through a hell he had given others, but never experienced himself, not even with Mia's predecessor, Ava Gardner. His friends tell me he was never in love with Mia, that it was a case of an aging Romeo who suddenly realized that most of the women he knew were over fifty and the men more than sixty. He was forty-nine when they met and perhaps he was flattered that a girl of nineteen was in love with him. Possibly he needed another daughter. Whatever it was, they swear he was not in love with her. I believe he was, at the beginning anyway. I can still hear Mia telling me breathlessly in the 20th Century-Fox commissary, "I've just had a call from the man I love." I had heard some rumors and queried, "Frank Sinatra?" "Yes." It was a clear, confident affirmative. Then she told me about how he was flying her to Palm Springs every weekend in his very own plane, the expensive pieces of jewelry he was buying her, how she had always loved his records, and really and truly, he was quite the most fascinating man she had ever known. She had met him on his set while he was finishing up *Von Ryan's Express*—which earned him another million dollars from his percentage—and she was Allison in *Peyton Place* on the sound stage next door. And right away she knew it was love and immediately dropped John Leyton, with whom she appeared in her first film, *Guns at Batasi*, whom she had only *thought* she loved. John was in the film with Sinatra and had made the introduction.

My story, with my announcement that they would marry, was front-paged in many parts of the world. Frankie learned of my exclusive before it appeared in my Hollywood newspaper and denied every word of it in strong language. The drama editor ran his denial, for which he later apologized in print, side by side with my story. Frankie stormed at Mia for talking to a reporter, especially this one. He had not liked me since I paragraphed his obnoxiousness to the press during the divorce from Ava Gardner, pushing reporters around and smashing or threatening to smash the cameras of the photographers. I had championed the girl from North Carolina, and at that time it was as good as slitting my throat as far as Sinatra was concerned. I was sorry for him when Frankie, Jr., was kidnaped and wrote him a letter of sympathy. I also contradicted in my column some of the skepticism that the kidnaping was a hoax. It didn't make sense and I said so.

When the columnists, myself included, were printing that Mia and Frankie were reconciling, an imp of doubt was always on my shoulder, because I knew how much Mia had punctured Frank's godlike image of himself. "How much longer can he take it?" I asked frequently in my column and on the *Merv Griffin Show*. Also, how much longer could Mia be happy with Frank's cluttered way of life, bored by his elderly friends, and ill at ease with the uncouth drinking pals? She made an irreparable mistake early in the marriage by trying to reform him. Soon after the nuptials, when he was gambling heavily in the casino at the Sands Hotel in Las Vegas and she had been waiting patiently on the sidelines, she touched his craps-swinging arm and said, "Let's go." He flung her hand off angrily and shouted, "Look, don't tell me what to do. Don't try to change me."

She became thoughtful and soon afterward left for London to make her film *Dandy in Aspic* with Laurence Harvey. Her husband did not want his wife to work, but had agreed reluctantly that at the most she would make one film a year. In the brief period of the marriage, she was always working. Knowingly or unknowingly, she had written an end to the marriage by dancing with Robert Kennedy at the Courrèges fashion party at The Factory and cheek-to-cheeking with Laurence Harvey, during their film in England, while the signatures were still wet on her marriage license. Sinatra disliked Senator Kennedy. He believed he was responsible for his exclusion from the White House after President John Kennedy was inaugurated. Frankie had worked hard to get him elected: speechmaking, raising money, providing stars for the political rallies, and lining up some of the top performers in show business for the Inauguration. Robert Kennedy, as Attorney General, knew Frankie's name had been mentioned in connection with various gangland figures, and he persuaded the brother he worshiped that Sinatra as an intimate was wrong for the Presidential image. It was about this time that Peter Lawford (then married to Pat Kennedy), who had been planning to charter a yacht with Frank in the Mediterranean, quietly withdrew from the ranks of the Clan.

Mia's much-publicized photograph with her long thin arms in a tight clamp on Harvey's neck while they danced and danced annoyed Frankie. His anger was not that she was dancing with Larry—he had told him to look after his wife in London—it was the too-friendly picture that he thought would cause gossip. It did.

If Mia had confined her tormenting of Sinatra just to working nonstop and dancing with other men in fashionable discotheques, she might still be his wife. But she committed the unpardonable sin. It was all meant in fun but she ridiculed him in front of his friends. It might have been Mia's way of proclaiming her independence, that she was a valuable person in her own right, that she would not toady to him as the others did. "Yes, Frankie," "Yes, Frankie," "Of course, Frankie," "Yes, Frankie." Mia, rushing in where angels would not have dared to tread, said, "No, Frankie," and "Don't be silly, Frankie." No one can make fun of Frankie. Sammy Davis, Sinatra's most loyal henchman, had made a few harmless jokes about the Clan during his night-club act. It had taken all their mutual friends including big, burly night-club owner, Jilly, and diminutive Danny, of Danny's Hideaway in New York, to intercede, before Sinatra would readmit the talented entertainer into his close circle.

But Mia had gone too far. She had lanced his sensitive armor in every possible chink. (The person closest to you always knows where they are.) What made her think he would take it forever? Mia is not stupid, only young and inexperienced and unable to understand or cope with a man like Sinatra. Mia's mother was right when she said, "If he marries anyone, it should be me." She would have made him a better wife than her daughter. If Mia had been older she would have remained silent during a weekend in Palm Springs at Frankie's home, when, as usual, he had wanted to entertain his guests with one of his movies. Mia, bored to tears, wanted to go out. She emitted a whoop of derision when her tired, harassed husband announced the plan for the evening and, according to one of the guests present, said, "Oh, no. We've all seen it at least five times. Let's go to the Purple Room," naming a popular spot in Palm Springs. They say that Frankie turned purple, but he has never been heard to swear before ladies, and they went to the Purple Room.

Mia was just as bored with his, to her, elderly friends on the yacht he chartered for two weeks, during her vacation from the *Peyton Place* series, which he had insisted upon. They played backgammon interminably, rarely went ashore. Sinatra, a fanatic about his privacy, used to stay at the Waldorf in New York because "I can't stand being mobbed and there are lots of exits." He curtailed the cruise by three days when a member of the crew was drowned. But Mia was not then Mrs. Sinatra, and you know how it is with a girl before she has married the man. She minds her P's and Q's.

It was an awkward situation for all of the twenty-five guests when Frank invited Mia to spend Christmas of 1967 at the Palm Springs compound. They were seemingly reconciled, but actually not; Frankie had been perturbed when he heard of her constant weeping and depression after their separation. It was Christmas and he was worried that she might do something desperate, so he asked her to join them.

Mia doesn't know yet what life is about, although she is learning the hard way. She is half child, half woman, sometimes ten years old, clapping her hands gleefully and jumping up and down, and sometimes a serious forty. Smart, dumb, and sometimes quite profound, with the uncorrupted wisdom of a child. Her moods are mercurial, changing constantly. She chopped off her lovely long blonde hair to chastise herself as women have done for centuries. Her chief characteristic is honesty. She never compromises with what she thinks is right. She is by turn realistic or living in a world of fantasy. And this is what attracted Sinatra, but it was one thing for her to be honest about life and another to have the person closest to his vulnerable hide be so honest about him.

As with the Cary Grants, the Sinatra marriage might have been saved if Mia could have worked with Frank in his film *The Detective*. It was not a big part, but the idea was intriguing—to play his mistress—and she had never in her hippiest girlhood dreams envisioned costarring with the magical Sinatra. For Frank, it was a way of getting to see his bride. For once they would be working as well as living in the same city. When she had taken off for London and *Dandy in Aspic,* Sinatra, tied to the United States with recording dates and a Florida night-club engagement, had moaned to pal Sammy, "I need this like a hole in the head." All during her filming in London, Mia, who was and perhaps still is in love with Frankie, flew to Florida for weekends to be with her husband. She was in a constant state of exhaustion, and the marriage was on and off several times.

Sinatra had broken his brief engagement to Juliet Prowse two years previously because she refused to comply with his demand that she give up her career. He stated categorically at the time, "I'll never marry an actress. I went through it once." After two weeks of silence from Sinatra, the unhappy Juliet decided her career was less important than the marriage. She called Frankie with the happy news that she had reconsidered and would be a wife to him only. Nancy Sinatra, Jr., gave me her father's reply, when she visited me at my Malibu Beach home and everyone was wondering whether he would really marry Mia. I gathered from Nancy that the family would have preferred Juliet. "When Juliet called my father, he said, 'Forget it, baby,' and hung up."

When I saw Juliet in London in the fall of 1967 when she was the toast of the town in *Sweet Charity,* she told me, "Just before he married Mia, Frank took me out to dinner. I had the impression he was weighing me against Mia. He seemed to be thinking, 'Which one would make me the best wife?' I was ten years older than Mia. She was too young for him." Mia was younger than his daughter Nancy, and he struggled with his conscience and the possibility that his children might turn against him, but when he told them he must marry Mia, they replied, "Whatever you want, Dad, we want for you." It would have been better if they had put up a fight.

The marriage was in desperate straits as Frankie, whose chief characteristic is impatience, waited for Mia to finish her picture for Paramount, *Rosemary's Baby,* to join him in *The Detective.* Sinatra was four weeks ahead with his film. He can never be bothered to do second or third takes. He will discard some of the script before the end of the film, and when he is told they are going beyond time, "Now we're on time," he will say, scattering the pages. Roman Polanski, the director of Mia's film, was four weeks behind schedule—four weeks is nothing for Polanski, who was at least four months late with his *Vampire* film. The impatient Sinatra went to the studio and demanded, "Tell me the truth, when will Mia be through?" "Not for another month," he was told, which meant she would be too late for his film. He thanked them with deceptive courtesy and then began nonstop harassment of his exhausted young wife, ordering her to "ankle the film," which is what he does when he has "had it" with a picture. He flabbergasted Stanley Kramer, the producer of *The Pride and the Passion* in 1956, with six more weeks of production in Spain, by telling him, "I've had it. I'm jumping out, so sue me." There was a contract but suing would not have helped Kramer finish his expensive picture, and he patched it up without Sinatra, who is always bored and edgy if the film has a long schedule.

Mia has been raised in a family of professionals—her father, the late Johnny Farrow, was a director. Her mother is actress Maureen O'Sullivan. It was unthinkable for her to leave the film with her starring role unfinished. She tried to explain this to her angry groom, but he wouldn't listen. If she loved him she would walk out of *Rosemary's Baby* and join him in *The Detective.* It was as simple as that. "What shall I do?" Mia cried to her producer. "I love my husband, but I can't do this to you and Paramount." Sinatra had an angry one-sided quarrel in Palm Springs with Robert Evans, who is the young head of production at Paramount. Bob is a diplomat and managed to keep his temper. But it was too much for Mia. Her throat was bothering her, she was near collapse, and she was in and out of the hospital. On the set she wept constantly. She lost weight, when there wasn't an ounce to lose. For the scene outside the Time-Life Building in New York, she had to look tired and drawn, and she didn't need make-up. A woman in the crowd, noticing her condition said loudly, "Look what Frank Sinatra has done to the poor girl."

She begged the producer, "Please make Roman work faster." But she wouldn't quit. Perhaps at the back of her mind she thought, If my marriage is going to break up—which seemed likely—I'll need a career. She wanted to keep her marriage contract with her husband, but she also wanted to keep the contract with her career. The ambitious girl was playing for big stakes. She's like the young Hepburn, some of the same talent, the same tactless honesty, the same outspokenness. And the same knowing where she stands and what she wants. The part could make her a top star—and it did. If she left the production without completing her role, she knew she could never work again. So she stood her ground, albeit shakily, and bent and almost broke under Frankie's pressure.

I doubt whether she will ever again be the breathless little girl in the studio café who told me how much she loved Frankie. She had loved him, but everything had gone wrong. She had thought, mistakenly, that she could do anything with him, as a young wife can with a much older husband; but Sinatra has become more domineering with the years, and it is not his nature to tolerate opposition and criticism. They will be friends and he has a sense of responsibility toward her. She can always stay at his homes as long as she does not ridicule him and his friends, but the grand passion was over even before she divorced him in Mexico. And perhaps it's just as well for both of them. Frankie can continue to be undisputed king of his kingdom, and Mia, with all the publicity and her acting talent and her hard core of strength, will have a fine career.

His friends say he has never really loved anyone except Ava Gardner, for whom he made the supreme gesture of divorcing his childhood sweetheart, Nancy, which meant that while he could still see his children whom he adores, the devoted father was no longer living with them under the same roof. His fights with Ava were different—the kind Elizabeth Taylor had with Mike Todd and is still having with Richard Burton, lusty and laced with liquor. But even Ava could not take his way of life and his irritability and changes of mood, although she was very moody herself.

It is unbelievable, but true, that Sinatra has excluded from his circle of friends and acquaintances Brad Dexter, the actor who saved his life when he was going down for the third time in the treacherous sea off the coast of Kauai in Hawaii. "I didn't even get a card from him at Christmas," Brad told me.

It is an amazing story. It was Sunday. Frankie was wading near the shoreline with Ruth Koch (whose husband, Howard, was producing the film *None But the Brave*). Brad, a good swimmer, cautioned them not to go far out because the water was tricky. Sinatra will fight a drunk in a bar, but not an angry ocean, so he stayed close in. Suddenly the two paddlers were hit by a gigantic wave, knocked down, and the fierce undertow sucked them out to sea. Within seconds they were three hundred yards out and calling feebly for help. Brad was walking back to the house they were renting on the beach, when he heard someone shout, "My God, Ruth and Frank are drowning!" "When I reached them, they were almost gone. Frankie was whispering with a sort of incredible wonder, 'I'm drowning.' He couldn't see anything. I've seen people drown and they lose their eyesight and go blind—and he was completely white."

Dexter spent fifteen minutes in the sea that had now swept the three of them farther out, holding them both up, alternately turning them over to slap them on the back, keeping their faces out of the water. "I was getting very worried, and then the giant Hawaiian surfers arrived with their big surfboards. They lashed Frankie and Ruth to the boards and took them in." They were so concerned with the errand of mercy, they forgot Brad, who was left fighting for his life in the ocean. "Have you ever had total fatigue?" he asked me in his office at Paramount, where he is now a producer. "I had it then. You don't care what happens to you. You just want to sleep. But I didn't want to die. 'Hey, fellers!' I shouted, but they didn't hear. I vaguely saw a big rock and automatically struck out for it."

Everyone in Hollywood believed that Sinatra would take care of Dexter for life. If it had been Howard Hughes, you know he would have set him up in his own studio. "We never talked about our working together and he didn't give me, and I didn't want, money," the big husky actor told me. "But a year later he asked me to play a role in *Von Ryan's Express*. After that he thought I should become a producer. I worked for Frankie for ten months without pay and that was all right, because I wanted to learn on my own time." Dexter found a property—*The Naked Runner*—to produce with Sinatra as the star. He found a director, Sidney Furie, the young Canadian who had made a name with *The Ipcress File* with Michael Caine. Frankie had never heard of Furie and had to be persuaded to accept him.

On the fifth day of shooting in England, at a location scene two hours by car from London, the impatient star ordered a helicopter that would, he was told, cover the distance in fifteen minutes. "There was something bugging him that morning," said Brad. "It was foggy, and it took forty-five minutes to get there instead of fifteen. As soon as he landed, Frankie jumped out, started cursing everyone, including the pilot, and demanding, 'Why in hell did I come here?' Mr. Furie tried to explain that no one could control the weather. 'I don't give a shit,' said Sinatra. 'I didn't want you in the first place and you can get the hell out of here.'

" 'Listen,' said Sidney, 'the only reason I'm doing the picture is for Brad. He'd better straighten you out or you get yourself another director.'

" 'Look, Frank,' I said to him, 'I promised Jack Warner and Ben Kalmenson [the studio production chief] I'd control you.' He turned on me, 'And if *you* don't like it, *you* can quit too.' " It was a man striking out at the world because a trip had taken thirty minutes longer than promised. "It was my first disillusionment with Frankie," said Dexter.

But there was worse to come. After twenty-six days of shooting he said, "I've had it." He was leaving for America, he told the almost unhinged producer. "He promised reluctantly that if we needed him, he'd come back. We needed him for only three days, I told him on the phone. But he didn't come back." Not three days for the man who saved his life. "The picture was emasculated without the central character, but Sidney and I did our best to put it together with other actors, and with bits and pieces of scenery." When Sinatra learned that filming was continuing without him, he called from California with an ultimatum to Dexter: "Stop shooting or get out." "I couldn't do either. I felt my obligation now was to the film. He sicked his lawyer onto me. I realized then that if I wanted to be a producer, I couldn't work under Frankie's domination. There was no real fight, no argument. We never had words. He knew my feelings, but it was tough luck for Sidney, who'd just finished a film with another difficult actor, Marlon Brando, in *The Appaloosa*. He told me Marlon had almost driven him mad and then to have to go through all this!"

Sinatra has not communicated since with the man who saved his life. He has not answered his telephone calls. Recently when someone mentioned Brad, Sinatra said, "Who's Brad?" It's a pity that Frank banished Mr. Dexter to the outer sphere of his displeasure. He is one of the few who could calm him down when his rages got out of control.

"I've only punched two people in my life," Frankie told Rosalind Russell. "So," he asked her, "how come I have this reputation?" "I've sat with him in bars," Rosalind assured me, "and belligerent guys would come over and say [she acted the scene for me], 'Say, my wife tells me you're a great lover.' 'Please go away,' Frankie will say without looking up. 'Oh, yeah? They say you're a tough guy. You don't look so tough to me.' 'Look, creep, go away,' Frank will say, still trying to avoid a fight, knowing what the press will do to him if he swings. The guy keeps insulting him." Then suddenly Frankie stands up straight, and his eyes are like blue knives, and the man doesn't have to be told any more. But the stories persist and it is hard to find the truth through his bodyguards and the crust of his friends.

He has always surrounded himself with sycophants who "yes" him. When he first came to Hollywood you had to plow through twenty people to reach him. He was less complex in those days. He was not so domineering or angry. He'd break dates with the press without explanation, but when you finally got through he'd be charming, casual, and even flirtatious (I was younger then), and he had not yet started to write off the people who committed wrongs or imagined wrongs. Some of his best friends have graduated to his "drop dead" list.

"Where was Jack Entratter when Carl Cohen was trying to kill me?" he demanded after the shocking fracas in Las Vegas. They had been friends for thirty years, but not any more. Sinatra feels that Entratter, who was one of the owners of the Sands Hotel before selling to Howard Hughes and who remained in an executive capacity, had let him down. But Entratter was not there at the time. It wasn't the same for Sinatra with Hughes as the owner. He tried unsuccessfully to contact Howard by telephone to check in with him as the stellar attraction at the Sands. I doubt whether Howard would return a call from the President of the United States if he didn't feel like it, and he didn't feel like talking to Sinatra, who was furious.

Like so many stars, he cannot bear to be rejected, which is perhaps why he so often rejects others. To teach the new owner of the Sands a lesson, Frankie made a deal to appear at Caesar's Palace.

Everything is known in Las Vegas, and when Frankie applied for more credit beyond his limit of $200,000 at the Sands, he was refused. The scene with Frankie shouting obscenities and threatening to break people in half read like Dante's *Inferno*. If I were a psychiatrist, I would say it suggests the frustration of a thwarted man who didn't really want to fight. He will when he has to, but he hopes he won't have to. Ever since the knockout administered by Carl Cohen, who runs the Casino at the Sands, it has been open season on Frankie. His threats have been proved a joke. "Actually," one of his cronies told me, "and don't you dare use my name, Frankie knows he's a little guy, he's getting older, and I think he would hate to fight. He could get hurt."

Sinatra is three people and only Dostoevski could do justice to the subject. As his personality is split, so are his friends. On one side there are respectable, intelligent citizens such as the Bennett Cerfs, Armand Deutsches, Garson Kanin and Ruth Gordon, Rosalind Russell, Claudette Colbert, the William Goetzes. In the middle are the few remaining members of the Clan: easygoing Dean Martin, happy-to-please Sammy Davis, Joey Bishop, who bases his humor on his misfortunes. And there are the boys in the back room, the unlettered swingers, spearheaded by Jilly, at whose emporium on the West Side Frankie practically makes his home when he is in New York. They have a satisfying time playing tough guys getting drunk, making noise, raising hell, and breaking things, far into the night, finally staggering to bed feeling they have accomplished heaven knows what. He loves each member of each group with a benignly paternal affection. He is 100 per cent loyal to them all, as long as they accede to his wishes, even in small matters. For instance, he never says, "Will you have dinner with me?" It's "You're having dinner with me." If you don't, he will probably strike you off the good-guy list.

While he was filming *Ocean's 11* in Las Vegas with the Clan (Dean, Sammy, Joey, and Peter Lawford, who was then a member in good standing), he was asked to make an appearance at a big social charity bash at the Desert Inn. He didn't want to accept because he was appearing twice nightly at the Sands. After some persuasion, he consented, and once Frankie has said yes, you know he's going. The press agents involved waited for him between shows to take him over. As he was about to leave, he saw Sammy and said, "Come over with me and give me support." Entratter, a small distance away with the press agents, was embarrassed, because from all he had heard of society people who pay large sums to attend charity shows in Las Vegas, they are prejudiced against Negroes. There was a whispered conference. They agreed the way out of the dilemma would be to explain the situation to Sinatra and ask him to forget Mr. Davis. "If Sammy can't come, I won't," he said flatly, and didn't. This is one of the few times he has not appeared after making a promise.

During *Ocean's 11* he was visited a great deal by his good friend, the then Senator John Kennedy, who came in friendly and easy to see his brother-in-law, Peter Lawford, and the other actors. "A photograph with Sinatra? Sure," said Kennedy, "but not now, tomorrow, when I'll put on a tie."

Frankie first came to Hollywood in 1941, when Bing Crosby was the top record seller, to make *Las Vegas Nights* following his enormous hit at the New York Paramount Theater on Broadway. His efficient press agent, George Evans, whom he fired later for some imagined wrong, then rehired many years later, had organized the bobby soxers who swooned and carried on for their idol. It was Evans who encouraged them to rush down the aisles in droves. It set a precedent for Elvis Presley, the Beatles, the Rolling Stones, and all the groups. The RKO publicity department did not believe that the extravagant adulation was on the level. To make sure of an ovation for Frankie they hired five hundred girls to stand by and scream at the Pasadena station when Frankie arrived. Five thousand showed up, and it was on the level.

Frankie bought a house in Toluca Lake, a fashionable suburb of Los Angeles, and there, in spite of an occasional rumor of a romance, he lived happily with Nancy. It was where his youngest daughter, Tina, was born. His relations with the press were good, until he fell violently in love with Ava Gardner and accused the reporters and photographers of persecuting him.

He has provided handsomely for Nancy (who I think still hopes he will return home one day), for their children, and for his parents. If you were to choose the one characteristic of Sinatra that stands out above all others, you would have to say, "This is a man who loves his family." It's the strongest part of his heart and mind. He's pure Italian—mama and the kids. His moods are Italian—violent anger when he dislikes something, and as violently loving when he loves you. His eating habits are Italian. He eats pasta by the bucket load.

He is basically, as Miss Russell said, a sentimental slob who is too impatient ever to be a happy human being, who is a miserable and lonely man in spite of all his fame and the people who come with it (there is a billionaire in Florida who has a large ringside table whenever he performs), and yet Sinatra will call people he knows not too intimately late on a Saturday night, just to talk, and you know he is unhappy and lonely.

With his craggy, nicked, worked-over face, he could have been another Bogart on the screen if he'd been smarter in his public relations and if he had given as much attention and concentration to the longer job of making a film as he does to making a record or a television show. It's too bad, because he proved in *From Here to Eternity* that he has the stuff from which great stars are made.

But he could not cope with fame, the adulation, and the power. It was too much for the aggressive, skinny kid from Hoboken, New Jersey, who became a mixed-up tin god in Hollywood.

6)

The Iron Butterfly

Julie Andrews became a star in Hollywood while Doris Day was retiring as "The Girl Next Door." There is always a scrubbed young face that epitomizes purity and sweetness on the screen. From Mary Pickford to Rin Tin Tin; Shirley Temple; Lassie; June Allyson, who was complemented by "The Boy Next Door," Van Johnson; Debbie Reynolds, the eternal Girl Scout; freckled Doris; and now, Julie. The public must have its daily dose of sugar. The nice ladies of the screen are usually the hardest to know, and Miss Andrews is the woman nobody knows. She has worked all her life and never lived. She is cautious. Every action is controlled. Every word carefully weighed. She is encased in an iron sheath of charm that is impossible to penetrate. I have never been able to cut through the metal, and neither has anyone else, to my knowledge.

"I never really knew her," said Alfred Hitchcock, who spent three closeted months on the sound stage with her making *Torn Curtain*. Ebullient producer Ross Hunter, who had Julie for five months in *Thoroughly Modern Millie*, glowed, "I love her. She's the greatest performer I have ever worked with, always on time, always knows her dialogue, and always ready to help the picture. But I never really knew her."

Some of the British colony in Hollywood called her "The Hockey Stick," meaning a determined English schoolgirl who goes all out for sports. I call her "The Iron Butterfly."

Robert Wise, her director for *Star!* and *The Sound of Music,* the most successful film in the history of motion pictures (it has made about $125 million), explained her popularity with the public to me. "It's her smile, her honesty, her lack of subterfuge and phoniness. She has contact with the audience. She's the kind of lady who would never blow her temper in public." When I pressed for more details of what he knew of her private life, Mr. Wise, who worked with her for a total of two years, confessed that he had rarely seen her away from the studio.

James Garner, who costarred with Miss Andrews in *The Americanization of Emily,* pondered the question of her personality and advised me, "If you're looking for something you don't see on the surface, stop looking. You won't find it." We both agreed that what we see on the surface we like.

"Have you ever seen her lose her temper?" I asked.

"Never," he replied promptly. "But I can usually tell when she is put out."

"How?" I persisted.

"By a sort of tightening up, and even more reserve."

I have seen her "put out" twice. She never really forgave Jack Warner, in spite of the smiling smoke screen, when he chose Audrey Hepburn for the film version of *My Fair Lady* instead of Julie, who originated the role on Broadway. I didn't believe her publicly professed pleasure that Audrey had won the role. Her real emotions exploded, albeit charmingly, when she made a speech at the Academy Awards accepting the Oscar as Best Actress of 1964 for *Mary Poppins.* After thanking everyone she sweetly thanked Jack Warner "above all the rest, for making this award possible." If he had signed her as Eliza Doolittle as she had wanted with all her professional heart and soul, she would not have played Mary Poppins, but she still would have won the gold statuette as Eliza, for which Audrey was not even nominated.

Hollywood opinion was outraged with Warner's rejection of Julie. But Jack had paid $5.5 million for the Alan Jay Lerner-Frederick Loewe stage musical and thought he was doing the right thing by putting an established actress with Rex Harrison, who had not wanted Julie in the Broadway production. During the stage rehearsals Broadway buzzed with rumors that Julie would be replaced. Moss Hart had seen her in *The Boy Friend* and had chosen her for the role. But this was on a different level and her limitations were showing. She simply could not grasp what Eliza was about. There were stories of Julie collapsing in tears, the only time I have heard of Julie weeping. Something had to be done before the show opened and Moss did it. He pleaded, "Let me have her for several days alone," and spent the days and nights hammering his conception of the part into her head. It worked, and we had a new Broadway star.

But films are something else. No one knew if she had the magic that must emanate from the screen to the audience. Julie had been in Hollywood in 1956 to appear in a television show with Bing Crosby and had caused not the slightest ripple. She disliked Hollywood then, she told me in her musical voice. As far as Hollywood was concerned, it was mutual. It was a double stroke of luck for Julie when Mr. Warner refused her for his film. Not only would she not have made *Mary Poppins,* but she could not have starred in *The Sound of Music,* which overlapped in production with *My Fair Lady.*

I didn't know she was annoyed with me until she refused an interview. I had committed *the* crime. I had peeped into her private life and stated in a magazine story that she was separated from her husband, Tony Walton, who had been her childhood sweetheart and whom she had married at nineteen after some girlish flirtations with "an acrobat" and an "older man." She would never go into it more than that.

When I wrote my story, Julie and Tony had already been separated for a year, not only by distance but in marital fact. He had designed the sets and costumes for *Mary Poppins,* and all was merry as a marriage bell while they lived together in Hollywood. With her success the atmosphere changed, as often happens when the wife is enormously successful and the husband has to decide whether he will live in his wife's shadow or, as in the case of Tony, ply his trade elsewhere. For Mr. Walton, elsewhere was New York and London.

Julie's reply to the rumors of a breakup was to look sweetly amazed. She had previously told me with sincerity and warmth, "The rumors aren't true, although we're apart a lot. This of course creates some problems." They had a joint agreement, she revealed, not to make demands on the other. "This way we have the best of all worlds," which she found rather marvelous. In a similar interview with Phyllis Battelle, the columnist had noted that Julie sorted her thoughts carefully before she spoke and when she did, the words came tumbling out "swiftly and precisely." Precisely. This girl always thinks twice before she speaks, and the spontaneous words that tumble out are the careful result of what she has decided to say.

Tony came back occasionally to visit their child, Emma Kate, but I was sure of the separation and the ultimate breakup of the marriage when Julie bought an expensive home in Beverly Hills. I thought, why would she be putting down roots in California when only the year before she had bought a big house in a London suburb that she and Tony had not yet lived in? I made some discreet inquiries—everything concerning Miss Andrews has a top-level aura of discretion—and learned my hunch was right. They were separated. This was soon after the release of *The Sound of Music,* in which she played a novitiate nun. Julie was worried. A torn marriage would tarnish the image of 100 per cent purity and womanly understanding mixed with a dash of charming heedlessness that she was projecting so beautifully in the film.

This is a normal anxiety for the saints of the screen. It was because Ingrid Bergman had been presented to the public as a wholesome, pure personality that the flight from her husband, Dr. Peter Lindstrom, and her letter to Roberto Rossellini—"I'm just a little Swedish girl and I love you"—was judged so harshly at the time. Elizabeth Taylor can do it and the world will say, "But, of course," but not Julie or Ingrid, who, before Rossellini, had so recently starred as Saint Joan, the Maid.

Lucille Ball hesitated for years before breaking up her marriage to Desi Arnaz. It was fine to fight on their TV show, because it was all in fun and always came out right at the end. But a real-life divorce from Desi could shatter the profitable fun and friendliness in the series. In addition, there was the horrendous task of dividing the community property. This fact has clamped many a battling Hollywood couple in unbearable tandem for years before the lawyers finally sort everything out.

Sometimes the celluloid sweethearts of America are grateful when a gossip columnist hints there is something amiss with their supposed bliss. Not too long after Shirley was married to actor John Agar—I attended the magnificent ceremony in the Wilshire Methodist Church in Los Angeles—there were rumors of trouble. It seemed impossible that the Good Ship Lollipop was foundering. But I checked—their best friends or press agents are usually the best source—and I was reasonably sure it was true. Not long after my story appeared, I was horrified to find myself at the same table with Shirley at a party at Holiday House in Malibu. But Shirley greeted me affectionately and was most friendly. I nearly fell into the soup when she said quietly, "I'm very grateful to you for the story." "You are?" I said wonderingly. Usually they scream about how they'll get you if it's the last thing they do. "Yes," she continued, "it will prepare the public for my divorce."

Miss Andrews was not grateful. She has her own method of preparing her public, and it did not include a blunt unauthorized statement from a columnist. I believe my story retarded the actual announcement by a couple of years. *The Sound of Music* received mixed notices. Judith Crist in the *New York Herald Tribune* slashed it to bits, but it was doing tremendous business. Julie waited until the film was in its third year before coming into the open with a brief paragraph written by her press agent. "The varying demands of our careers have kept Tony and me apart for long periods of time, thus placing obvious strains upon our marriage. It has therefore become clear that a divorce will be in the best interests of all concerned." With the usual addendum that they respected each other and would always be good friends.

Julie is expected to marry Blake Edwards, her director for *Darling Lili* and also for *Say It with Music*. Blake, who started his Hollywood career in high style with Cary Grant and Tony Curtis in *Operation Petticoat*, hasn't had a hit since *The Pink Panther*. His film for Warner's, *The Great Race*, with Natalie Wood and Tony Curtis, was a $16-million disaster. *The Party*, with Peter Sellers, was a fizzle. To direct Julie is a tremendous break for Mr. Edwards, and if the films are successful, he will be on top again. But working with the woman you are planning to marry is sometimes bad for the production. I remember Kirk Douglas' howls of anguish during the filming of *Strangers When We Meet* with Kim Novak, who had announced her engagement to its director, Richard Quine. Kirk didn't have a chance and neither did the film.

And while Julie and Mr. Edwards hold hands and appear to be in love, I am wondering whether he will still be head man in her life if he doesn't come through successfully as her director. It isn't that she would love him less, but it would be hard to fit a director who failed into her successful career, as it was with Mr. Walton, and as it has proved difficult for so many actresses (and actors) before her—Doris Day with her first husband, and Shelley Winters with hers.

Julie hasn't had time to become a woman of the world, and I doubt whether she would ever want to be. She is limited in some areas because the blinders of work since childhood have kept her straight ahead on the narrow road of ambition, not diverging to the right or the left. She was supporting her family with her voice when she was twelve. Her discoverer was a theatrical agent, Charlie Tucker, who took a generous portion of her earnings for his services. "Uncle Charlie," she called him. She dropped him when she made *Mary Poppins* and signed with the all-powerful MCA. Her real name is Julie Wells. Her parents divorced when she was four years old and she took the name of her stepfather, Ted Andrews. Dancing and singing in *Humpty Dumpty,* the Christmas pantomime at the London Hippodrome in 1948, she met her future husband. She was thirteen. Tony was fourteen. At one time in a semiexpansive mood, Julie said of Tony, "He has never let me down." Has she let him down? I won't attempt an answer. A career is like another man in a woman's life, and vice versa. You can't hurt a marriage if it's good, and when a woman prefers a career to her marriage, it means the marriage wasn't very good.

As a child on the road in vaudeville, the little girl from the prim suburbs of London was always working and always polite to the other performers. A nice girl never loses her temper; a nice girl knows her songs and her dances; she is never rude. She always smiles prettily and says good morning and good evening. She does her very best. When I asked Robert Wise if he thought she had changed much between the three years of *The Sound of Music* and *Star!* he replied, "Not really. Perhaps she has become more confident. With the first film, she would suggest, 'Could we?' In *Star!* it was 'Why don't we' or 'I'd like to do that number again. I'd like to make it warmer.'" Always polite, but now more positive.

Except for becoming more reserved and more confident, Julie is one of the few stars I know who has not changed at all. There is the same honesty and sincerity and unsophistication. When she heard during *Thoroughly Modern Millie* that Ross Hunter loved tapioca pudding, she had her wardrobe woman, who was a good cook, make him tapioca pudding until the stuff was coming out of his ears. She rehearsed on her own time with Bea Lillie, who had not made a film in years, and whom she had admired as a child. Julie came to the studio on Saturday, her day off, to read off-camera dialogue to the other stars who would shortly have to report for other assignments. At the very beginning the director suggested it would be easier for Julie to perform on a closed set. She replied, "No, I'm flattered that people want to see me."

"She's basically the nicest girl in films and has no idea she's a big star," Mr. Hunter told me, dreaming of the big *Millie* grosses. One time I saw the thirty-four-year-old actress tripping toward the sound stage fresh as a new morning with the sun glinting on her head. "Your hair looks lovely," I told her. "I just washed it," she laughed, running her fingers through her short locks—just the way she does on the screen. You can't tell where the actress ends and the woman of real life begins. The entire package is 100 per cent wholesomeness. The girl you would like to find next door. Once she confessed, "I'd love to go to night clubs and parties, but I'm always too tired." The last part of this sentence is a clue to the part of her personality she keeps hidden. She is tired all the time. A psychiatrist will tell you that perennial fatigue is an indication of concealed anxiety.

Behind the wholesomeness and the composed exterior, Julie Andrews is overanxious and worried. Three years ago she started twice weekly visits to a psychiatrist in whose waiting room she had her first accidental meeting with Mr. Edwards. Julie explained to a friend why she was undergoing treatment: "I want to find out about me." A good reason for a person who has bottled up her feelings since childhood. Also a psychiatrist is like a confessional box. He will not reveal what he hears. Secrecy about her emotions is of the utmost importance to Julie. She must maintain the façade of a completely controlled woman, the ideal of British suburbia. You do nothing to cause anything but the nicest comments on your behavior. You do all the right things. Julie was asked once, "Don't you ever get mad?"

"When I do," she replied primly, "I stand in front of a mirror in my bedroom and rant at myself." Thank God for that. I had thought she was not human. At least she explodes at someone, even though it is herself. Alone, she can release some of the tension and the superhuman control she maintains when others are around.

She never complains about her work although she worries about every new project. This is understandable in view of the fact that she has rarely had a flop. Almost everybody has one sooner or later, and each time Julie starts a new project she wonders, "Will this be it?" She has been in show business long enough to know that it can happen, and she is in mortal dread of it happening to her. *Torn Curtain* with Paul Newman for Hitchcock was not successful, and she was almost, but not quite, unladylike about the experience. "She was miscast," Hitchcock told me. "They said 'she's hot' and they pay me a lot of money and I thought, if she's so hot, she might be good for the film. She was not." I asked Julie, "If anyone but Hitchcock had asked you to do the film, would you have accepted?" She thought carefully, then said, "No," adding, "It was a bad picture."

This is strong language for Miss Andrews. *Hawaii,* which paid Julie her first million dollars on the screen, was a poor picture in my opinion, and bad for her image. Julie Andrews groaning in childbirth and throwing up at sea was wrong for the actress who is at her best dispensing great gobs of open-faced friendliness and that marvelous smile.

I believe that Miss Andrews is striving for more depth in her private life. Recently she received a letter from a girl who was doing a piece on Julie for her high-school paper. "Are you really Miss Goody-Two-Shoes?" the skeptical student asked.

"Oh, dear," said Julie. "What do you do with this kind of image?"

The question is, can she change it? I don't think so.

7)

Marlon ("School's Out")

Marlon Brando has a sense of humor that can be funny, child-like, or sadistic. One of his practical jokes changed the course of my life. It was 1952 and I was between marriages. A very rich man whose wife had recently died was courting me. He had not been happy with his wife in the last years, but he had married her when he was nineteen—he was now in his late fifties—and was used to being married. He told me he had been in love with me since I had met him with his wife during the war, on the Super Chief to Los Angeles. The way was clear for him to marry me and I was willing. Only one thing bothered him. I had always seemed so dedicated to my Hollywood career, so ambitious in my work.

"Would you be happy without your column?" he asked, after telling me he wished to make me his wife. He had a twenty-six-room apartment on Fifth Avenue in New York and an estate in Connecticut. He and his late wife had loved to travel, and he wanted to repeat the whole pattern with me.

"Oh, yes," I assured him vehemently. I liked him, although I was not in love with him, but I thought, with all that money I could easily make the transition; and I was, oh, Lord, so weary of the agents and the actors and the prying into other people's lives.

"Let's talk about it over dinner," I said, taking him possessively by the hand and leading him to the dining room. I had an excellent cook, and I knew I could swing it before we got to the dessert. We had just sat down when the phone rang. I can never resist the compelling call of a telephone.

"Excuse me, I'll be right back," I said, kissing him on the cheek and dashing into the next room, which I used as my office.

"This is Marlon," mumbled the unmistakable voice. "I thought you'd like to know I'm getting married tonight." He hung up before I could ask where and to whom. "I've got to check it through. I won't be long. Why don't you start on the soup?" I told my future husband. For the next three hours I was calling everyone I knew who might have information on the marriage and/or Marlon's whereabouts. I telephoned all over Hollywood, trying to find his close friends Jay Kantor and Wally Cox. They were in New York, I learned. I called New York. I called and called and no one knew anything and I could not find Marlon. When I finally gave up, my millionaire had finished a solo dinner and was leaning back in an armchair in the living room. He smiled at me and said sadly, "You see what I mean. This is your life. You would never be happy without your work." My assurances fell on deaf ears. We still saw each other when I was in New York, but there was no further mention of marriage. At one of his lavish cocktail parties, I introduced him to his present wife.

Marlon was not getting married that night. His secret ceremony with Anna Kashfi did not take place until four years later.

Marlon's humor is mostly of the little-boy kind. He will stick a piece of paper into the side of his shoe, raise one leg over the other so that you see it, and when you bend down to read what is written on the paper, you will find "What the fuck are you looking at?" He watches you through half-lowered lids, then giggles like a kid.

When he was training to portray a paraplegic for his first film, *The Men* (he came to Hollywood in 1949 when the advent of television was causing apprehension among the film-makers, and Gable had slipped into middle-age), Marlon, the new young glamour boy in reverse, to understand his role, lived at the Van Nuys Hospital for Paraplegics, spending his time in a wheel chair in and out of the hospital. On one occasion, returning in a taxi, as the driver was setting up the chair for the cripple, Marlon jumped out and ran off on his own steam. For extra surprise, he performed a brief tap dance before disappearing into the hospital. Another time Marlon was in the wheel chair in a Ventura Boulevard bar with some of his cronies when a do-gooder lady came in. She did not recognize the actor, but she wanted to help the poor paraplegic. "You can be healed if you have faith," she told him earnestly, and she read to him from the scriptures, which she just happened to have with her. Her face shone with uplift until Marlon sprang from the wheel chair exuding frenzied glory, and raced up and down the bar, then collapsed with laughter into the chair.

When he was filming *Sayonara* in Japan, his constant arguments with the director, Joshua Logan, had delayed the film, but they had finally neared the finish line. Only three more days. "That morning," Mr. Logan told me, "Marlon came in with his right arm in a sling. You can imagine our consternation."

"Don't blame my stand-in," Marlon said, "we were just wrestling around. It's my fault. I started it."

"Is it broken?" Logan asked anxiously.

"I think so," he replied.

Marlon was in every remaining scene, and the director thought he would have to shut down. "Can't you remove the sling for a few minutes at a time?" Josh begged him.

"No, the doctor says I must keep my arm in the sling at all times or I'll be crippled for life."

"If I change the setup so the sling doesn't show, could you move your fingers a little bit?" Logan pleaded.

"Well," said Marlon, "I reckon I could," twitching his

fingers violently and roaring like a twelve-year-old. The joke, Josh told me, took two years off his life.

Marlon was sipping tea in the foyer of the fashionable Prince de Galles Hotel in Paris. A passing waiter inadvertently poured some boiling hot water onto Marlon's lap. He jumped up, yelping with pain. The waiter was all apologies. After Marlon sat down, shifting his pants from the injured area, he said reflectively, "I'd like to write the headline for this story—Brando Scalds Balls at Prince de Galles."

Brando enjoys his pranks, but when they are perpetrated against him, it is a joke of a different color. He bleeds a bright red. He will never forgive Truman Capote, who he says tricked him into devastating self-revelation and wrote every word verbatim for *The New Yorker*. The talented little gnome with the high squeaky voice is the darling of the international jet set, and Marlon was flattered when Truman made the journey to Japan in 1956 to pay his respects to the star he admired above all others. Marlon, pleased with the lavish compliments, reciprocated, telling the author how much he enjoyed his writings and talked and talked. Marlon seemed depressed. Capote wondered, "What do *you* have to worry about?" He told Marlon of his own anxieties and his strange childhood, and about his mother. Marlon was sympathetic and told Truman of his childhood, and about his mother.

There was never a notebook or a pen or pencil. Truman has total recall and a perfect ear for dialogue. It was all on such a friendly basis. Sometimes the questions were so probing they aroused a slight suspicion in Marlon's mind. He had read some of Truman's brilliant dissections of celebrities.

"Don't worry," squeaked his new friend, "I'm not going to write any of this." But as soon as Capote reached home, he put it all down on paper. And when the amazingly accurate piece in *The New Yorker* appeared, only Capote's conversation about his own family was omitted. Marlon went into shock, as much by what he considered the betrayal as by the microscopically cruel story.

While he never reads anything about himself in the columns, and if anyone brings him a newspaper with an item about him he covers his eyes with his hands and insists, "Take it away," he read every word of the Capote story. He raged and swore he would find the little bastard if it were the last action of his life. Later, when he had cooled somewhat, he was asked, "What will you do when you get your hands on him?" Marlon thought a while, then said, "I'll beat him to death with a wet noodle." I've never heard of Marlon resorting to physical violence. He's as gentle as Sinatra is violent. I once saw him pick a bee off a chair, cup it in both hands, and release it outside the sound stage.

My first encounter with Marlon was during his New York stage appearance in *A Streetcar Named Desire,* when I had asked Jessica Tandy, his costar, to introduce us and he had depressed me by asking her if I were her mother. I hadn't known that she disliked Brando. His pranks had sometimes ruined her best scenes. One evening she noted great restlessness with the people in the audience, and some giggles, when they should have been absorbed in what she was saying. She turned around and a nonsmiling Brando had stuck a cigarette up one nostril.

Because Mr. Brando has not made himself available to columnists ("Why are they so interested in me?" he demanded of a press agent during *Morituri,* and his court battles with Anna Kashfi), I have done the next best thing, talked with his friends and associates to understand what goes on behind the mumble and the sullen exterior. Everyone with whom I spent long hours agreed that Brando is self-destructive.

"Marlon is four people," said one of his intimates. "The Prankster, The Brooding Man, The Freedom Fighter, and The Disappointed Actor."

There is a fifth man, the self-indulgent Marlon. He indulges his desires of the moment, no matter what they are, although always trying to maintain a façade of inscrutability. He used to drink beer. Now he prefers vodka, but he doesn't want anyone to know, so he drinks it from a tea cup. When he wants a woman, he has to have her. He used to say, "I can knock off any dame in a couple of hours." He means what he says when he says it, but can change his mind later, and he can admit a mistake. Unlike Sinatra, he does not behave as though he were god.

Sam Spiegel, who produced *On the Waterfront,* told me, "I have always liked Marlon very much. He was a tortured man in the early days and he was great on the screen. When he ceased being tortured, he had to pseudo-torture himself in order to function." Sam had him in *The Chase* in 1966, and the pseudo was showing. "But he tried," said Sam, who rarely says anything bad about anyone. It was a different Brando. At times I thought he was sleepwalking. He gave an adequate performance, but the soul wasn't there. "He was a shy star when he was successful," said Mr. Spiegel. He is still shy but less successful.

Marlon was to have starred in *Lawrence of Arabia,* but Spiegel wanted a new face for Lawrence and he created a new star, Peter O'Toole. Without naming names Sam sighed, "You make a star, you make a monster."

If Marlon is more confused now than when he started as a stage actor in New York, he can blame Hollywood, which gave him too much fame and money too quickly. He has a life-size guilt complex about all this. Deep down, he is appalled at the ease with which he made it. His sense of righteousness (he was born with Satan on his ear) is outraged when his acting is praised, when he knows it was lousy. He is intelligent and doesn't believe he's worth the money or the attention. There is nothing of Cary Grant's carefulness with a buck about Marlon. At one time his bill for flowers to the ladies he courted was $1,500 a month. He's a spender and often hard up for ready cash in spite of the million dollars he received for *The Fugitive Kind,* based on Tennessee Williams' *Orpheus Descending,* which he refused as a play. It was the first million dollars ever paid a movie star. Later Universal paid him a million dollars for his Pennebaker Film company. The deal included X number of films from Marlon, including the ghastly *Countess from Hong Kong*, which no one forced him to make, but he yearned to work with Chaplin. Perhaps he thought the spluttering spark of his own talent could be reignited by Chaplin's genius. He didn't know that Chaplin's lamp had also flickered low. If Marlon had not insisted, the film would never have been made. Chaplin owned the *Countess* for thirty years and had been waiting all those years for a Brando.

It was a bad experience for everyone except Chaplin, who adored his bad film. He laughed at every scene on the sound stage and roared with mirth over the rushes in the Pinewood studio projection room. When I was on the set I felt the tension: Charlie acting out the parts, the two principals (Marlon and Sophia Loren) watching without enthusiasm. Usually there were several of Charlie's nine children on the set (most of them appeared in the film), and always Mrs. Chaplin, the former Oona O'Neill. After a scene Charlie would turn to her for approval. She always gave it.

I was not there when Marlon, playing The Prankster, stopped his leading lady cold during a love scene, looked searchingly up her nose, and said, "You have black hair in your nostrils." She never really liked him after that.

When Marlon was ill and in the hospital, the cast and crew took up a collection to send him a basket of flowers. Sophia was the only member of the company who did not contribute. She has never been a hypocrite.

Brando disliked Chaplin after he realized the awfulness of the film. Behind Charlie's back he ridiculed him, and behind Marlon's back Charlie did imitations of his leading man that were not flattering. Charlie once said to him, "If only you could dig down into yourself and gather the talent you possess." But because of his drive toward destruction, apparently he won't do it, although I am sure it is still there.

Marlon's treatment of women would have interested Freud. He seems to enjoy humiliating them even when he needs them. I remember a story in London with a by-line by Josiane Berenger, a French fisherman's daughter. Marlon and Josiane had met at a cocktail party in New York and like all the women there, she had tried to attract him. He ignored her, rudely and deliberately. When she was about to leave, he blocked her departure. "You're coming with me," he told her flatly. On their second evening together, he told Josiane to prepare dinner for three. The guest, according to her story, was the girl whom everyone knew he had been previously romancing.

He is fascinated by dark brunettes, and he has four children to prove it: a boy and a girl from Movita, the Mexican actress, which marriage was recently annulled; a son with Tarita, the pretty Tahitian girl he met in his *Mutiny on the Bounty* disaster (Movita was in the 1935 version with Clark Gable and Charles Laughton); and Christian, from his marriage to Anna Kashfi, whom he believed was an East Indian when they married. Later a story appeared in a London newspaper that her parents were Welsh and she was about as Indian as Paddy's pig. When reporters pressed Marlon for a statement, he told them what to do with themselves, but he prodded Anna to reveal her origins to his press agents.

"Go on, tell them."

"You son of a bitch," she replied. "When they ask you, you say it's none of their business, but you want me to tell them so *they* can tell the press." And she told Marlon what *he* could do with himself. It coincided with what he told the press. The amusing side of this sad little story is that he had originally wanted to marry the mother of Christian in Arizona but, at the time, mixed marriages were forbidden in that state and the ceremony took place in California.

After the child arrived, it was a question of a little time before they separated and divorced. He loves his children and spends considerable time with them. How he hated his appearances in court battling with Miss Kashfi for the physical custody of Christian, whom he had removed from her home! He was working in *The Chase,* and every time he left the set for any reason, the process servers grabbed him. It did not help his performance in the film.

I'll be surprised if Marlon marries again. He is very sensitive, and I doubt whether he could take further humiliation of this kind. "My kids are getting old enough to read," he said recently, "and I don't want the other kids to say to them, 'Your father is a kook.' "

Movita is the woman Marlon needed most. She is only about six years older than he is, but she mothered him from the time they met when he was a very young man. During the filming of *On the Waterfront* in New York, when he was thirty years old, Movita decided she had had enough of the relationship and left him. Marlon was frantic.

Whether Sam Spiegel is right when he says that Marlon gives a better performance when he is deeply unhappy, he *was* magnificent in *On the Waterfront*. Even the grunts were great. Now, most of what he does on the screen is a caricature of his former greatness and he knows this. It tears Marlon apart to give a bad performance, but he can't seem to stop the steam roller.

"And yet," Stanley Shapiro, who wrote and produced *Bedtime Story* with Marlon and David Niven, said to me, "dramatically he's the most talented performer on the screen." Stanley found him cooperative, although other directors have told me he is not. I think it depends on the degree of his trust, and he has trusted very few people in recent years except Elia Kazan and Chaplin, who almost ruined him.

"He loves chaos," said Sidney Furie, who directed him in *The Appaloosa*. "You simply can't get past 'B' in a conversation with Brando, and you can't get him to discuss a script rationally."

Another associate of Marlon's puts this down to a natural slowness. "He's like a string of beads held upside down and you can only count one at a time. Marlon can only grasp one subject. If you want to confuse him, talk about two things at the same time."

According to Mr. Shapiro, he's very intelligent. According to Mr. Furie, "He's disorganized, no discipline at all, a procrastinator. One little scene that should have taken us a few hours to film took ten days. Every day he had another complaint—his tummy ached, his head ached—you should have heard the moans. What a performance! Then he'd be searching for his lines. Anything to procrastinate."

Sometimes, working in the snow, he'd creep up behind an unsuspecting bystander and hit him on the head with a snowball. How Marlon laughed! He would insult the producer with "What the hell do you know?" in front of the crew, laughing when the director shouted, "You may be the star, but you're full of crap." And yet Marlon could also be charming. There was the party on the location in Utah, and the star, all scrubbed up and neatly dressed, danced with everybody's wife and they loved him.

Meeting Mr. Furie in London recently, Marlon surprised him with his friendliness. "It takes me a long time to get to know people," he told him. "I thought you were a phony, a liar, a dirty double-crosser. I discovered you've got the great visual sense of the good directors. Let's do another film."

"Never!" Sidney told me.

On one end of Marlon's scale is talent. On the other, all the destructive elements of his nature which sometimes overbalance the talent and cause him to forget his lines, although his acting technique will see him through. The first time he forgot a line, when he was an enormously important star, the director said, "It's all right, baby, we'll do it again." He thought he was helping Marlon by coddling and spoiling him. "We'll break it up and do it from another angle," he said. But if instead of pampering him the director had bawled him out, had made him study, he might not be in the fix he is today.

Marlon is the original hippie. He was twenty years before his time with his torn shirts, leather jacket, dirty sneakers, and his hatred of authority and affluence. His father, Marlon Brando, Sr., looked like a conservative banker when I met him one lunch time at Paramount.

"How on earth did you have a son like Marlon?" I couldn't help saying. He smiled like a banker who has just refused a loan.

Like many of the stars, Marlon has been good to his parents and his sisters. When he made a hit in Hollywood, he employed his father (who was a salesman of limestone products when Marlon was born in Omaha, Nebraska) to look after his finances. The only time they had words was caused by the confusion over their names. The senior Marlon sometimes received his son's letters. He was always scrupulously careful to send the wrong mail to his son's office. One day he inadvertently opened a letter. After glancing at it—it was from a girl—he wrote across the envelope, "Sorry, Bud, I opened it by mistake." Marlon was furious and came storming at his father.

"This is awful. This has got to stop. You must change your name!"

"Look, Bud," said Dad, "I've had it for thirty-five years longer than you have. If there's going to be any changing, you do it."

The stories of Marlon's slobbiness have not been exaggerated. Neither have his table manners. On location in the desert for part of *One-Eyed Jacks,* father and son were staying in a motel together and Marlon was doing the housekeeping. His father made the mistake of opening the refrigerator and the stench was something awful. He moved out.

Marlon can be a complete gentleman at table when he feels like it. At other times he's like a runner waiting for the signal, then stuffs the food in with both hands. He is always on and off a diet. He believes grapefruit sections at the end of a meal counteract the caloric content of what he has just eaten. To do the job properly, it would have to be a grapefruit as big as the Ritz. He lost ten pounds at the elegant Buxted Park reducing establishment in Sussex, England, before the London and Paris premieres of *Countess.* Then put some back on after the film was launched and sank soon after. He hates being fat, and it is part of the self-indulgence-destructive pattern that he can only control the food intake in spasms of self-hypnosis.

He had a birthday while making a recent film and, as always in sentimental Hollywood, they brought out, on cue, a big cake with candles and sang "Happy Birthday, dear Marlon." The birthday boy was offered a slice. He was on one of his diets and said no.

"Aw, come on." (You know how they plead.) "It's your birthday. One slice won't hurt you." They kept at it and at it with Marlon saying, "No, fellers, no. Really, no." Then suddenly he grabbed a large slice and jammed it down his throat. "When I open a refrigerator door," Marlon says ruefully, "nothing is safe, not even the pipes."

Away from the screen Marlon enjoys impersonating characters, some invented, some based on real people. His favorite role is himself, an exaggerated caricature, with the mumble and bewilderment larger than life. When he is traveling, he likes to appear as a movie version of the FBI—the snap-brim hat, the trench coat, and dark glasses. He believes he is unrecognizable. The "disguise," like Greta Garbo's weird clothes and big floppy hats, merely draws attention to him. He prefers to live in flea bags away from home, although he has a beautiful Japanese-style home in Beverly Hills. (I'd hate to see his ice box there.) When he registers in the second-rate hotels of New York, London, Paris, and Rome, he whimsically signs in as Lord Greystoke, the ancestral name of Tarzan of the Apes, who as you remember came from an aristocratic family in England and was lost in the jungle and raised by the apes. It is amusing, people tell me, to hear the hotel help calling Marlon "Lord Greystoke" or "Yes, your lordship."

He impersonates people because he feels inadequate socially and he is embarrassed by his lack of formal education. His coterie consists of his agent, his make-up man, Phil, who reads scripts with him, and the make-up man's wife. Also his secretary, who has been with him since 1957. This is a predictable pattern with the insecure stars. They feel more comfortable with their press agents and agents and make-up and wardrobe people, whom they can order around, and who will not judge them from a high level, with whom they can let their hair down. It gives them a feeling of being "Duke of my own Domain," as Marlon stated to Mr. Capote. Marlon did not finish high school; he never had the education that his intelligence rated and which might have given him the discipline he lacks. So he imitates the people he admires who are educated. He has lately been aping the producer George Englund. He admires George enormously. He attempts to think like him and dress like him—from being a slob he became a dandy with custom-made shirts and suits. He uses George's phrases, he quotes the same elaborate words—he won't say "lie," it's "prevaricate." He uses George's gestures, and he is such a great inherent actor that he actually *is* George Englund.

During *Streetcar* he became Stanley Kowalski in real life to a revolting degree—the same scratching of his rear and picking his nose, the awful clothes. In *The Young Lions* he dyed his hair blond to look like the Nazi officer he was playing, and while he hates Nazis, he couldn't help making the role sympathetic. Shelley Winters once assured me that actors cannot bear to be hated, and Marlon is no exception. He will take advice about his roles from pipsqueaks. He chooses the movie, then asks for opinions from his companions. In *Mutiny on the Bounty* he should have played Captain Bligh. He made Fletcher Christian foppish and feminine, which Marlon is not. Men react to his virility as much as women do, which he resents (as did Errol Flynn, who disliked being a phallic symbol—although, like Marlon, he used it to good advantage). It drove Errol to drink and Marlon to eating. He wants to be loved and he can be sympathetic and pleasant, but he also believes in some violence in his films. He told Josh Logan at the beginning of *Sayonara*, "I've got to have one brutal scene in every picture." In the last scene Marlon was to find his friend, Red Buttons, and Miyoshi Umeki, the Japanese girl Red had married, dead in a suicide pact. He had wanted to play it tough and domineering, pushing through the crowds of watching Japanese, to burst in on the tragedy. Logan wanted a hush of impending disaster. "That's the most stupid, ridiculous thing," Marlon raged. He finally agreed to do it if the scene was shot two ways. "All right," said Logan, "but let's do it my way first." Marlon came quietly through the silent people, and when he saw his dead friends, he murmured, "Oh, God." It was the most effective scene in the film, as Marlon agreed later. He can go from reverse into low gear without going into neutral. After the shower of critical acclaim for *Sayonara*—four Academy Awards and listed among the ten best pictures of 1957—Marlon wrote Logan a letter saying that several times during the making of the film he thought Logan a bloody idiot, but that in every case Logan was right.

The director would have liked some of this during the making of the movie, when he was painfully aware that his star was making dreadful grimaces at him. "Marlon has the greatest innate talent of our time," Mr. Logan assured me emphatically. "He's a special kind of man with a special kind of ability. He can play anything. His trouble is he believes everyone is trying to belittle him. He hates authority. He distrusts anyone with power—the producer, the director, the writer, the politician in Washington. He only trusts the poor and the unsuccessful. In *Sayonara* we put him with twenty young Japanese girls and at times he was happy." He had told Mr. Logan, "I'll only make the film if I marry the Japanese girl at the end," although this is contrary to the James Michener book. He was playing an American Army major and to marry a Japanese girl would, he thought, help to break American prejudice against miscegenation. It was a gesture against the omnipotent white race.

He is an idealist. He is happiest giving help to the downtrodden Negro. During the civil-rights protests in Washington and Mississippi, Marlon called all over Hollywood, from Charlton Heston to the then sixteen-year-old Portland Mason, asking them to join him in the marches. Charlton went. Porty's parents said, "No, she is too young."

Marlon has been deeply involved in the civil-rights question. Whether he really feels the injustice, as I think he does, or is merely bugging The Establishment, as some of his friends believe, is open to question. He gives money and he will march, but when one of his two partners in Pennebaker Productions suggested a practical way of helping the poor Indian by starring in a film for them (the Indians have a big film industry), Marlon would not. The exasperated associate said, "Marlon, stop worrying about 100 million starving Indians and worry about two Jews who are your partners."

But, after the assassinations of Dr. Martin Luther King and Senator Robert Kennedy, he appeared in projects for various liberal causes.

Marlon is against capital punishment and spent time and money on the protracted Caryl Chessman case. On the night of the execution of the convicted rapist-murderer, Marlon went to San Quentin and picketed outside the prison walls with the other mourners.

Marlon reminds me of a Dickens character. He is so busy giving help in the abstract that he forgets the people under his narcissistic nose. When Richard Harris was to die in the blazing boat in one of the several endings for *Mutiny on the Bounty,* Marlon would not report for work until it was cut out.

" 'I'm the star,' " Richard told me he said, " 'and the star must have the best scenes.' " Perhaps he is right. But the way he went about it was wrong, acting up like a naughty child. The behavior pattern is usually more adult when the ladder to stardom has taken more time to climb. Marlon came out of the stage version of *A Streetcar Named Desire* without the aging process of trying to reach the top. He was Instant Success. He did not know how to react to the Instant Love of the multitudes. He was unsure about himself, and he could not accept the love, indicating, "If they like me, they can't be much good." He wants to be loved, but he is too insecure to accept the gift. The one person he respects above all others is Elia Kazan, the director who made him a star. The reason, in my opinion, why he canceled his promise to star for Kazan in *The Arrangement* was not only that he wished to devote his time to meaningful films, but because he was afraid that if he failed with Kazan there would be nothing left.

8)

Gorgeous George and
Other Lovable Characters

"You are playing with fire," I warned George Hamilton. "You will be in the public eye all the time. You can't take her up, then drop her. It will boomerang." George slowly raised a highly manicured hand to slick down one side of his shining black hair and grinned boyishly.

"You're cute," he said, "you never give up. That's what I like about you."

George genuinely liked Lynda Bird Johnson. As he genuinely liked the Duchess of Bedford's attractive daughter, Catherine; as he enjoyed being with Charlotte Ford. Also Merle Oberon, Gloria Swanson. And me.

Charlie, as the President enjoyed referring to him, is the type of man who always is seen and reported in the company of a well-known woman. Some of these men might even marry the women. I feel they must have a poor opinion of themselves, believing they won't be noticed and admired unless they are bracketed with important women. "Look," they are saying in effect, "look who I've got, look who likes me." So you know the girl must be either a famous beauty or related to a famous man or woman.

In the girl department you can't do better than being seen with the daughter of the President of the United States. And

George ran it for full career mileage. His press agents usually knew when and where he would be with Lynda Bird. He'd say, "This is between us, hey?" and managed to keep a straight face. But they knew the score, and I usually knew just by lifting the phone and calling the Hollywood office that George was in the White House, or New York, or when he was going to the ranch in Texas. No one had to be told when he went to church with Lynda and her family. The world's press fed it to the world.

During this period, every time I saw George, whom I have known since he was seventeen, I asked, "Are you going to marry her?" He always laughed good-naturedly and said, "You know I can't answer that."

Much persevering revealed that "She's a very charming, intelligent girl." Then he would subside into a silent reverie that indicated there was more he could tell me if only Lynda were not the daughter of the President. It drove me almost mad, especially when he teased, "You know any announcement would have to come from the White House."

When the "Will he marry Lynda?" furor was at its height, his press agents in Hollywood naturally wanted the true story and an executive in the office asked the direct question. "George replied," he told me, " 'I enjoy being with Lynda, but I don't want to get married. I don't want to get locked in.' "

The astute p.a. kept this statement confidential and went along with the guessing game, telling inquiring reporters, "I don't really know. I've never asked him."

It kept the publicity pot—I almost said plot—boiling. A press agent in the New York office was more candid. He also knew that George was not in love with Lynda and had no plans for marriage. He bet me $10 to my $5 that the ceremony would never take place.

I have never underestimated the power of a woman, and I was betting on Lynda, who, from all Washington accounts and from what I saw of them in Hollywood, was mad about the boy. Her father was not, as everyone seemed to know, and that was manna from heaven for George, who was determined to see Lynda and still maintain his bachelor status, plus the publicity he loves and makes no bones about. "It's an actor's lifeblood," he told me many times. The question was, how long could he maintain the delicate situation?

It exploded in his face in the summer of 1967 when Lynda Bird came to London where she stayed at the home of the American Ambassador and his wife for several weeks. It was expected that George, who was perambulating around France and Spain, would fly at once to England to see Lynda. He had made longer flights to be with her in the United States. But he knew that time had run out. He must either put up or shut up. And he was not ready to propose. While Lynda went to parties in London, George allowed himself to be photographed with well-known beauties in Europe. After one of their many telephone calls, he flew in on a Sunday and took Lynda to dinner at the Trattoria Terrazio in Soho with Sammy Davis and Peter Lawford. The next morning he checked out of the Connaught Hotel and flew back to Spain. Whatever they discussed that evening, it did not include plans for marriage. They both knew it was over although when he returned to the United States, George continued to be mysterious about whether he was or was not seeing her— until the stories of her attachment to Captain Charles Robb appeared in the public prints and then there was no need for him to say anything.

I was present during Lynda's first visit to George's twenty-room home, Grayhall, in Beverly Hills. It had been built by Douglas Fairbanks, Sr., for Mary Pickford in the early days of their marriage, before they bought Pickfair, where they reigned as King and Queen of Hollywood until the inevitable divorce. I had been in New York and London and had heard the Lynda-George rumors. I decided to see George as soon as I was in Hollywood again. I spotted him the Monday night of the Variety Clubs Banquet for Prince Philip, who was raising money for his favorite charity, the Boys Clubs of England. I snaked through the other guests (who had paid

$100 and more to attend the affair), tapped George on the shoulder, and said, "I'd like to see you very soon. How about lunch on Wednesday?" (I have learned over the years to be definite, never "Let's get together sometime.")

"Okay," he replied, "I'll call you."

"Give me your number," I said. If he didn't call me by Wednesday morning, I was going to call him.

On Tuesday night I was watching the local news on television and nearly fell down when the commentator announced that Miss Lynda Bird Johnson was coming to Hollywood on Thursday and would stay in the home of Mr. Hamilton and be chaperoned by his mother, the handsomely dark Anne Spaulding Hamilton. This was more than I had hoped for. His call came at eleven o'clock on Wednesday morning. He arranged to meet me in front of the Beverly Hills Hotel, then take me in his rented 1967 Rolls-Royce to his house in the hills behind the hotel. (My poor sense of direction is well known. I have started on many journeys and never arrived. Even in a house I don't always know where the exit is. I say good-by and stride into the closet.)

"When I heard that Lynda was coming, I thought you'd cancel," I said when I was safely inside the house.

"I did think of canceling," he confessed, "but I discussed it with Lynda—she read some of the nice things you wrote about us in the *Washington Star*—and she said it was okay."

I asked careful questions, always trying for the big story. George laughingly fielded those that touched on the possibility of marriage, but he could not resist telling me of all the plans he had made for Lynda's long weekend with him. "On Friday, I'm giving a cocktail party to introduce her to my friends. It has to be private, of course," he said, looking reflectively at me, "only for my friends." This seemed to depress him. Then he brightened and said, almost defiantly, "You're a friend and you're invited. You'll be the only member of the press there."

Marvelous, I thought, it would be another scoop. I have always preferred the excitement of an exclusive story to some of the fanciful stuff that goes into a column. George filled me in on the details of the party. Also the names of the people he was inviting to the dinner for twelve he was giving for Lynda at his home on Saturday night. He sent for his cook to give me a detailed account of the menu. Then he took me upstairs to show me the suite of rooms he had allocated for Lynda. I could barely wait to get home to wire the story to my syndicate.

Somewhere between the time he invited me and the actual cocktail party, George must have realized that among his intimate friends were some other members of the press. When I arrived, I found Mike Connolly, the late gossip columnist for the *Hollywood Reporter,* Army Archerd, the gossip columnist for *Daily Variety,* elderly society columnist Cobina Wright, whom George had often escorted to parties, and several other assorted members of the fourth estate. It was difficult getting into the house through the platoons of television cameras from all the networks and the dozens of photographers and reporters blocking the entrance. "Well," I thought, "he couldn't really keep this party a secret." But I was completely disillusioned when the ever suave and smiling George brought Lynda to the front door and opened it wide, and posed and posed with her for the whirring and clicking cameras. He answered questions while Lynda Bird smiled shyly, and when she was asked what she thought of George's rather unusual house, she replied, "It's like a movie set." "The thing about George," his Hollywood press agent told me, "is that he would poll the world for advice and then ignore it. He would tell us no publicity and then he himself would invite the press."

George, who is an agreeable person to have around, is totally ambitious. During the exciting eighteen months of being seen with Lynda, his career zoomed. When the guessing game was over, there was only one way for it to go. Without the possibility that George would be the President's son-in-law, the press literally yawned in his face. There was a slight flare of interest when it was known, and he let it be known, that Lynda Bird, a gracious girl, had invited him to her wedding to Marine Captain Charles Robb. At the time, George was starring on the road in *Bye Bye, Birdie.* It was not to be "bye bye, George." How to make the wedding in Washington with the publicity that is mother's milk to this boy and make it back in time to Chicago for the show? He was pricing Lear jet rentals to stand by in Washington to fly him back to Chicago when his kindhearted producer gave him the night off and he was thus able to stay for the reception as well as attend the nuptials.

George isn't in too many films these days. And the lack of clamor for his movie services could also be because his recent movies were flops. His *Jack of Diamonds* was dreadful. And it was a question whether his *Long Ride Home* with Glenn Ford for Columbia could be released. Actually he hasn't made a good film since *The Light in the Piazza* in Florence, Italy, with Olivia de Havilland and Yvette Mimieux. He was good as the lightweight, elegant, man about town. (George was the first to wear Cardin suits—long flared jackets and wide lapels.) Another thing worked against George. He became the butt of too many jokes. This is a fungus to be avoided if you want to be accepted as a serious actor or actress. Jane Russell's bust was a good peg for her career at the beginning. She wasn't a bad actress, but the bust was a bust for longevity in pictures, and as soon as she left the warm haven of her contract with Howard Hughes (who is nearing the end of his payments of $1,000 per week on her 20-year-payment stretch with him), she skidded downhill on her film front.

Every comedian was making jokes about Hamilton's high-life romance—Red Skelton, Jack Benny, Johnny Carson, Merv Griffin, and Bob Hope, who is a master of the satirical quip. George was begging for it when he brought the glamorized Lynda to Hollywood's most publicized event, the Academy Awards. He had called George Masters to come posthaste to the house to fix her hair and make-up (Masters charges $100 a visit and is worth it). All eyes were on Lynda at the big show, but I was wondering what the President was thinking when Bob joked, with 60 million people watching and listening, that someone had given the President, but not Lynda, a watch, as she already had a Hamilton.

Lynda was beautiful that night with the inner glow of a woman who is with the man she would rather be with than any other. George was happy to have so much enthralling limelight, and he smiled at Bob's humorous remarks. I doubt whether LBJ did. He had not wanted his daughter to appear so publicly with Hamilton, who was in trouble with the newspapers over his draft status. George had overplayed his hand. His blatant publicity tactics had irritated the press who made a Roman holiday of his military deferment. It is true he was and is supporting his mother and for a time his two brothers, but did he have to do it in such extravagant style—a butler, a cook, a gardener, cars, a movie-star home, his poor old mother clothed in Paris gowns, his gambling losses in the casinos of Las Vegas and London. Perhaps he thought he could get away with it because he had always led a charmed life. His father was Spike Hamilton, a famed band leader of the '30s and '40s, and life was good. And when it was not, George had always managed to live elegantly. His brother, David, told me, "George is the kind of person who, if he were marooned on a desert island, would come back to civilization on a yacht with three pretty girls." You can bet they would be rich and/or well known.

Hamilton's career problem—he is not a bad actor—is that he wants to be Cary Grant. Many have hoped and failed, including Tony Curtis, whose home, when I visited him during his marriage to Janet Leigh, was filled with photographs of Cary. The impossible dream nearly ruined Tony. There is only one Mr. Grant. The imitation can never be as good as the real thing. And Tony almost committed career suicide with some of the absurd comedies in which he was about as funny as a maddened elephant and as much like Mr. Grant as I am.

The cold draft on the career of Mr. Curtis occurred by coincidence at the same time as the hiatus in Rock Hudson's popularity. Rock, who was then Roy Fitzgerald, had started at the Universal Studio in 1948, a few weeks before the arrival of Bernie Schwartz, who was to become famous as Tony Curtis. They were the last actors in Hollywood to receive a star build-up. With the advent of television, Hollywood abandoned its people who were not under contract. Tony and Rock were both handsome. Neither could act, but they had charm and eagerness and what they had came through on the screen. At lunch time they were usually in the studio café keeping a sharp lookout for the press to whom they were enchantingly honest and natural. They have come full circle because they are again available to reporters and eager for the publicity that had originally brought them to the attention of the public, with its cash-and-carry rewards.

It isn't only the publicity. You can rave about new personalities until the cows come home, but unless there is a film continuity (and they don't all have to be good, but they must keep hitting the public with them), they will not be stars. They call someone a star today after his first film. No one is a star until he or she has appeared in at least five films. To be a star you must also know how to handle yourself with the public and press because there is no one to do it for you. Today the major studios and independent producers sell the picture, not the star. In the old days the pampered darlings were coddled, studied, nursed along and given the best available protection. In the '30s and '40s, if a star had one hit every six months, he could keep going. Bosses like Louis B. Mayer, Cecil B. de Mille, and Jack Warner would stand for no nonsense, not even from Gable or Tracy or Bette Davis. If they refused a film, they were suspended. There was enormous discipline. Today there is none.

In recent years Tony and Rock have been swimming in perilous waters and it seemed that they might be submerged. Whether or not they make it to shore again depends on several really successful films now. Tony was good in "The Boston Strangler," Rock fine in "Ice Station Zebra."

But the first dip into Hollywood with Universal as lifeguard was refreshing fun. They were as happy as two kids on a first trip to the beach. Tony, with his merry smile, dark curly hair, and blue eyes fringed with black lashes (he would have been pretty, but for his unmistakable masculinity). Rock was as rugged-looking as his new name, and this was deceptive. Beneath the façade he is soft as a new tabby. They both fell in love early in the game. Rock was smitten first. We were in a passageway in the old publicity department which you entered from the street (it was as it had been in the days of the founder, "Uncle" Carl Laemmle, Sr.), and Rock poured out his feelings for Vera-Ellen, a dancer-turned-actress, a painfully thin girl who didn't think much of Rock's prospects as a future provider. "She doesn't want to marry an actor," Rock moaned. "She thinks the acting profession is too precarious." His anguish made him tremble. Later, when Rock was number-one at the box office for five years, I wondered what Vera-Ellen, who married a not-so-rich member of the great House of Rothschild, was thinking.

His fame did not swell Rock's head as it seemed to swell Tony's. But even Rock finally shed the man who had discovered him, agent Henry Willson, as Tony had dropped his discoverer, Joyce Selznick. Rock had married Mr. Willson's secretary, Phyllis, a few days before his thirtieth birthday and as suddenly dropped her via divorce. The marriage was always considered a marriage of convenience to give the retiring Rock a girl to love and to look after him when no one was watching. He gave her a generous settlement. There was no name calling in public. Everything was handled as discreetly as Rock wished it. And he kept Willson on for a long time afterward, only leaving him when they both thought they had gone as far as they could together. I believe they are still friends. Rock is not a man to forget the person who made him.

Tony is on the short side, and he can snap and yap at people's heels like a small dog, where a St. Bernard would sniff and walk away. For every injury, imagined or real, Tony assumes a fighting pose. Some years ago he was in Boston for a premiere. He was all dressed up and wearing the round silver cuff links given him for Christmas by his wife. Getting into the limousine through the crush of humanity after the show, he noticed that one of the links was missing. It was a pair that had been made especially for Tony. The loss plunged him into depression. The car stopped at a light, and, looking out the window, Tony saw a young man holding the missing silver link. He jumped out, shouted "This is mine," and snatched it from his hand. The lights changed and Tony examined his prize. It was the last Lifesaver in the packet, covered with the silver foil. He managed to laugh.

Tony was paid $300,000 to star in *Lady L* at Metro. The story developed problems and the project was abandoned after it racked up a wasted $1 million. Tony took it personally and told me at the time he was suing them. He must have received some good advice because to my knowledge, the case never came to court. He did not realize how lucky he was. *Lady L,* made years later with Paul Newman and Sophia Loren, laid a monumental egg.

Tony was an important figure during the actors' strike of 1960. Meetings were held at his home, and he led the fight for the less fortunate actors, prodded by his then very left-of-center wife, Janet, who, I suspect, knew more about the subject than her husband. They parted soon afterward, when Tony went to South America to make a film with a seventeen-year-old actress, Christine Kaufmann, whose father had been an officer in the Luftwaffe during World War II. His friends were surprised that Bernie Schwartz from the Bronx would fall in love with a German girl. Proximity on location brings actors and actresses together every time unless the marriage with the wife or husband left behind is really solid. Tony's marriage with Christine seemed happy for several years. He refused to dine at houses where he was not seated next to his wife, aping Douglas Fairbanks, Sr., and Mary Pickford. Christine gave up her minor career when she married Tony, and presented him with two more daughters. (He had two girls with Janet.) In return Tony showered his young wife with furs and jewels and a palatial home she did not want. It was too much housekeeping, although what else was keeping her busy, I don't know. Part of her spare time was spent in Marvin Hime's jewelry emporium in Beverly Hills, where I saw her several times discussing her own designs for expensive gems. One diamond necklace looked like a $250,000 number, but Tony could afford it. He made a fortune from his percentage of *Trapeze* with Burt Lancaster and from other successful films. At one time his salary came to $750,000 plus a percentage of the film.

During the marriage with Christine, Tony became more difficult with the press, but he and I had always been good friends, or so I thought. When I was in London in 1965, Tony was filming *Arrivederci, Baby,* one of his disastrous comedies, in the South of France. I was planning to visit him there. I learned the company was coming to London to finish the film. Good, I thought, I won't have to fly to France. When the company came to England, I made a date to lunch with Tony at the studio. I was to be picked up by car at noon and taken to Shepperton where he was working. At five minutes past twelve I was called by his press agent's secretary, who informed me that Tony was ill and the lunch was canceled. I don't believe in sudden illness when the patient is a star. I was determined to find out what had happened. I went to the studio, forty-five minutes from London. Tony was in the café at a far corner table finishing his lunch with a group of chums. "Tell him I am here and expect to talk with him," I told the worried press agent. Before leaving the café Tony stopped to kiss me. "Be sure now to come over to the set." I promised. Ill, my eye!

I caught him between takes and we discussed, among other subjects, Lauren Bacall's recent interview with *Time* magazine in which she put herself in the same age group with Mr. Curtis, who was forty. Miss Bacall was forty-one, but the juxtaposition had annoyed Tony. He said she was a middle-aged woman trying to hang on to her glamour. It was a good quote and would cause comment. I scribbled away under his nose so he would know exactly what I was planning to write. Miss Bacall was appearing in *Cactus Flower* on Broadway, and when I saw her in the show she looked so attractive and elegant that I felt I must say so in a later column, adding, "I don't care what Tony Curtis thinks, she's beautiful." This brought an indignant letter from Mr. Curtis. After stating that I had forced him to say these awful things about the actress, he added, "I have been told that Errol Flynn chased you off the set and I couldn't imagine what any woman could have done to cause this. Now I know, kiddo." There *had* been a chase with Errol, but it was I who had chased Errol—out of my home when he called on me without an invitation after my first interview with him at Warner Brothers Studio in 1936.

While Tony is more or less predictable, Yul Brynner is not. I knew him very well while he was repeating his stage success in *The King and I* at 20th Century-Fox. The film was a hit and Yul was in great demand. When Tyrone Power died suddenly in Spain in the middle of filming *Solomon and Sheba,* Yul demanded and received $1 million for stepping into the breach. They would have done better to have abandoned the film. It was a costly failure.

Yul is far from through. He seems to be working all the time, but he is not the great drawing card he once was. When his career went into a lower key, he became oversensitive with the press. There was a story of a fight with a photographer in Mexico. He could smell out an unauthorized camera and everything would stop until it and its operator were removed. During *Morituri,* Marlon Brando allowed selected reporters and photographers on the set. But not Yul. It was poetic justice when Katharine Hepburn ordered him off the set when he took some unauthorized candids of her during their *Madwoman of Chaillot* film.

Once, in New York, when he was annoyed at something I had written in my column, he told me, "Check with me when you hear any stories about me."

"But you are always traveling and I don't always know how to reach you," I replied.

"Just pick up the phone, ask for Switzerland, and say you wish to speak to Yul Brynner," he replied. It must be nice to have that kind of ego.

9)

Caesar Sellers

One of Peter Sellers' early films was titled *Up the Creek,* and lately some people have wondered if he is. Actors have to be a bit nutty or they couldn't perform. To keep changing into someone else and to believe you are someone else can be confusing. At the beginning, before the actor makes it, he is usually humble and quite charming. When the need to cover up no longer exists, the real man comes out. Sometimes it would be better if he didn't.

When Mr. Sellers started his career, he was just a voice, heard but not seen. I didn't know him then, but I am sure he was lovable and anxious to please. When the voice materialized into a star, the problems and pressures made him moody and difficult. Even in the early days of his marriage to the beautiful blonde, Swedish Britt Ekland, she was powerless to bring Peter out of his dark spells, she told me. Any incident can cause them: a disagreement with a director, a request to interview him, a gossip item, or he wakes up on the wrong side of the bed.

He is happiest on his boat. As he says, "It's the only place where I can relax. There is no one there but the water." He hates large parties, but he will go to small gatherings with Princess Margaret and Lord Snowden, who find him amusing with his impersonations of Winston Churchill, Brigitte Bardot, and Senator Everett Dirksen.

Discussing the more plebeian gatherings, Peter said, "You have to sit there and make small talk, which I can't do, and everyone expects me to be funny, to tell a joke."

He did not object to Britt's career, but he did not want to get caught up with it. She found it simpler to work when Peter was away on his boat. He was irritable when he was there for the interviews and photographic sessions to promote her films. He made *The Bobo* with her against his better judgment. After the critics murdered it, Peter sent a horrid telegram to the producer, who has it framed in his office.

People say Peter changed after his serious heart attack in Hollywood while he was making *Kiss Me, Stupid* with Kim Novak for Billy Wilder. He loathed the picture and he battled with the director. His illness removed him from the film, which was a blessing for everyone, especially Peter. But the *Stupid* picture was not the only cause of Peter's illness or his subsequent unhappiness in *I Love You, Alice B. Toklas* or his disappointment in *Casino Royale,* a multimillion-dollar nightmare for the producer, Charlie Feldman, who took the brunt of the criticism for the delays.

"I didn't complain about Peter then and I won't now, even though he rewrote the script fifteen times. The only way to make a film with him is to let him direct, write, and produce, as well as star in it," the producer said to me shortly before his death. Mr. Feldman, a soft-spoken, handsome man with a deceptive air of vagueness, thankfully gave an end-of-the-film party. Peter was not there. He was recovering his equilibrium in solitary confinement on his boat. The normally debonair Charlie aged ten years during the nine months of filming, with five directors and a dozen stars, some in brief roles and some of whom were paid off with a Rolls-Royce.

Peter was just as involved with all aspects of *The Bobo.* He invaded director Robert Parrish's territory to such an extent that when Charles Champlin reviewed the film in the

Los Angeles Times, he listed Mr. Sellers in the credits as co-director.

The only way to make sense of Sellers is to start at the beginning of his career. He was in the R.A.F. in World War II in a camp in India, saving the Empire. He was twenty years old when the war ended. He is now in his mid-forties. His parents had been in show business and his vaudevillian grandmother had introduced "Splash Me" and "Have a Dip" at the turn of the century, so it was natural for Peter, when he realized he had a talent for mimicry, to entertain his fellow flyers by giving imitations of them and the various Indians he had met. That is where he picked up the Indian dialect he used so successfully in *The Millionairess* with Sophia Loren.

After we had won the war and lost the peace, Peter earned his living as a voice on radio. He could imitate just about anyone. It was as though he had a tape recorder in his head, taking down the exact nuances and inflections. He might have remained a disembodied voice forever if Mike Frankovich, then head of European production for Columbia Studios, had not been driving to the London airport to catch a plane to Rome to look over some of the studio productions. Mike turned on the radio in the car and listened to a play, broadcast by the BBC. At the end the announcer amazed him by saying, "All the characters were played by Peter Sellers."

"We were doing *Fire Over Africa* with Maureen O'Hara at the time," Mike told me, and he required seven actors to dub the dialogue. "I needed English and American voices of all classes. When I returned to London, I called Peter and asked him to do the seven voices and paid him 250 pounds for the lot." (On the devaluated pound this amounted to $700.)

In 1956, Peter was the voice of Winston Churchill in *The Man That Never Was,* which starred Stephen Boyd. But Peter wanted to be more than a voice. He wanted to be everything, most of all, to act. He was soon appearing on stage with Spike Mulligan and Harry Secombe in *The Goons,* entrancing audiences with his imitations and ad libs, changing the dialogue every night and driving his co-actors batty, as he did later in *Lolita*. You never knew when he could add a bit here, eliminate something there. After some roles in British films Peter persuaded Walter Shenson, a press agent who wanted to be a producer, to give him a role in *The Mouse That Roared* for Columbia. He was adorable and talented and everyone loved him, and he became an international star.

Alex Guinness had given up the comedies in which he played several characters and this field was wide open for Peter, who jumped in with all his voices and took on so many people in his pictures that we soon forgot that Guinness had ever been a versatile actor.

But even then Peter was considered a bit eccentric with his mad passion for cars and for taking photographs. During the *Lolita* period he was invited to lunch at the James Mason home in Beverly Hills, and Mrs. Mason told me afterward that he spent the entire time lying flat on his back on the floor taking photographs of his leading lady, fifteen-year-old Sue Lyon. Soon after he was divorced by his wife. She married the architect he had commissioned to redesign and redecorate their home in Hampstead, a suburb of London, where Peter had lived with her and their two children, pre-*Lolita*. It was a blow to Peter's ego which, as usually happens, was swelling with success and adulation.

Blake Edwards directed *The Pink Panther* and *A Shot in the Dark,* and this statement by Sellers will give you some idea of his two personalities. "The best experience I ever had with a director was with Blake in *Pink Panther* and the worst experience I ever had with a director was with Blake in *A Shot in the Dark*." After *Shot* they swore they would never work together again. But "never" in an actor's dictionary means tomorrow if it suits him. As Jack Warner always said of certain actors, "Never let that son of a bitch come back to the studio—unless we need him."

Mr. Edwards directed Peter in Hollywood recently in *The*

Party, where they were the best of friends and Peter was a lamb to work with, but still sometimes difficult with the press. A colleague of mine asked him on the set, "Why do you have all that dark stuff on your face?" Peter, made up to look like an East Indian, darkened even more with anger. "If you don't know why I have this stuff on my face, you have no right to interview me," he said, and ordered him off the set shouting after him, "Go ahead, print all the dirty things you want to." The reporter is still mystified. As the film failed, I doubt whether Peter and Blake will work together again. But you can never be sure.

During a brief estrangement with his astrologer, I was told that Peter discussed his problems with his "familiar." I asked Diane Cilento what a "familiar" was and she replied, "A cat." In witch circles a trusted cat is a "familiar"—someone from another sphere with magical knowledge. You see what I mean about actors not being like other people.

I had my first real talk with Peter at a small gathering hosted by the late British film producer, Jimmy Woolf, who had bought the film rights to Lionel Bart's *Oliver,* a stage hit in London. Jimmy's original idea was to have Laurence Harvey play Fagin, but Mr. Frankovich would not go for that. "Either Ron Moody, who created the role, or Peter Sellers." Because Ron Moody was unknown in America and Sellers was a big star, Jimmy agreed on Peter. The party was to celebrate the deal and have Sellers meet some of Jimmy's associates and friends. I was in London and invited. Peter was absolutely charming. He said exactly the right thing to everyone, and he smiled benignly at me when I told him I was a fan of his. I went into rhapsodies about his brief role in *Lolita,* especially the ping-pong scene, which is the funniest piece of comedy I've seen in my whole life (except, perhaps, for the early Chaplin two-reelers).

Peter did not play Fagin. "He simply could not make up his mind," Mr. Woolf told me later. One man's demands are another actor's chance, and Mr. Moody is the screen Fagin.

I am a friend of Mr. Sellers' press agent in London, and he

has always told me lovely things about Peter that I usually print. Soon after Britt had the baby, I was invited to see Peter in his suite at the Dorchester Hotel and he was friendly and articulate. We talked about the roasting he had received after his quoted indictment of Hollywood when he arrived back in London on a stretcher—"Hollywood is not a place where a man of my creative ability can work."

"How ungrateful," everyone said. He had been pronounced dead six times at the Cedars of Lebanon Hospital, and, but for the special equipment owned at that time only by the hospital, he would not have lived to die another five times, let alone survive.

During our talk at the Dorchester, Peter swore to me that he loved Hollywood, that he had never said he would not return, that he had been misquoted, and that he had only disliked the conditions of working in Hollywood and having too many people on the set which made it impossible for him to concentrate. He had been most grateful for the care he received when he was in the hospital, and for the letters from all over America wishing him well. He talked delightfully about his baby daughter, and I wondered what wicked person was spreading the awful stories about him.

Casino Royale had an enormous nut to crack to make back the money it was costing Columbia. It had been budgeted at $8 million. It had consumed ten by the time I was in London, and there were many months to go. I wanted to talk to Peter about the film, "But not on the set," I said. "He gets so wrapped up in the action that it is impossible to talk with him."

Our date was set for his dressing room at eleven on Tuesday morning. It was now Friday. On Monday morning, because I am thorough, I checked with Columbia's press department on Wardour Street to make sure everything was still on. "Eleven in his dressing room," I was assured. I called them again at 5:55 P.M. before they all went home. I called Peter's personal press agent. "Perhaps you'd better come, too," I suggested.

"No need to," he said cheerfully. "I've just talked to Peter and he is looking forward to seeing you."

One last call before the car came to take me to the studio. I rechecked with Columbia, and for double certainty I called the unit man on the set. "Peter will be waiting for you in his dressing room," he promised. The unit man met my car at the gate. He seemed uncomfortable, but not worried.

"Is Peter in his dressing room?" I asked while he helped me out of the car.

"Er—yes," he said hesitantly.

"Come on, let's go," I said.

"Er—well—he says he'll see you on the set instead," without quite looking at me.

"Oh, no," I cried.

"Don't worry," he assured me. "I'm to tell him you're here and he'll come immediately to the set. He doesn't work until after lunch and you will have plenty of time with him."

He led me to the set, put me in a chair, and left me. Half an hour later he returned, smiling. "He's coming right away."

At 12:20, Mr. Sellers appeared. I made a run for him, but stopped in my tracks when he said, "I'll be with you in a minute. You don't mind?"

"Well, I've been waiting an hour and a half," I said, hoping my irritation didn't show.

He went to the director and told him he had thought of something new for the Highland fling number they were shooting with real Highlanders. Peter got in with them and showed them how to do it, and stood by while they filmed it, take after take, as he thought of new ways of Highland flinging. He was still encouraging them when I walked off the set at one minute to 1:00 P.M. for my lunch date at the studio with Ursula Andress.

Woody Allen is easier to get along with. Woody is Peter's double. The resemblance is so startling that on one occasion, when he walked into Britt's bedroom with Peter behind him Mrs. Sellers sat up and said, "Hi, Peter."

Woody was also in *Casino Royale* and was also staying at the Dorchester. He had been in London three months waiting for his two weeks before the camera while Peter rewrote the script, advised everyone on his role, and even sat in on the cutting, but Woody did not mind the wait. He loved London, he told me. "They have all the four seasons in one day." His enjoyment had been heightened by a story that had convulsed everyone except Mr. Sellers. One of the very top executives of the New York Columbia office was in London to see what in heaven's name was happening with the picture and the studio's money. He was also staying at the Dorchester. He saw Woody in the lobby and sat down with him, pouring out his problems with Peter.

"It's terrible," groaned the executive. "Look, Woody, I don't know how to tell you this, but Peter doesn't want you in the picture. But with all the trouble he's giving us, instead of getting rid of you, we really should get rid of him."

"Yes, you should," said Woody. "You can't put up with that sort of behavior. Get rid of him." And he walked away. The face was Woody's, and the voice was Woody's, but the taller body was unmistakably Peter Sellers'. This is the chief reason he did not return for the new ending.

A man who worked for Sellers tried to explain him to me. "He once told me, 'I don't have any friends. I suspect everybody. I have the feeling that because of my success and fame they want to use me so, until I know them well, they are suspect.'" The former employee added, "He has a set of ideals and values that are impossible for others to live up to."

There is one man in England whom he trusts completely, a Mr. R. D. A. Wills, who runs the Sellers empire. He has made Peter a rich man, and this has not been too easy because the actor is a generous man. He showered Britt with jewels and furs during their marriage, and he spends a fortune on his cars and photographic equipment. He is always coming up with a new car. "Is it the 102nd or 103rd?" I will ask, and he smiles. Last week a Mercedes, this week a Ferrari, and when he wants a new car he's a child who can't wait. While he was filming *The Party* he had a sudden passion for a Pontiac, but this was to be no ordinary auto. It had to be the right color, have certain tires, air conditioning, and a certain kind of brakes, and he wanted it yesterday. His agent drove all over Los Angeles and found one to Peter's specifications. The star was thrilled, ecstatic. He jumped in and between takes drove happily around the block. When work was done, he left last week's car on the lot and drove today's to the home he rented on Bedford Drive in Beverly Hills. He rushed inside to get his camera equipment and took endless photographs of the car until the light failed.

The next week he called his agent and told him, "I hate this terrible car. I've got to get a Corvette. It must be white, with hard and soft top, FM-AM and all the extras," and he wanted it now. The bemused man called all over town. No one had a white Corvette with all the extras that Peter wanted. There were cars available, but not the exact auto Peter yearned for, like a pregnant woman wanting a pickle. A dealer called Detroit and The Car was flown out that day for Mr. Sellers.

Peter will spend money extravagantly when he is pleased, not otherwise. He is not a prankster like Brando, but he has his own method of proving a point. While making *Casino Royale* he ordered forty-five suits from London's "in" tailor, Doug Heyward. Peter told Doug to send the bill to the *Casino Royale* production people. They sent it back with a letter saying they had already ordered the clothes for Mr. Sellers for the film. When Doug complained, Peter told him, "That will teach you never to make anything without a contract." He then paid the tailor.

A top producer said to me recently, "The price is more important to Peter these days than where he works and what he makes." I don't agree. I think this very talented actor is concerned about each film, and in recent years overconcerned. If Mr. Feldman suffered while millions of dollars drained away during *Casino Royale,* he could partly blame himself. He had been somewhat worried when Peter took the bit between his determined teeth during *What's New, Pussycat?,* Peter's first film after his illness. The main role had been written by Woody Allen for Warren Beatty, a close friend of Charlie's. After several months of procrastination, Warren decided it was not for him and after some rewriting the part was accepted by Peter O'Toole. Feldman, who used to consider Sellers his good-luck charm, asked whether he was well enough to play a small part in the picture. Peter was trying to follow doctors' orders—"resting and staying in bed and taking limited exercises," but he was itching to face the cameras again and besides he was now married to a young beautiful girl and he wanted to drop the invalid image. If he worked one or two hours a day, he was sure he could do it and his doctor agreed it would be healthier for him to work than fretting himself into another heart attack.

From one or two hours a day, for three weeks with a moderate fee, the ad-libbing, inventive Sellers was working five and six hours for several months with a corresponding raise in salary, adding bits of business here and someone else's dialogue there, climbing all over the sets and the cast until his "cameo" unbalanced the picture, which might account for the New York reviews—so bad they were front-paged in the London evening newspapers. Sometimes, as with *Valley of the Dolls,* a movie can receive such bad reviews everyone is curious to see it. *Pussycat* was a smash in New York. I've heard good and bad about the other cities, but with all the "record-breaking" accounts handed out, you can never be sure.

One of Peter's problems is that, like Robert Mitchum, he wants to be loved and will do almost anything to please you. Peter is terribly hurt when stories of his irritability and temperament get into the newspapers. He usually slams off to his dressing room, sits there sulking, and has to be coaxed to come back to work. He believed he had an enemy on the set of *I Love You, Alice B. Toklas* who was leaking items to the press. It could be true. There is always at least one jealous person who will tattle the latest shenanigans of a not-too-popular star.

During the first six weeks with *Alice B. Toklas* Peter was obviously unhappy about something. He was sometimes late, holding up production, which no studio can afford in this day of enormous film costs. One morning when Peter was late again, his irritated costar, Miss Jo Van Fleet (who is a fine actress and fairly difficult in her own right), told Peter it was disgraceful for him to hold up the company. He flew into a rage and bawled her out before everyone, saying she was unprofessional to do this to him—*she* was unprofessional!—adding, "and nobody likes you." She ran sobbing off the set.

Peter admires pretty young girls and they admire him, so it was not surprising that young Miss Leigh Taylor-Young came vociferously to his defense after reading accounts of the temperament displayed by Peter during *Alice B. Toklas*. The most publicized incident was Peter's distress when the script girl reported for work in a purple dress. Purple is Peter's unlucky color, and via an executive he demanded she change into something else immediately. There was a sort of hush until she reappeared in green which, thank heaven, is a lucky color for Peter. When the story appeared in print Peter stormed, "I don't know why they attack me. Perhaps it's because there is no one else to attack right now."

He may have been right. Barbra Streisand had left town after *Funny Girl*, and, incredibly, Peter's picture was the only film in production in all of Hollywood.

But his behavior sometimes begs for criticism, as the famed French director Gerard Oury can testify. Oury is one of the most successful directors in France. His film *La Gran Vadrouille* made $15 million in France alone. Oury, married to former Hollywood actress Michele Morgan, a big star in France, wanted an Italian, American, and French star for his new film, *The Brain*. To play all the roles he needed someone like Peter Sellers. A top American producer who is a friend of Peter's and of Oury's promised the latter, "I'll arrange a meeting." He called Peter, who was in Paris, explained the situation, and said, "He'll tell you the idea. If you like it, I'll arrange for Columbia to take over all the English-speaking countries."

Peter met Oury at the Plaza-Athénée Hotel. He would give the French director an hour, but he was so delighted with Oury and his film idea he remained until three in the morning.

"This story is ideal for me," he told the pleased director. "I was born to do it."

Then Oury made his first—and fatal—mistake. "You must see my picture *La Gran Vadrouille,*" he said to Peter, who was pacing excitedly up and down the room.

"As soon as possible. How about tomorrow morning?" enthused the actor. Peter wanted to absorb every nuance of Oury's masterpiece, and he brought an interpreter to the projection room. He watched gloomily until the end and then jumped up and shouted angrily, "If there's one picture I hate in the whole world, it's this one. I would never work for the man who made it." He stalked out without shaking hands or saying good-by to Oury or the interpreter. The American producer laughed when he told me the story.

"It's like the Chaplin film where the rich man takes the poor man home every night when he's drunk, then throws him out in the morning when he's sober. Peter is just as unpredictable," summed up the producer.

Another producer, Joe Levine, loves Peter and thinks he is the most discerning actor in the business. The star and one of the Mirisch brothers came to a privately owned projection room in Hollywood one evening to see a foreign film. The print was not available, but Peter had come to see a film and by God he was going to.

"What else do you have?" he demanded.

They had a print of Mr. Levine's picture *The Producers,* which had been shown to the trade reviewers the evening before and had not yet been picked up.

"I'll see it," said Peter.

He was enraptured by the film starring Zero Mostel, and

with no one prodding him he spent $1,000 on trade-paper advertisements extravagantly extolling it. "Last night," he told the trade, "I saw the ultimate film ... *The Producers* ... Brilliantly written and directed by Mel Brooks, it is the essence of all great comedy combined in a single motion picture. Without any doubt, Mel Brooks displays true genius in weaving together tragedy-comedy, comedy-tragedy, pity, fear, hysteria, schizophrenia, inspired madness and a largesse of lunacy with sheer magic. The casting was perfect. Those of us who have seen this film and understand it have experienced a phenomenon which occurs only once in a life span." Signed, Peter Sellers.

I'm glad he did not see it in the morning.

Peter's passion for perfection applies to his private life as well as to his work. He must excel in both areas. He was thirty-nine when he married the twenty-one-year-old Britt in 1964, but he was not going to let the difference in their ages hamper him in any way. His astrologer had predicted he would marry a beautiful blonde young Swedish girl whose initials were B. E. He telephoned her when he found she was also staying at the Dorchester and invited her to his suite, where he promptly told her, "I am going to marry you."

After they returned to England following his heart attack, he reprimanded his astrologer. "How is it you didn't know I was almost going to die?" The stargazer is said to have replied that he *did* know but if he had told Peter he would have dropped dead on the spot from shock.

So, because he wanted to seem as youthful as his bride, Peter, who always worried about his heart (his father had died of a heart attack), lost weight too rapidly, which helped to cause what he had feared to happen.

When Peter was dying, his agent came to see him. Peter, who wants every new thing he sees, gaspingly admired the agent's cuff links. The agent took them off and gave them to him. Not long ago Peter admired the agent's new car and begged to take it for a spin in London. Afterward, when it was not presented to him as a gift, there was a break in their working relationship. It was probably coincidence, but Peter is like a child who wants your toy or he won't play.

He has seemed happier since the parting with Britt, but he is still up one day and down the next, and he is still dieting. Peter left six lives on the surgeon's table at the Cedars of Lebanon Hospital. He has three more to go. To enjoy them I suggest a return to the tranquil man he was when he was only a talented voice. He'll live longer.

10)

Fatty

Richard Burton uses it as a term of endearment. He loves his plump wife. "Fatty." The adjective is indicative of the relationship between the most unexpected lovers of our time.

"He likes me on the dumpy side," Elizabeth stated in a recent magazine article.

Fat or thin (and she has been thinner since her partial hysterectomy), makes no difference to her realistic husband. If she were three times the size, he would love her three times as much. It is what she represents to him that is important. In Elizabeth he has realized all his dreams.

"I have been searching for this woman all my life," he told me not long ago.

When he was a beautiful man of twenty-three, he predicted his future to Claire Bloom during their first appearance together on the West End stage in *The Lady's Not for Burning*. Seventeen years later, perhaps for the last time, Claire was Richard's leading lady in *The Spy Who Came in from the Cold*. The role was too small for Elizabeth, or Miss Bloom would not have been allowed within a mile of the film. Unlike Richard's first wife, Sybil, her successor has taken no chances of losing the actor, with his notorious roving eye, and she was on the set all the time that Claire was on call for Richard.

"He hasn't changed at all, except physically, but that was natural as he was older," Claire told me. "He was still drinking, he was still boasting, he was still late, he was still reciting the same poems, and telling the same stories as when he was twenty-three. They were both rather aloof to me," Claire added with some amusement. "In all the months' shooting in Ireland, I was never asked to dinner by the Burtons." It didn't bother her. "He was interesting years ago, but now I found him rather boring, as people sometimes are when they get what they have always wanted."

"And what did Richard want?" I asked the actress who acted with him in three films and several plays, including *Coriolanus* Ophelia to his Hamlet, and *Twelfth Night*.

"A beautiful wife, money, and a great career. In the early days," she added reflectively, "he would have included a wish to be the best actor in the world. It was obvious he was going to be a huge star, which is not quite the same as being a great actor. He has confused them. He thinks they are the same."

It was Richard who told me of the famous actor (who I imagined was Laurence Olivier) who cautioned him in a cable from London at the height of the Richard-Elizabeth-Sybil-Eddie furor: "You must decide what you want to be— a household word or a good actor."

"Why not both?" Richard wired back.

Is there anyone who has not heard of him? I smile, remembering the concern of his then press agent, Arthur Jacobs, who warned him when he took off from *Camelot* in New York for *Cleopatra* in Rome, "I hope you realize that Elizabeth will get all the publicity. You must watch out for yourself."

"Don't worry," Richard replied jauntily, "I can take care of myself."

Elizabeth was beautiful in *Cleopatra*. Today she certainly isn't homely—her violet eyes will always save her—but sometimes her neck seems to disappear and she must be photographed from a certain angle to hide the jaw line.

Richard's kidding-on-the-square affectionate description is a classic: "Her arms are too fat, her legs are too short, and she is too big in the bust." It suits him to have her this way, like a man who is always making his wife pregnant so she will never have the chance to look at another man. Because make no mistake about this always-in-the-news couple; if there is any throwing out to be done, it will be Elizabeth who will do it. Richard plays his role of rough, tough guy to please his wife, but he is actually a gentle man with occasional angry outbursts.

Elizabeth, who has no qualms when she wants a jewel or a man or a yacht, was determined to get him. She was out of love with Mr. Fisher who, like the *Dummkopf* the couple sometimes call him, had dropped his singing career to trail in Elizabeth's shadow. During *Suddenly Last Summer,* soon after the marriage to Eddie, she had burst into tears and sobbed, "I made the greatest mistake of my life." She realized she was not in love with him, and Elizabeth has to be in love or she cannot breathe.

I was in Rome several times during the long filming of *Cleopatra.* (I was there so often that when the two press agents on the picture wrote a book about their experiences, I was listed in the cast of characters.) Early in the production I lunched with an impatient Burton at the studio. He had been bought out of his *Camelot* musical, then, as often happens, he sat around for several months filling in the time of waiting with his hobby of girl chasing. There was a lovely model, I remember, who had followed him from New York, and scads of other girls. It has always seemed strange that Richard, who is such a lover-boy in real life, comes across so coldly on the screen.

During *Ice Palace* at Warners in 1959, he told a chum, "If there's a dame on this set I can't screw, my name's not Richard." With this type of roving Romeo, you could never be sure if he is boasting or if it is a fact. Any girl who worked

with him—from Claire Bloom to Jean Simmons in *The Robe*
—was automatically suspect in the Beverly Hills-Bel Air
drawing rooms where they were hung, drawn, quartered and
envied by the bored wives of filmland's executives. And yet,
in Richard's films, the passion and his real-life warmth did
not and still does not come through. The thin screen has been
as effective as lead, separating the romantic Richard from the
people in the audience. It took the affair and the ultimate
marriage with Elizabeth to change his image from a good
stage actor who had lost his appeal on the screen, into a sex
symbol with women clutching and clawing him outside the
stage doors and at the few premieres he attends with Elizabeth. They were almost crushed to death arriving at the Boston airport and hotel after their wedding in Canada, as they
were four years later at the New York premiere of *Doctor
Faustus*. Screaming fans were trampled underfoot and photographers lost their cameras as the frenzied mass of hysterical
humanity charged upon the terrified couple.

If Elizabeth had her way, she would never subject herself
to these demonstrations from the public. She would never
see the press. But Richard is more practical. He realizes they
must sometimes be available and he is easygoing and loves
people, whereas Elizabeth loves Richard first, and what is left
over she gives to her family and her animals. The wise press
agent never asks Elizabeth to do anything for the picture.
Elizabeth's initial reaction to any request is "Oh, shit!" She
is an advanced student in the use of 4-, 5-, 6-, 7-, and 8-letter
profanity.

At the start of *Who's Afraid of Virginia Woolf?* Elizabeth
asked Ernie Lehman, "Why do you think I can play Martha?"

The tactful producer, who had also written the screenplay,
prefaced his reply by saying, "Among other reasons, I think
you have a great deal of Martha in you."

"Oh," said Elizabeth, "you mean because I use four-letter
words?"

Then up spake Richard, "I cured her of all that."

"You bet your ass you did," retorted Elizabeth. "That was a *three*-letter word," turning to Lehman triumphantly.

Richard's pornographic vocabulary is more vivid than Elizabeth's, who learned the words from three of her five husbands, and he uses them to his wife's delight when they scream at each other which, before the last operation, was fairly frequently.

But while Richard is the slave, he can be the master in the areas of their careers. After her preliminary "Oh, shit," she will accede to his suggestions that she see *The Times* of London and New York, *Look, Life,* but not *Time*—and never ever after the devastating review of *Doctor Faustus* with its crushing finale: "When she [Elizabeth] welcomes Burton to an eternity of damnation, her eyeballs and teeth are dripping pink in what seems to be a hellish combination of conjunctivitis and trench mouth. Mercifully mute throughout, she merely moves in and out of camera range, breasting the waves of candle smoke, dry-ice vapor and vulgarity that swirl through the sets."

But in the beginning was *Cleopatra,* and any account of Elizabeth and Richard must start in Rome in 1960. Elizabeth had not wanted to make the film and Walter Wanger had originally earmarked it for Susan Hayward, who was a big star following her successes in *I'll Cry Tomorrow* and *I Want to Live.* But *Cleo* was to be a $10 million production with Rouben Mamoulian directing, Stephen Boyd as Marc Antony, and Peter Finch as Caesar. With the publicity garnered by Elizabeth after she dragged the dazed Mr. Fisher from her favorite bridesmaid, Debbie Reynolds, she was a bigger star than Susan, and the actress who played Cleopatra must not only be the most beautiful woman of her day, but she must have the drawing power of Elizabeth Taylor.

"She doesn't want to do it," her agent informed Mr. Wanger.

In Hollywood, as elsewhere, if they want you and you don't want them, the price goes up. One million dollars against

10 per cent of the gross would have been a gross mistake to refuse. For extra loot Elizabeth insisted that Eddie must be part of the package. The studio readily agreed to pay Fisher $1,000 a week plus an expensively furnished office. His main job would be to get his wife to the set on time. Everyone knew that when Elizabeth was not overly enthusiastic about a film she could act up and cause delays, as she had during *Butterfield 8,* for which she won the Oscar because she should have won the year before for *Cat on a Hot Tin Roof* but was punished for disrupting Eddie's marriage to Debbie. You know how it is in Hollywood. You rarely win for how good you are *this* year, and Elizabeth had been so ill in London, and Eddie so worried, and the whole world had held its collective breath while she struggled to live.

Joe Mankiewicz, Elizabeth's favorite script writer-director (he succeeded Rouben Mamoulian on *Cleopatra*), helped her with the marvelous speech, made after her recovery, in which she was humbly grateful to be alive. You had the impression that her life would be quieter, more conservative. I am sure she meant it at the time. But Elizabeth is a woman who has always followed her whims. A queen without a conscience. She does what she wants to do and to hell with what people think. She has ignored public opinion from the age of seventeen when she was engaged to millionaire Ed Pauley's son and soon after dumped him on his father's beautiful yacht in Florida. At that time Walter Winchell tagged her "The Most Beautiful Woman in the World." She has been in headlines ever since. She has always followed a straight line to her desires, and some have been pretty wild.

When Burton was finally told to report for his assignment as Antony, he celebrated the night before with a massive pub crawl in Rome. How this Welshman can put it away! The only man who can beat a drinking Irishman is a drinking Welshman. Elizabeth has stated in her account of the romance that it was Richard's hangover that first attracted her to him.

They had met during her marriages to Michael Wilding

and Mike Todd, and he had made no impression on Elizabeth, but he had noticed her, to put it politely. An eyewitness on the set believes the swiftness of her assault on Richard was to punish a recalcitrant admirer. Regardless of the cause, Richard wasn't having any. An affair, yes, but nothing serious. He was a good family man, and besides, he loved Sybil, who was quiet even when he created arguments, stomping out of the house and returning with the dawn; and if she suspected he had been with another woman, she said nothing.

"I shall never leave Sybil," he told me. "She loves and understands me, and thinks I'm a genius."

Later, when the whole world was wondering will he, won't he, and Eddie Fisher had made a crass ass of himself in New York informing the press there was no trouble in his marriage and calling Elizabeth in Rome to corroborate his fiction, I was in Rome again and had a long talk with Richard. I had promised I would not mention "The Affair." Before leaving however, I said, "It sometimes takes a few days before all my newspapers can use a story. Is there any likelihood of something happening in the next few days to make my story out of date?"

He saw through my nonsubtle subterfuge and roared with laughter. "If you mean," he snorted, "am I going to divorce my wife to marry Elizabeth, the answer is no!"

The *New York Mirror,* which was then very much in existence and running my column, used half its front page in big black letters to proclaim the vow of Richard's fidelity. Sybil was even more emphatic. "I will never allow the father of my children to be Elizabeth Taylor's fifth husband."

I was amazed when Sybil announced she would divorce Richard. I knew she had not wanted a divorce. I learned later it was a last-ditch attempt to bring him back to her and their two daughters.

While Richard sometimes calls Elizabeth "Fatty," he has always called his first wife by the affectionate diminutive of "Syb," and Syb knew Richard did not want a divorce. When the blaze with Elizabeth had become a forest fire, she had suggested casually that if he really wanted to leave her to marry Elizabeth, she would not stand in his way.

"No, no, Syb," he reassured her, "I could never divorce you."

To show his love for her, he bought her a pretty brooch for a few thousand dollars. At the same time, he bought Miss Taylor a diamond necklace that cost $100,000. His wife, of course, did not know this and if she had, she would have said nothing. She is an intelligent woman, and all she was concerned with at that time was getting her husband back.

While he vacillated, unable to desert Elizabeth or to break up his marriage with Sybil (at this period he was flitting from one to the other, assuring them each she was number one, how happy he'd be if t'other-dear-charmer-were-away sort of thing), Elizabeth proved her love for Richard by taking what she described as an overdose of chili beans which caused her to be rushed to the hospital.

At this point, Sybil, still determined to be the understanding wife, left Richard in Rome with Elizabeth. Her husband had always come back to her. If she went away, perhaps he would follow her. What she did not understand was Elizabeth's tenacity.

Poor Richard was spinning even more from his dilemma than from the drinking and the dodging of the papparazzi, who had taken up permanent positions in trees along the Appian Way and were peeping into bedrooms with long telescopic lenses. If Sybil had remained in Rome she might still be Mrs. Richard Burton instead of Mrs. Sybil Burton Christopher. When *Cleopatra* was finally in the can at an ulcerous cost of $35 million, Elizabeth went to her chalet in Switzerland and Richard went to his. Sybil took up residence on Central Park West in New York with her children. And again she wrote Richard that if he really wanted a divorce, she would not stand in his way.

More protestations from Richard that he did not want a divorce. Then, great news for Sybil. Richard had signed to star in *The Night of the Iguana* to be made in Mexico. His wife expected that on his way to Mexico he would stop in New York to see her and their children. Instead he went straight through to Mexico with Elizabeth. This was now a serious problem for Sybil. But she knew he loved her and the children. She knew he always came back to her and she wrote him another letter, stronger than anything she had written before, putting it on the line. Did he want a divorce? This surely would bring him back. One of her close friends told me how shattered Sybil was when she received Richard's reply that a divorce perhaps would be best for all concerned, that Elizabeth loved him more than anything on earth and that he loved her.

The new marriages proved better for them all than anyone could have prophesied. Sybil is happy with her young husband and their daughter. She has made a huge success of her Arthur discotheques (which she would never have started if she had been Mrs. Richard Burton). She met Jordan at Arthur when he was a member of "The Wild Ones."

Richard is happy with Elizabeth and told me, "If I am away from her for two hours I get worried and restless. I would die without her." Like all men in love, he endows her with all the qualities he wants her to have. But love is one thing and good business another. After they had costarred in several films, he laughingly complained to me, "I told Elizabeth we shouldn't do any more together. They'll be calling us Laurel and Hardy. 'So what's wrong with Laurel and Hardy?' she said. 'They did okay, didn't they?' "

He was still saying, "I could never kiss any woman but Elizabeth on or off the screen," but some of their recent films together failed badly and Richard persuaded his wife they must divorce their acting careers.

Fortunately there was no suitable role for Elizabeth in *Staircase,* about two homosexual barbers, nor previously in *Where Eagles Dare.* She will sometimes do a film on her own if it can be done in the same city. But mostly she prefers to be on the set with Richard, and even during his interviews. After chatting with Elizabeth in her dressing room during

Taming of the Shrew in Rome, I wandered over to Richard's, who wanted to say hello before I left. One of his greatest charms for a woman is that he is always interested in you. He remembers what you talked about the last time and he flirts with you, and if you are beyond a certain age, or any age, it's rather pleasant. He was saying to me, "If I weren't so happily married, you wouldn't be safe in this room with me," when Elizabeth floated in.

I thought, "Oh, my God, if she heard that!" and said hastily, "We were just talking about our children." Then Elizabeth and I got into a ridiculous argument about whether her children were better-looking than mine.

Some of Richard's acquaintances believe Elizabeth drinks only to keep up with him. This could be true. By nature she is an eater, not a drinker. The two rarely go together. Richard's favorite tipple is a boilermaker—whiskey laced with beer. Elizabeth prefers vodka or champagne or beer, and sometimes beer mixed with champagne (they call it Black Velvet in England). They are both addicted to Bloody Marys. I do not believe this, but a friend of Richard's once swore to me that there is an unwritten understanding with Elizabeth and the studios for whom she stars that a case of French champagne must be delivered to her daily.

Unfortunately the intake is now showing on Richard's once beautiful face, as all the guzzling is spoiling the beauty that vied with the immortal Helen's before Elizabeth's appetite ruined it. The fragile face of a decade ago has been fattened by the chili beans flown over the pole from Dave Chasen's to London and Rome, the Irish stew from Dinty Moore's, the steaks from Gallagher's, the *cassoulet* (a bean and sausage casserole) from L'Etoile, British sausages from a pub in London, and cheesecake from Lindy's. Nothing fancy for Elizabeth. Her almost sensual love of eating could have been caused by the admonition to be careful with the calories when she was a child actress, as with Judy Garland, who also became fat as soon as she could order her own meals.

Elizabeth had gained a lot of weight when I saw her at the

world premiere of *Doctor Faustus* in the university town of Oxford in England. It was an awful evening—cold, raining hard—and Elizabeth did well to wrap up against the weather. She was enveloped from neck to toe in a voluminous black velvet coat lined with white mink that fanned out to form a large collar. You could glimpse the enormous emerald and diamond necklace, which matched the diamond and emerald tiara and the diamond and emerald bracelets and rings. But you could not see the huge egg-sized emerald surrounded by large drop diamonds that Elizabeth was wearing in the center of the necklace. She was a standing $2 million monument. In contrast, the Duchess of Kent, representing royalty, wore a flimsy print gown; her only jewelry was simple diamond earrings. The Duchess looked elegant, Elizabeth like a woman who had made it rich and was wearing all her possessions on her ample back.

Don't get Elizabeth wrong. She has many other jewels, including the recent $303,000 diamond acquisition. Jewels are a mania with her. For a woman who has such good taste in gems, it is surprising that she dresses so badly. Those loud patterned pants that do nothing for her rear end—"Richard chooses them for me"—the orange serape, the shapeless things that make her look as broad as she is tall. I had wondered whether the jewels meant security for Elizabeth. They do not. With a reported $23 million banked in Switzerland, she will always be rich. It isn't the value of the gems that excites her. It's having them. She learned to love the glittering baubles during her marriage to Mike Todd, who was the first person in her life to tell her off, but who loved her madly and showered her with gifts. Mr. Todd, afraid perhaps of ever losing his beautiful wife, gave her a present every day. It could be a jewel, a painting, a car, a dress, a yacht, a fur coat, or a bunch of flowers. For his staff he had a big bulletin board on which to pin ideas for presents.

A friend of mine was visiting Mike and Elizabeth at their villa at Cap Ferrat in the South of France. Debbie and Eddie had just arrived to be their house guests. Mike was telling them about the new emerald he had just bought "Mrs. Schwartzkopf," the name he loved to call his black-haired wife. "Run up and get the emeralds, dear, so Debbie and Eddie can see them." They were sitting around the pool. The villa was on top of a hill and it meant a long walk up to reach the house.

"Yes, Mike," she said like a little girl, and she ran up and down the hundred steps and breathlessly showed her emeralds. Since then she has made it a point of honor to try to extract a jewel from the director or producer on each of her films.

Richard loves to indulge the woman who brought him so much, including their combined income of $6 million a year, not counting the enormous expense account they receive, as much sometimes as $10,000 a week. He buys her a piece of jewelry with every film. He was reprieved slightly during *Boom* (from Tennessee Williams' *The Milk Train Doesn't Stop Here Any More*), when Elizabeth, playing the richest woman in the world, had the famed jeweler Bulgari on the Via Condotti bring a selection of gems to the location in Sardinia for her to wear in the film. It seemed her own collection was not enough for *the* richest woman. Elizabeth went into ecstasies over a beautiful brooch in the presence of director John Heyman, who had won her for his film over tremendous bidding for her services.

"Oh, it's so darling," Elizabeth said in effect, turning the jewel in her hand so that it was a live thing in the Sardinian sun. "Oh," as Mr. Heyman was slow to catch on, "I wish it were really mine." He caught on. What was $60,000 more or less on the budget?

His reward was a hug and a promise that she would love to make another film for him. In her second film for Heyman, *Secret Ceremony,* he made sure she would play a poor girl, a prostitute, minus jewels, but Elizabeth managed to swing some Paris gowns as the imagined mother of rich Mia Farrow.

Elizabeth did almost as well with *Who's Afraid of Virginia Woolf?*. She managed to get a pair of ruby and diamond earrings—"One from you, Mike [Nichols, her director], and one from you, Richard." But when she sent word to Jack Warner that she wanted an $80,000 matching brooch to go with them, he replied, "I'm paying her $1 million and 10 per cent of the gross. Let her buy her own brooch."

For one moment of bliss I had a chance to make off with Elizabeth's emeralds. I was preparing my story of the *Faustus* premiere in my room at the Randolph Hotel in Oxford when there was a "tap tap" at the door. Two of the Burton minions—I will not mention their names as it might get them into trouble—tiptoed in like guilty conspirators. One of them was clutching an ordinary-looking box. He sat down on my bed and, with a dramatic flourish like a magician, opened the box. "She'd kill me if she knew I was doing this," he whispered, "but I thought you would like to see the emeralds." He allowed me to try them on, and for a few minutes I was bright green all over. I could have fed all of starving India and myself forever and ever, and for a fraction of a second I measured the distance to the window, but I knew I could never make it.

The entire Burton retinue, without which the Burtons never move a step, was in Oxford. Richard Hanley, who started as Louis B. Mayer's secretary, was taken over by Mike Todd, then by Elizabeth and Eddie Fisher, and is now executive assistant to Elizabeth and Richard; John Lee, who is Hanley's assistant and vice president in charge of southern fried chicken, which Elizabeth adores; Bob Wilson, who was best man at their wedding when he was Richard's dresser and now has the title of personal aide to both; Dick McWhorter, who is coproducer for their film company; Ron Berkley, Richard's make-up man and dresser; Claudie, who travels with Elizabeth to help with her hair—for important occasions Alexandre, the famed hairdresser of Paris, is on hand. He was in Oxford as he was in New York for the premiere of *Faustus,* and why did he make such a mountain of her hair? Liz looks better with a simple hairdo. Also in Oxford were business associates from all over the world—her lawyer from

New York; her press agent from New York; Richard's agent from Hollywood; Elliott Kastner, the producer for his following film, *Where Eagles Dare,* who had come up from London for five minutes of Richard's time before Elizabeth demanded his return for lunch, and when Elizabeth demands, Richard obeys.

It was a great occasion for Richard, who spent six months at Oxford taking courses in English drama and literature while he was in the R.A.F. nearby. He was not a graduate or a student of Oxford as generally believed. With the University emptied because of the war, the men training in nearby camps were invited to participate in classes and lectures. It was the return of the barefoot boy, and he invited all the available members of his family to the event—his brother Ivor and his wife Gwyn, his sister Cis. He had sent his brother and sister-in-law to Italy to fetch Liza Todd Burton, ten, and Maria Fisher Burton, seven, with their nurses and governesses, and all were staying at the centuries-old Bear Inn. Elizabeth's two sons by Michael Wilding, who attend The Milford School in England, were also there. Elizabeth is the Eternal Mama. She loves her own and all children and all small animals and cannot bear to be parted from them. And some of the London reporters and press agents were there, and I caught the longest cold of my career, trying to catch up with the Burtons, who had promised me an interview.

I had been put in the wrong hotel, but word came that a car was waiting to take me with Professor Coghill, Richard's teacher during the six months at Oxford, to The Bear. The professor by mistake marched me upstairs into Elizabeth's bedroom. She was dressing and was naturally startled and annoyed.

"Where's Richard?" I stuttered.

"In the bar," she said coldly.

Actually it was no novelty for me to see Elizabeth dressing. A week after her honeymoon in northern California with Nicky Hilton, she had returned somewhat depressed to her mother's home to have photographs taken in her wedding gown. Something had gone wrong with those taken at the reception at the exclusive Bel Air Hotel given her by Conrad Hilton and the mother of Nicky (his other wife, Zsa Zsa, was also there). My housekeeper was off for the day, and when Mrs. Taylor asked me to come to lunch with Elizabeth, I took my four-year-old son, Robert, with me. Afterward we all went upstairs for Elizabeth to change for the photographs. She was just about to strip when she realized a male was in the room.

"Little boy," she said to Robert, "would you please wait outside?"

When I called or visited Mrs. Taylor, she gave me a blow-by-blow account of Elizabeth's dreadful honeymoon with young Hilton. During the first part, in California, he had played golf all day, and on the boat to Europe and in Monte Carlo he gambled all night. The unhappy experience landed the most beautiful girl in the world in a hospital in Chicago, where I contacted her and she cried her heart out on the telephone.

It was a tougher woman I faced in that bedroom at The Bear. I went to the bar and found Richard, his face flushed, friendly as always, and as always waving a glass and making speeches to an admiring group.

I managed to get in a few questions, but it was embarrassing and difficult with so many people around and so much noise.

"How about Elizabeth?" I whispered during a lull.

"You know how long it takes for her to dress and get her hair done," he said, "and we have to leave soon for the premiere."

Fortunately for my time in Oxford the Burtons arrived early at the theater through the wrong information that royalty was already there. I tapped Richard on the shoulder (he was only just recovering from the *faux pas* of asking Anthony Quinton-Hogg about his Maltese wife under the impression he was Lord Boothby) and said, "Take me to Elizabeth." She corroborated an amazing story I had heard earlier in the day that the captain and the chef on the Burton yacht, the *Ka-lizma,* had been feuding and the captain had proclaimed, "He goes or I go."

When the chef was ordered off the yacht, his wife, who served as a maid, took Elizabeth's small Corgi, Thomas à Becket, named for Richard's film with Peter O'Toole, inside her coat with her. She claimed later that Liza had given the dog to her. Before the animal was returned (after several trips by lawyers and company employees to the South of France, the home of the fired couple, then to the chalet in Switzerland), they had spent about $10,000 to recover tiny Thomas.

Elizabeth, as is well known, has always loved animals. I first knew her in the Fabulous Forties when every film made money in the lush war years, when she was twelve years old and starred in *National Velvet.* Louis B. Mayer, she told me breathlessly in the commissary at Metro, had given her the horse from the film and she had it stabled in the Malibu hills and she could barely tear herself away to come to work. She told me then of her pet chipmunk, Nibbles, and later presented me with the charming little book she wrote after Nibbles died.

I thought she was carrying her love for animals pretty far when she rented another yacht, the *Beatriz,* at a cost of $2,800 a week, while the *Kalizma* (named for their daughters, Kate, Liza, and Maria) was being refurnished, and anchored it on the Thames to use as a floating kennel for her four dogs and two cats while they lived at the Dorchester with their retinue. They could not bring the animals into London because of the six-month quarantine laws. But they could have left them in Switzerland where they keep a large staff at the ready, during the three months of filming in England. This sort of waste causes revolutions. But money is no object for Elizabeth. She flings it around and believes it is good for the economy.

While Richard was starring on Broadway in *Hamlet,* they spent almost $6,000 a week for the several suites of rooms, with the liquor and food to match, at the Regency Hotel on

Park Avenue. Two large rooms were turned into a wardrobe for Elizabeth's furs and clothes. (At one time she maintained a suite at the Beverly Hills Hotel on a year-round basis, just for some of her clothes.)

Elizabeth has raised Richard to her own financial film level of $1 million per picture. Whether he would receive this on his own steam when Elizabeth is in retirement (which she has so often told me she plans in the near future) is very much open to question. Elizabeth is indolent. She would rather not have to get up so early to work, and all the make-up and the hairdressing are a bore for her. She has been trying to retire for more than fifteen years. She would give up acting and open a hat shop in London, she told Michael Wilding, after whisking him from under the confident nose of Marlene Dietrich.

"I can't make up my mind whom to marry, Elizabeth or Marlene," he confided at the time. He was mad about Marlene. I used to see him waiting for her inside Max Factor's where she would go to get her wigs dressed at one time; and, while he hated shopping, he always went shopping with Marlene. Mr. Wilding wouldn't hear of such a sacrifice from Elizabeth, and they both returned to Hollywood where she worked and he made unsuitable films which ruined his acting career.

Mike Todd persuaded her to do *Cat on a Hot Tin Roof*, but she had his promise that she could retire when it was finished. It was the last film on her contract at Metro. She completed it after his death because "Mike would have wanted me to."

I have always thought some of her serious illnesses were caused by traipsing all over the world with Todd, while she was pregnant with Liza, to promote his film *Around the World in 80 Days*. It hurt me to see the rain drenching her distended body at the royal premiere in London. She still suffers pain from a bad back. But "everything for my man" is the secret of her success with them. When Eddie Fisher was at the lowest ebb of his career (he had been the heel in the affair and his popularity had dwindled to zero), he finally landed a two-week appearance at the Empire Room in the Waldorf-Astoria Hotel. But he was a dead issue as far as the press was concerned, and no one wanted to interview him without Elizabeth.

"It's not my opening," she explained. "I don't want to take anything away from Eddie."

No Liz, no interviews for Eddie. "Okay, what shall I wear?"

"Your tightest dress."

On opening night she invited sixty celebrities to be her guests, including Sir Alex Guinness, Molly Berg, Prince Aly Khan, Gloria Vanderbilt, Lauren Bacall, Jason Robards, Mai Britt, etc., etc.

She has worked so much in recent years because it helped Richard. But how much longer can they mesmerize the public and the producers who have been so willing to pay them millions and millions of dollars? With the exception of *Virginia Woolf,* the recent product has not been successful. *Faustus* was a total disaster. *The Comedians* and *Reflections in a Golden Eye* and *The Sandpiper* were dreadful. Richard told me *Taming of the Shrew* earned $18 million. He can weave a fanciful story, and I'd like to see the balance sheet. This could explain their present nonstop working schedule. They are obviously making as much money as possible before time runs out. Richard is not a fool. He is cognizant of the fact that the million-dollar ride on the gravy train might be ending.

"I will retire before I'm forty," Elizabeth, who is now thirty-seven, promised me during the filming of *The Taming of the Shrew*. "But before I go, I'd like to do a play with Richard."

I hope it won't be *Macbeth,* although according to Mr. Burton, they have a backing of $4.5 million to do it as a film. Laurence Olivier could not raise a quarter of this when he wanted to portray Macbeth on the screen.

"Elizabeth would be so good as Lady Macbeth," Richard purred to the press. As of now, he plans only to direct. He told me not long ago that his wife had improved him as an actor! I did not care for Miss Taylor as the "Shrew." During the periods of the picture when she managed to diet, she looked lovely, but it was the same sort of high-pitched shouting that she emitted in *Cleopatra*. Lady Macbeth requires a more exalted standard of acting.

If the Elizabeth-Richard screen saga is really ending, Elizabeth will find it easier to depart. She has suffered much illness and much tragedy. I was among the sympathizers outside the hillside home in Beverly Hills when they told her Mike Todd had crashed to his death in *The Liz*. I can still hear her loud sobbing. And she has given much in the name of love. Richard was a good actor and some people believe he still is. He will be a writer, he says, but unless he abandons the bottle, I doubt whether he will make it to old age.

I envision one day walking down a street in London and a fat, middle-aged woman will pass me, and unless I look very closely, I won't recognize her as the most publicized woman of our time.

Elizabeth and Richard have perhaps earned a rest, but I cannot imagine they will ever stop making news. Of one sort or another.

11)

Marilyn

In a hospital you always know when an operation is scheduled. The nurses congregate in little groups and there is much coming and going into the patient's room. The atmosphere is almost ghoulish, but it is not meant to be. It's like a bullfight before the first event. There is an element of risk. Will everything go smoothly in the operating arena? Will the surgeon do a good job?

On the morning of April 28, 1952, there was less speculation and more excitement than usual in the corridors of the Cedars of Lebanon Hospital in Los Angeles. The surgeon was one of the best in the country and a top member of the Board of Governors. His patients were among the richest and most glamorous in Hollywood. But this patient was the most glamorous of all. Marilyn Monroe.

Only seven weeks before, on March 10, while she had been acting in her first starring role for 20th Century-Fox, *Don't Bother to Knock,* the door had burst open on one of her two deepest secrets—the nude calendar for which she had posed in 1950. It had proved so popular with discriminating art lovers during 1951 that it had been reproduced for 1952. A reporter was tipped off that the incredible body sprawled on red velvet in a combination of Manet's "Olympia" and Goya's

"Naked Maja" belonged to the luscious blonde star just emerging on the Hollywood film horizon. The disclosure and her explanation, "I did it because I was hungry," which was not true, had catapulted the former Norma Jean Baker to the heights of notoriety. This was before the wholesale undressing-to-the-buff of ambitious actresses for *Playboy* and other magazines. In the early '50s, for a star to be seen in the nude, was shocking and titillating. And now, the twenty-five-year-old cause of all the furor, her glamorous torso covered with a thin cotton hospital blanket, was being wheeled into the operating room. A young nurse in the group by the door was heard to giggle, "I wonder if she really *is* blonde all over"— repeating one of Marilyn's own remarks.

The surgeon, his assistant, the anesthetist, and the three nurses were ready. The cotton blanket was removed. The actress was lifted onto the operating table. A nurse started to arrange the operating sheet, with its open gap for the area of surgery, around the fragile flesh of the unconscious actress. She stopped abruptly when she saw three pieces of scratch-pad paper Scotch-taped to the stomach of the patient. The anesthetist was ready, and it was not until the operation was over that Marilyn's message was given to the doctor. In her scrawling illiterate handwriting she asked the doctor to be sure to read her note before operating, she begged him to cut as little as possible. That she might seem vain but that didn't enter into it. The fact that she was a woman was most important to her and meant much to her and she couldn't beg him enough to please save what he could, that she was in his hands, that he had children and he must know what it meant to her, and she knew somehow that he would and she thanked him in advance, over and over again and in the name of God he would not remove her ovaries. And she begged him to do all he could to prevent large scars, and she thanked him with all her heart.

A few days later when Marilyn was due to leave the hospital, she confessed to the doctor, "I'm afraid to leave, I can't pay my bill." The doctor, like all men who ever met her, was imbued with the desire to help and save her. He said, "Look, Marilyn, you're very important to 20th Century-Fox. Ask them to pay the bill." "Do you really think they would?" she asked in disbelief. "I'm sure of it," he replied. She telephoned the studio and the bill was paid.

She was no sooner home than her second secret was blared to the world. When Marilyn had signed her first contract in 1946 at Fox, she had stated in the biography every newcomer must fill out, that she was an orphan, that both parents were dead and that was the reason she had been raised in an orphanage and various foster homes. The truth was that her mother, Gladys Baker, was in a mental institution. Her father, Edward Mortenson, had met Miss Baker in the United States in 1923 after deserting his wife and family in Norway. Marilyn's mother was working in the cutting department of a Hollywood studio with frequent time out in mental hospitals. Mortenson was killed in a collision between his motorbike and a Hudson sedan in 1929, three years after Marilyn was born. In 1946 to admit you were illegitimate could ruin any chance of making it on the screen.

When confronted with the fact, Marilyn, as before, admitted it. If she were starting her career today, the nudity and the illegitimacy would have raised only an infinitesimal eyebrow. It is now almost fashionable in film circles to admit to being illegitimate or being unmarried to the father of your child. When Ingrid Bergman gave birth to a son before her marriage to Rossellini in the early '50s, it was a six-foot-headline shocker that shook the world and seemed certain to finish her as a film actress. In the realistic '60s, early poverty and misfortune are a plus for a film career. It is almost impossible for a rich, socialite actor or actress to make the grade. Dina Merrill is beautiful and has proved she can act, but her mother is Mrs. Marjorie Merriweather Post, one of the richest society women in the country, and Dina has not yet had more than medium success in her career. Amateurish Princess Lee Radziwill started at the top and there was only one way for her to go. She is beautiful and with practice perhaps could act as well as a Marilyn Monroe or an Ava Gardner or a Rita Hayworth, but there is too much refinement, not enough letting go. Grace Kelly, with her façade of aristocratic coldness, was a peasant, sexy dish underneath the clean-cut features. Ask any of her leading men. *All* the sex symbols were endowed with a large portion of earthy coarseness. Marilyn had the most. She never met Grace, although they had the same agent. When Miss Kelly's engagement to Prince Rainier was announced, Marilyn telephoned her and said, "I'm so glad you've found a way out of this business."

I met Marilyn during the late '40s in the Café de Paris at 20th Century-Fox. There had been some excitement in the newspapers about her: the publicity tour for Lester Cowan's picture, *Love Happy,* with Groucho Marx, where she was photographed from top to bottom and her witty remarks had been quoted; a lead in a nine-day "B" picture, *Ladies of the Chorus,* at Columbia; and stories of a romance with powerful 20th executive Joe Schenck, who had been instrumental in getting her first abortive contract at the studio in 1946. I watched Marilyn pause at the entrance of the café. She was accompanied by a young man (she always made her entrances with a man, even if he was just the office boy, to indicate her popularity with men). In one hand she held a big book. The free hand furtively creased the skirt of her thin beige suit between her buttocks, to emphasize them. The jacket was cut in a deep U so that you could see the rising mounds of her breasts. Every part of her shook when she walked. I thought she was tarty, pretty, eager to answer questions. I asked her what the book was about. It was *The Basic Writings of Freud.* She didn't look like an intellectual and I asked her, "Are you really reading it?" "Oh, yes," she breathed, and opened her blue eyes to the widest extent. She had a beautiful brow. It had not always been so beautiful. I knew her agents in those early days, Helen Ainsworth and Harry Lipton. They had suggested she remove the frizzy hair around her hairline before signing at Columbia for *Ladies of the Chorus.* Her hair was naturally curly, baby soft, and hard to manage. A new hairline was drawn for her at Columbia and the excess fuzz removed with hot wax, later by electrolysis.

Changing hairlines was common in Hollywood. Tyrone Power's was almost on his eyebrows and he was getting nowhere in his career. The higher forehead made it possible for him to be the hero instead of the villain. When Harry Cohn gave Rita Hayworth a contract, he told his make-up department, "I've just signed a girl named Rita Cansino from Fox at $50 a week. For God's sake, give her a higher hairline." Marilyn's new wide brow transformed her from being merely attractive into a beauty. But she always had a problem with her hair. She had resisted dying it blonde. Her hair broke under the continual assaults of peroxide. What a pity she was too soon for the wig era. Always concerned with how she looked, Marilyn washed and set her hair every day. Her greatest treasure was her beauty-parlor-size hair dryer. She lugged it to every city she visited in the United States.

There was fine, downy, blonde hair all over her face, which, although covered with make-up, gave a luminous quality to her skin on the screen. She would spend hours experimenting with make-up—putting it on, taking it off. She was never really sure she was beautiful, and she thought her nose was unattractive, a piece too long. Photographers learned to take her full face. When she was powerful, she killed every "still" showing her in profile. On the photographs she liked, she placed a star. Instinctively she knew where to turn when she saw a camera. Her eyelashes, upper and lower, half an inch long, were completely white and had to be dyed constantly. Her fingers were tiny and ineffectual. Her fingernails, often dirty, were chewed to the quick. Like Cary Grant, she had a bad chin. Stars of old were conscious of their defects. Claudette Colbert believed one side of her face was better than the other, as did Vivien Leigh. Everything on the sets had to be changed to fit the better side.

But at the beginning with Marilyn, there were no complexes. She was sweet, sensitive, and frightened by her lack of education and experience as an actress. She was easy to understand, no neuroses. For her first film role in *Scudda Hoo! Scudda Hay!* early in 1947, she was paid $125 a week, which was more than she received as a model. She spent most of her salary for lessons at the Hollywood branch of the Actors Lab, which came to be known as The Group. John Garfield was a member, also Morris Carnovsky. For *Ladies of the Chorus,* in which Adele Jergens played her mother, Marilyn was paid $150 a week. But she was always broke. She needed a car and borrowed $500 from her agents for a down payment on a used Ford convertible. The debt spiraled to $1,500. "She paid it all back in time," Mr. Lipton told me. Part of the debt was for braces on her teeth which protruded. She was put together with spit and yet she was irresistible, at the beginning as well as at the end.

She took the first of the pills, which were eventually to kill her, in 1948, when she had returned to Fox for a bit in a Jeanne Craine film, *You Were Meant for Me.* Like *Scudda Hoo,* this role expired on the cutting-room floor. Marilyn was living in the Valley then in a cheap apartment. She was naïve, trusting, and, having married a policeman, Jim Dougherty, at 16, she knew she could trust the law. One payday at Fox— it was a three-day job and she was paid $75 a day—she found she did not have enough cash to get a meal and buy gasoline to take her home. She stopped her car at Hollywood and Vine and asked a policeman where she could cash her studio check. She showed it to him with her address to prove it was bona fide. "I think Penny's will cash it for you," he told her. She stopped at a drive-in, had her dinner, and drove home. At two in the morning the cop broke into her apartment and tried to rape her—it had happened before as a child with one of the boarders in a foster home. Marilyn's screams brought the neighbors who called a doctor to calm the hysterical girl. He prescribed a sleeping pill, a seconal, to put her to sleep. It was too easy later, when she could not cope with her fears, to calm her nerves with large doses of nembutals and chloro-hydrate, and she needed more and more and more as the pace and problems of her life whirled her off the planet.

After her new agent, diminutive Johnny Hyde, who fell in love with Marilyn and wanted to marry her, had landed *Asphalt Jungle* for her with John Huston at M-G-M, the press department, reviewing the film, wrote a combined letter to the top studio echelon suggesting Marilyn be placed under contract. It was a small role, but she had come across as a sex blockbuster. "She's *too* sexy," said Dore Schary, who had only recently succeeded in ousting Louis B. Mayer as the studio head. Perhaps he meant she was too cheap.

Joe Mankeiwicz didn't think so when he insisted Darryl Zanuck sign her for *All About Eve,* which starred Bette Davis. She looked like a burlesque chippie doing the grinds and bumps in *Gentlemen Prefer Blondes* with Jane Russell, although Jane did not. Only an inherent whore could walk like Marilyn and dress like Marilyn. When she attended a Hollywood function, the dress was brought to her in pieces and sewn into the curves of her body. You could see there was nothing underneath.

I remember the glittering red dress she wore to receive *Photoplay*'s Gold Medal Award as the Best New Star of 1953. (At the Foreign Press Award in '62, her sequined green dress was so tight, she couldn't walk; she could only manage a mincing hobble.) The crush of photographers and reporters has never been equaled before or after. Not even for Elizabeth Taylor. I realized then from the shoving and the hysteria that a new star had arisen in Hollywood and that she could make any demands and she would get them. One thing about Hollywood, once they are sure you are a star, every door opens, everyone is rushing to kiss your rear end, and how Marilyn flaunted her rear end! In her public-appearance gowns, you could see every crevasse. I hope I was not among the reporters who wrote "How shocking!" but I might have been, because I *was* shocked. I had never seen anything like it in public. She was the living end. Her private wardrobe was meager, except for a black mink she loved; the rest was mostly sweaters and skirts and down-at-heels pumps.

When you talked with her away from the camera and the

crowds, she was modest and as true as the platinum tint she came to use on her hair in the manner of a previous sex symbol, Jean Harlow. After her marriage to Joe DiMaggio in 1954, she raised her neckline because that was how he preferred it. He objected strenuously to her blow-up dress over the New York subway grating to publicize *The Seven Year Itch*.

I was sitting at a table in St. Marks Square in Venice on the night of August 6, 1962, after attending a performance of *La Bohème* in the exquisite opera house. An acquaintance joined our party at midnight and said casually, "What a pity about Marilyn."

"Don't tell me she tried to commit suicide again?" I asked. Only the week before in London I had told a reporter, "She'll commit suicide. There will be the one time when it will be too late to save her."

"She's dead," the man said.

I didn't believe it, but I rushed to the Danieli and asked the concierge if he had heard anything. She was dead—"the pills," as every Italian, English, and French newspaper stated the next day.

There was no discipline in her life. A man who knew her well told me that she was stupid, but I didn't agree with that. It was simply being unable to cope with the fierce worldwide fame with which Hollywood drenches its favorites. I was there at the beginning, the middle, and the end. I saw the deterioration. I saw the hope and the disappointments. The longing to give what the people wanted and at the same time, to become a complete person herself. She was also selfish, rude, thoughtless, completely self-centered. She kept people waiting for hours. I waited three hours once in the sitting room of her Beverly Hills Hotel bungalow, making forced conversation with Pat Newcomb, who had become her companion. When Marilyn appeared, made up to kill and wearing theatrical gold pajamas, she was so charming and friendly, all my irritation vanished and I was eating out of her hand as everyone else did.

In the early days, when the studio could send her off on
jaunts to publicize herself and their films, she was in Atlantic
City to judge a beauty parade, and I can still see her in the
car with the Mayor, with the front part of her dress nonex-
istent. Earlier in the day she was scheduled for a mass interview with the world's press, which had converged on the sea-
side resort. Hour followed hour and no Monroe. Men with
cameras and reporters with pencils were pacing angrily up
and down, and the man from *Look* magazine was howling to
the 20th press agent, "Who does she think she is? You can tell
her for me I don't want to see her now or ever." "We have
done everything to get that bitch here," he apologized. With
late people these are always the magic words and she appeared
almost on cue. The man from *Look* was so enchanted by
Marilyn, he turned to the press agent and stormed, "How
dare you call her a bitch!"

Look magazine in the early '50s instituted an annual cocktail party in Hollywood to announce some special awards for
film people. My N.A.N.A. boss, John Wheeler, was in town
and I took him to the party. John has always had an eye for
blondes, and he suddenly pointed to a fair head in the far
distance of the Crystal Room of the Beverly Hills Hotel and
demanded, "Who's that?" "Oh, a new starlet," I said. Would
he like to meet her? He would. "You are very pretty," he told
Marilyn, and predicted, "You will be a great success." She
thanked him prettily and modestly.

By the time Mr. Wheeler came to Hollywood again, Marilyn had evolved into the most glamorous film star in the
world. "That blonde, Miss Monroe," he said to me, "I'd like
to talk to her again." "I'll invite her to my home for a drink,"
I said. She had attended a party at my house not too long before, arriving when nearly everyone had gone and she had
kissed my seven-year-old son, Robert, who squirmed and was
oblivious to the honor conferred on him. Marilyn did not kiss
my ten-year-old daughter, Wendy. She always related to men,
not to women, if she could help it.

There I am pouring a Scotch and very little water for John

Wheeler in my Beverly Hills living room and waiting for Marilyn who was due at 6:00 P.M., 7:00 P.M., 8:00 P.M., 8:30 P.M.—and I am getting mad. That bitch was standing me up in front of my boss. "I'm calling the studio to see what in hell happened to her," I told John, who said not to go to any trouble, but I could see the air was out of his steam. "Where is she?" I demanded of someone in her dressing room. "Oh, she's coming," I was assured, "but this afternoon, she broke out in hives and had to go to the doctor." Marilyn's skin, paper thin, with the veins very visible, bruised easily and erupted into hives when she was nervous; and after she was successful, she became more and more nervous. At 9:15 when I was calling the studio to tell her not to bother, the doorbell rang. Marilyn. Breathless. Apologetic. She sat on the sofa very close to Mr. Wheeler, almost in his lap, and he found her adorable. She had a trick of making all men feel she could be in love with them and I think she could be, a sort of saving each one for a rainy day, for when things would get tough again in her life and she would need help.

Marilyn and Mr. Wheeler became good friends. When she was married to Arthur Miller and spending the summer of 1957 in Amagansett on Long Island and the Wheelers were in nearby East Hampton, they would frequently dine with each other. Marilyn liked champagne and loved caviar. The Millers were due at the Wheelers' one Sunday afternoon to partake of both luxuries when a servant from the Miller house called with a message from Arthur. Marilyn had suffered a miscarriage and he was rushing her to New York by ambulance. When Marilyn was well enough, she insisted on the champagne and caviar treat with the Wheelers at her New York home at 444 East Fifty-seventh Street. Whenever she saw me, she would ask after Mr. Wheeler, never John.

I pulled off the coup of the year by bringing Marilyn to one of the annual N.A.N.A. cocktail parties during the publishers' convention held late in April every year in New York. It was earlier in her career and she was on time, arriving when most of the guests—editors, publishers and their wives—

were still there. She was an enormous hit circulating around the suite in the Waldorf-Astoria, talking to the wives as well as their husbands. One man who drank too much—he was not an editor or a publisher, they never drink too much—sneaked up on Marilyn and unzipped her dress. She merely moved away with a vague smile and zipped it up again. But when I told Mr. Wheeler, he was furious and ordered the man out. Of course caviar and champagne were served in Marilyn's honor. This was the last of the N.A.N.A. cocktail parties. It could have been because of the zipper incident or it could have been because Mr. Wheeler felt he could never top his guest list.

I would always keep him informed of Marilyn's movements and what she was doing, except the time when she fell in love. In any case, John would not have believed it. The man was charming, and Marilyn succumbed to his gallantry and the rapt attention he gave her. His wife had gone on a trip to Europe leaving her husband in their Beverly Hills Hotel bungalow. Marilyn's was next door. Soon after, late at night, his doorbell rang. He was surprised to see Marilyn all bundled up in a fur coat. He was more surprised when, doing the polite thing, he asked her to step inside. She immediately dropped the coat and revealed herself stark naked. "I'm a man. What could I do?" the gentleman confided to a friend of mine. Marilyn was still married to Arthur Miller and he was also aware of the situation. But perhaps because Marilyn had helped him with her presence in Washington during the time of the inquiries into his Communist activities, when his passport had been taken away from him, or perhaps because he believed he could save their marriage by remaining silent, he looked the other way. When Marilyn was in the hospital for some real or imagined ailment—she was in and out of hospitals constantly at this time—she asked her new lover to come and see her or she would do something desperate. Everything is known in Hollywood and this was soon transmitted to the gentleman's wife, who put her foot down.

"If you see her in the hospital," she decreed, "I'll divorce you." He loved his wife and he knew she loved him. He did not go to the hospital, but he had not seen the last of Marilyn.

Some time later, Marilyn, who was living with her husband in New York, learned that the man's plane would have a half-hour stopover at the airport in New York. She came to the airport in a chauffeured limousine, fortified with a magnum of champagne and a large can of caviar. Eight planes had been grounded because of a bomb scare. I was among the hundreds at the airport waiting for the all-clear signal to take off for Los Angeles when I saw Marilyn's friend. Before I could say "hello," a gray-haired woman dashed over to him, Marilyn Reese, Marilyn's secretary, whom I could see he knew very well. She guided him to the exit where a blonde in beige from head to foot met him, flung one arm around his neck—the other was holding the champagne and caviar—and gleefully informed him that the half-hour wait had been expanded to five hours. "Let's go to the VIP room," she said in her breathless little-girl voice. He was willing, but TWA's Ambassador Club was packed. "Let's go to the International Hotel," she said while the man kept muttering, "All this is very confusing." Miss Reese telephoned for a suite at the hotel where they tucked into the caviar and champagne. Marilyn called Arthur Miller to say she'd be late getting home, acting as though five hours in a suite with a man she had reportedly had an affair with was a normal thing.

Some years later in London the gentleman said to me, "I do not understand American women. Over here we fook and we don't think anything more about it, but American women want to marry you. Me, I've always been married to my wife. Why should I have wanted to marry Marilyn?"

This question has been asked frequently about Arthur Miller's inability to write anything except an original screen script for Marilyn, *The Misfits*, during the four and a half years of their marriage. His enemies who dislike him for *After the Fall*, his view from the Marilyn bridge, accuse him of ego, of being flattered that the sex symbol of the world wanted him above all other men and legalized it on a hot summer day in White Plains, New York, June 28, 1956.

Nineteen fifty-six was an important year for Marilyn. She had made her best film, *Bus Stop,* for Joshua Logan, after an absence from Hollywood of fifteen months. She was bitterly disappointed that she was not nominated for an Oscar. It was one of the two things she wanted most—to be known as a good actress and to have children. Her ten-month marriage with Joe DiMaggio had yielded nothing but boredom. Like Cary Grant, he preferred to spend his evenings watching television —or he did during the marriage. I was on the lawn outside their rented home on North Palm Drive in Beverly Hills when she tottered by on the arm of her lawyer, Jerry Geisler, on the way to the divorce court—was she acting a stricken woman or was she really upset? If the latter, why the divorce, because Joe loved her and still does.

Even after the divorce from Miller on June 20, 1961, she saw Miller's children often. She taught his daughter how to make up. "They were my children," she told me pathetically early in 1962. His elderly father was her escort at President Kennedy's birthday affair at Madison Square Garden and at the party afterward. (I can still see her in the silvery see-through dress and hear her quavering childish "Happy Birthday, Dear President." She was terrified, but only the tremor in her voice revealed the ordeal to the glamorous audience.) The Millers had been her family and she would not allow a divorce to kill the relationship she loved. She saw them all whenever she was in the East, she told me seven months prior to her death.

But there was no sadness or thought of disaster for Marilyn in the first six months of 1956, although Hollywood was still in a depressed state from the competition of the TV aerials on the roof tops of the land. The film moguls had faced and come through panic before. In the transition to talkies in the late 20's, the early 30's, when the banks closed and there was no money for film production, and the customers could not afford the price of movie admission even though it was only 50¢ as against the $2.50 or more you must pay today. Marilyn's long absence from the screen had brought home to 20th Century-Fox how much their stockholders needed her. Something like one-half million dollars passed into Marilyn's hands, part of it for her Monroe Productions Company, part to pay back an advance from her agent, the mighty Charles Feldman.

There was nothing ineffectual about her business acumen and the way she used people to lean on, such as Milton Greene, who became her partner after he photographed her and whom she discarded without a backward look when Miller took over. There always had to be a prop for Marilyn, from Natasha Lytess, her first drama coach, to Paula and Lee Strasberg of the Actors Studio, to which she bequeathed some of the $1.5 million against a percentage (paid at the rate of $150,000 per year) she earned from her share of *Some Like It Hot*.

Bus Stop was finished before she took off from Hollywood to marry Arthur Miller in the East. "She was often late," Josh Logan told me. "She'd run in apologizing, take a look in the mirror, and then go through an agonizing process of getting herself in the mood." Billy Wilder went through hell with Marilyn in *Some Like It Hot*. Also John Huston, who directed *The Misfits*. He told me in Munich, when he was making *Freud* with Montgomery Clift, that Marilyn's lateness and inability to work made Clark Gable so nervous and restless that he insisted on doing the heavy horse handling that probably caused his fatal heart attack.

But "As Billy Wilder said," Josh remarked, " 'My Aunt Minnie in Massachusetts is always on time, but who will pay to see my Aunt Minnie?' I adored her. I resent terribly that she was maligned. This town belittled her from the time she got here. She was a beautiful, attractive sexual figure. They labeled her a dumb blonde. She was not educated, but she was intelligent. She longed to be an intellectual, otherwise, why marry Arthur Miller? The marriage was initially beneficial to them both. It gave her intellectual status and it flattered his ego. He wrote a terrible screen play for her, and his friends will never forgive him for *After the Fall*." In *Bus Stop* she had a champagne quality. In the middle of a scene, she would stop and everyone thought she had forgotten her lines, but it was her inner censor telling her to pause and think about the scene again. She was like a little fawn (someone else described her as a doe, she was shot at so much). So hurt. So used. She was bullied, threatened, used by everyone since she was a baby. It isn't true that she only loved herself. She loved the people who loved her. She was looking for direction and she never really found it. Marilyn was lost somewhere between birth and death. When *Bus Stop* was completed, Mr. Logan told his star, "You're a combination of Greta Garbo and Charlie Chaplin." She wept and replied, "You're the only person who ever said I was an actress." She gave Logan a party at Trader Vic's and presented him with her photograph in a silver frame and said, "It would look awfully well next to yellow roses."

They laughed when Marilyn, at the London press conference with Sir Laurence Olivier and Arthur Miller by her side, stood up to tell the reporters she wanted to play Grushenka in *The Brothers Karamazov*. I was there. Somehow I always seemed to be there. She would have been superb as Dostoevski's sensual, confused, heroine. She was born for the part, and Maria Schell with her assured smile was completely wrong, as I told her during a lunch at Warners where she was starring with Gary Cooper in *The Hanging Tree*, and she agreed with me.

June 1, 1962. It was Marilyn's thirty-sixth birthday. She was starring in *Something's Got to Give* at 20th Century-Fox. She had been late, mostly not reporting at all. And when she came, she would rush to her dressing room and Mrs. Strasberg had to coax her out. And then she was so frightened, she could not remember more than two words at a time. In the seven weeks of filming she had completed five days' work. The atmosphere was tense, but following the usual custom, they had a party on the set for her with a birthday cake and thirty-six candles and congratulations from her costar, Dean Martin, and Henry Weinstein, the producer, and George Cukor, the director, and the rest of the cast and crew. It was a brief ceremony, and afterward Marilyn walked out to the chauffeur-driven limousine provided by the studio—they mistakenly believed it would bring her to work on time. That night she appeared for a muscular-dystrophy benefit at Chavez Ravine baseball park and there was much joking and many photographs with Marilyn wearing a baseball cap.

Monday. June 4. Marilyn sent word to the studio that she was ill. The next day I was talking to the producer, and he told me they were planning to fire Miss Monroe. I called the *New York Mirror,* and on the streets that night the front page blared "Marilyn Bounced!" I was a reporter doing a job, but the stories upset Marilyn's press agent. I had seen Marilyn not long before at Trader Vic's in Beverly Hills with a group of people that included Frank Sinatra, who was one of her close friends. She had turned, seen me, and waved. I had thought of going over, but they all seemed to be having such a good time, especially Marilyn, who could get high on a glass of champagne. I remember thinking then, listening to her laughter, which was louder than usual, "She sounds desperate, she will soon be thirty-six—soon she'll be forty, and she'll hate that."

She was very thin in those last months. During the marriage with Miller she had wanted to be a housewife and had marketed and cooked—she loved spaghetti and had gained weight—but now she wanted to look gorgeous in the nude again. There was a nude scene in a pool in the film, and it was her idea to pose naked for the *Vogue* magazine photographer. The one thing she always had confidence about was her body. She knew people wanted to see her like that.

Friday, June 8. Marilyn insisted she was well enough to work and was determined to disregard the studio's notice to quit. But the studio had had it and hired Lee Remick to take over the part. Dean Martin refused to work with Lee on the grounds he had only signed to costar with Marilyn. He was obviously trying to get her back into the film. Everyone was suing everyone. Marilyn was sued by Fox for $750,000. Marilyn sued the studio. Dean Martin was sued by the studio and on June 25 he sued Fox for $6,850,000.

Wednesday night, June 20. Fox released Miss Remick from her contract. On Friday, July 11, Cyd Charrise, who had the second woman's role in the film, filed suit against the studio for $14,000, alleging this was owing on the $50,000 she was to be paid—she had already received $36,000. Defendants were 20th Century-Fox, Dean Martin, and Claude Productions—Dean's company. While all this was going on, three top executives from the studio called on Marilyn in the small Mexican cottage she had bought in Brentwood. (While she had been looking at houses, a man and his wife had answered the doorbell. The man was delighted when he saw it was Marilyn. The woman had screamed, "Get off my property." Marilyn was mystified by this kind of hostility.) The studio wanted Marilyn back in the film, then Dean would return, and everything would be fine. Marilyn, suspicious of their motives, was cautious. She did not want them to deny afterward whatever they said and offered. She had stationed a witness in the next room, leaving the door slightly ajar, to take down everything that transpired. Whatever promises they made her, they would have to keep.

Early in August, while waiting for the film to resume, Marilyn went in her limousine—she had kept the car and the driver—and visited her friends, the Dudley Murphys, at their Holiday House Motel overlooking the ocean at Malibu. Marilyn loved the beach and was a constant visitor to the Pat and Peter Lawford home in Santa Monica where other guests would sometimes include President John Kennedy and his brother Bobby. All the Kennedys liked Marilyn, and she would play with the Lawford children and be quiet and content. Before leaving Holiday House, the Murphys asked Marilyn to sign the celebrity guest book. Under "Residence" she wrote "Nowhere." Three days later she was dead. Marilyn: 1926–1962.

12)

Clyde and His Bonnies

One thing you have to say for Warren Beatty—he always keeps an open bed. Queen-size. Usually occupied. He starts with a preposition and ends with a proposition. But whether the girl is Julie Christie or a pick-up on Third Avenue, she gets equal consideration and attention. He likes women. Even when he leaves them. When the fire with Broadway star Barbara Harris was extinguished, he dispatched his personal press agent to take care of the actress at the Tony Awards, which she won for *The Apple Tree*. "She's nervous," he explained. He uses the telephone as a weapon of seduction. He curls up with it, cuddles it, whispers into it, "What's new, pussycat?" (He coined the phrase, and the picture was originally written for him.) When he mumbles, "How are you?" it's like a man on the verge of an orgasm. He uses the group to get the girl, separating her from the crowd, complimenting her for all to hear—"Have you ever seen such eyes!" His list of Girls I Want to Screw includes Mae West, Jeanne Moreau, and a Negress who paints. He's tender, romantic, and ruthless. He's Br'er Rabbit and Reynard the Fox, racing from the coop grinning through a mouthful of feathers, while the massacred chicks peep blissfully, "Please come again." He's childlike. He's crafty. He's locked into himself, full of nerve, verve, drive, follow-through. He seems languid, but it's a cover-up for his boundless energy. He has a cool head, and he is insatiable. He is also greedy for power, for accomplishment. He's a man on the run, a nomad who will check out of a hotel almost before he has checked in. He's ahead of the game. He's the inarticulate prophet of the sick Sixties, a flower child who didn't have to go to Haight-Ashbury, a night owl who boasts, "I've missed a million sunrises, but I've had some great conversations." He's today and tomorrow, with an old-fashioned hangover from yesterday. And he's afraid. He doesn't know who he is.

"He has a kind of innocence," Faye Dunaway, the film Bonnie to his Clyde, said, trying to explain him to me. She is one of the few to escape his lethal charm. He tried, but she said no. Nonetheless, he insisted at Warner Brothers, "I want Faye for Bonnie," while he was asking me and a hundred others, "What do you think of her?" He must always have reassurance. She was insulated against Warren because she was in love with Jerry Schatzberg, the photographer and director.

It seems almost easier for him to fall in love with a married woman. Leslie Caron was married. Natalie Wood was married. Vanessa Redgrave was not yet divorced from Tony Richardson. The Russian ballerina Maya Plisetskaya had a husband stashed away in the Soviet Union. Miss Harris was engaged to Arnold Weinstein. Julie Christie was devoted to Don Besant when Warren competed for possession. The girls he has loved, famous or unknown, are legion.

During a lull in *Lilith* he was in New York at Delmonico's Hotel on Park Avenue at Fifty-ninth Street.

"Let's take a walk," he said in his restless, disoriented way. A girl walked by. "Hello, pussycat," he called after her. She continued walking. "Go ahead, be stuck up," he laughed. Another girl walked by. The "hello, pussycat" treatment was repeated. She walked on. "Ah, well," philosophically, "you can't win 'em all." Three girls. "What are you doing later?" Warren asked them collectively. One girl turned. "Fresh," she spat at Mr. Beatty, who was not beaten yet. He looked down Fifty-ninth Street to Lexington Avenue. "They'll be coming out of Bloomingdale's now," he said, adding reflectively, "cute little bunnies." He took up his position on the corner of Lexington and Fifty-ninth. Success. "Where you from?" He gave the salesgirl his telephone number. As he said, You can't win 'em all, but if you keep on trying, someone will say "yes."

"Warren's secret?" Miss Dunaway smiled. "To start with, he is one of the most charming men I've ever met. He has a totally unconventional approach to women. It's a direct approach. He'll dare anything. He's tenacious, audacious. He plays it for shock. He has a boyishness, a vulnerability that is immensely appealing. He trusts his instincts. He doesn't waste time on amenities. He appeals to the feminine wish to be engulfed. He adores challenge." I can see Julie Christie smiling and saying, "True."

The scene is San Francisco. Julie, an original, who exploded into stardom with a swinging walk in *Billy Liar* in 1963 and became an international favorite two years later in *Darling*, was starring in *Petulia* with George C. Scott and Richard Chamberlain. Mr. Besant, charming, good-looking, had flown over from London. She loved Don and would like to have a child with him, she had told me in 1966 while starring in *Dr. Zhivago* in Spain. They are free souls of today's antiestablishment rebellion. Mr. Beatty was in San Francisco to visit his Russian girl friend. He meets Julie. He knows a cool pussycat when he sees one. He senses she is more with it even than he is. He is enchanted by her resemblance to an unmade bed. He tries to move in, but gets no further than her hand. She knows all about Mr. Beatty. She is not going to fall into *that* trap.

Mr. Besant returns to his art teaching in England. Warren, sniffing his opportunity, hangs around. (The Russian ballerina is twirling somewhere on the road.) Warren develops a sudden desire to study all aspects of *Petulia*. He is constantly on the set. But Julie is indifferent. He is getting no-where.

The premiere of *Camelot* in Los Angeles. Julie, whose film is also for Warner Brothers, is invited to attend. Don is not around and she requires an escort. "How about one of the press agents taking me?" she suggested. No, she was advised. "You must be seen and photographed with an important star." Several names were suggested, among them Warren's, who had eagerly acquiesced when asked about being included as a possible escort. She turned them all down, including Mr. Beatty. "Ha!" said the executive who had asked him. "You're supposed to be such a great cocksman but Julie Christie doesn't even want you for her escort to a film." You can imagine how galling this remark was to the Casanova of our day. "Where is she now?" he demanded. In Tijuana (Mexico) filming the last scene for *Petulia,* he was told. It was Thursday. The picture would finish Saturday.

The next day Warren casually asked the executive, "What are you doing this weekend?"

"Why?"

"Oh," replied Warren, "I think I'll go to Tijuana to try my luck with Julie again."

"You're wasting your time."

"I'll make a bet with you," grimly. "This time she'll know I'm around."

A week later the executive needed Miss Christie for some *Petulia* publicity chores. "Where is she?" he demanded of his publicity department.

"She's in Mexico," they told him. He tried a short cut. "Where is Warren Beatty?"

"He's in Mexico, too . . . with Julie."

Warren met his match in Miss Christie. She is as inde-pendent and as disdainful of old-fashioned responsibility as he is. She is four years younger (Warren was born in 1937, Julie in 1941), but even more than Warren, who marches to the beat of today's generation, she gyrates to the new sound of undisciplined self-expression. And she will not be pushed

around. Soon after flying from London to join him in Los Angeles—he had rented a beach house at Malibu—Warren was
asked to appear at the Tokyo premiere of *Bonnie and Clyde,*
which he had eagerly promoted all over the United States
and Europe when Warners did nothing, believing all they had
was a nice little picture. Warren's efforts were largely responsible for the film's great success. When he was telephoned
at Malibu to leave immediately, he said, "Just a minute."
The executive heard him ask Miss Christie if it was all right
if he went to Tokyo for a few days. She was angry. "Look, I
flew over the Pole to be with you. If you go to Tokyo, I'm
flying right back to London." Warren on the phone, "I talked
to J.C. and it's—er—complicated."

"We'll pay for Julie to go, too" ("although we didn't want
to because we were publicizing the picture, not the romance,"
the executive told me later).

"No. She doesn't want to go to Tokyo," said Warren. "She
wants to go with me to San Francisco." They went to San
Francisco. Mostly, Warren went to Europe to be with Julie,
or she came to California or New York to be with him. One
time she flew into New York and telephoned him at Delmonico's from the airport. It was rather awkward because at
that moment he was entertaining Barbara Harris. He went
into the other room to call a friend. "I need help. The situation is—er—complicated." I did not hear the sequel, but
Warren, while he gives an impression of helplessness, is expert at extricating himself from complicated situations.

Part of Warren's admiration for Julie has been that she
does not particularly want to get married. This suits him because while he sometimes talks of marriage now, even asking
his married friends, "What is it like to come home every day
to the same woman? Is it confining?" he would just as soon
stay single for as long as the traffic will hold. I almost believed
him when he told Leslie Caron, "If you want me to, I'll marry
you." But Leslie did not, and after costarring with him in
the disastrous film *Promise Her Anything,* she released her
lover from his lukewarm promise of marriage.

When Warren was named as the other man in the divorce action brought by Leslie's husband, British stage and screen director Peter Hall, she assured me that her marriage to Peter had broken up before the start of the romance. It wasn't true. Leslie had seemed the happiest of women when I lunched with her in England a few months before the rumors began. She was wearing a white, red, and blue sailor suit—Chanel or Dior, I've forgotten now—and it was very chic. Her face was set in the relaxed lines of a woman who has no worries. She had only one, in fact. She would like to work more, but there weren't many roles in English films for a French actress. She talked of her two children, whom she adored. She spoke lovingly and proudly of her husband. They divided their time, she told me, between their two homes; in fashionable Montpelier Square in London, and at Stratford-on-Avon, where Peter was in charge of the Shakespearean program. The Bard might have made something of *The Unfinished Love of Warren and Leslie*.

It began in the lobby of the Beverly Hills Hotel, where rich tourists and executives from the East stare at the film and television stars and starlets, usually heading toward the Polo Lounge for interviews or a rendezvous. Deals are made in the dimly lit cavern. Lives and careers are changed. Warren was with a press agent when he spotted Leslie. "Who's that?" he demanded. Ah, yes, he had always admired her as an actress. He was surprised at her sophisticated appearance. Like many others, he was still thinking of Mlle. Caron in terms of *Lili* and *Gigi*. "I really dig her," said our instant lover. He sprinted after her and panted, "I think we have a mutual friend," and beckoned to the press agent, who happened to be hers. He told Leslie he had always found her films very poignant, while his half-closed appraising eyes were stripping her naked.

That was the beginning, and it might have ended there because Leslie is a sensible Frenchwoman. But Warren, when hunting the quarry, is irresistible. He drenched her with attention, and was so interested in every little thing she said—

isn't the secret of charm listening intently to the other person?—and he was sympathetic about her present lack of films. She had danced and acted since she was thirteen, had starred in her very first film in Hollywood, *An American in Paris,* with Gene Kelly, had married and divorced Geordie Hormel of the ham family, and now while she was Mrs. Peter Hall and an "in" member of the intellectual set of London and Stratford, she wanted to work again. "It's tough," said Warren, plunging his myopic blue-green eyes into her unwary soul. The next thing we knew, Leslie was visiting Warren openly on the set of *Mickey One* in Chicago.

I had a drink with Leslie in the Polo Lounge, and she was tense and refused to discuss Warren or her disintegrating marriage except to say, "Everything is all right. Nothing has changed." The very next day the newspapers carried a story from London that Peter Hall had made their two children wards of the British court to prevent them from going to Hollywood and Warren Beatty, that he was planning to divorce Leslie and was naming Warren as corespondent. Leslie flew to London immediately. She would fight for her children, but she would not give up the man who had disrupted her life.

I was in London soon after and called Leslie. I was invited for cocktails to the house in Montpelier Square. The drawing room, with its red plush upholstery and gilt mirrors, Leslie told me as she smiled wanly, was copied from a famous French brothel. That was the only time she smiled. She admitted her feelings for Warren and his for her. He had told her, "I'm in love for the first time in my life." He said he had finally found a simple, quiet girl with no tricks, a straightforward woman with whom he could be completely natural. "I'm not ashamed of loving him," said Leslie, with enormous sincerity. "I tried to hide it at first, but it had to come into the open. Of course it has made my life difficult because I cannot give up my children and so I'm changing my plans. I was going to live with Warren in Hollywood, which is not the wicked city my husband seems to believe—my children would have gone to the same school as Gregory Peck's; I have seen it, and it's a marvelous school. But now I'll live in England to be near them, and Warren has agreed to live here. When I have my divorce, we will be married."

It was a marvelous interview. I wrote the story with tremendous care so as not to upset Mr. Hall. I pointed out that when children are parted from a mother or father they love, later when they grow up they resent the parent who caused the separation, especially from a mother, and Mr. Hall should think carefully before risking such a disaster. I received a letter from Leslie thanking me—"You're a real friend"—and promising never to forget my help.

When I was in England the next time, I was interested in getting a follow-up story, the date of the marriage to Warren, how he liked the idea of living in London, etc. I heard that Leslie was flying to the United States and that Warren would be with her. They were now free to marry, and I was convinced the trip was a honeymoon. I was in a limousine taking me to Otto Preminger at the Dorchester Hotel, with his press agent, when I exclaimed, "What am I going to Otto for when I should be on the way to Leslie!" We changed direction. Montpelier Square. Leslie's small daughter opened the door. "Where's Mama?" I cooed.

"She's out." I knew it was true because little children don't lie.

I settled in the car for a long wait, but a few minutes later a taxi stopped at the door and Leslie stepped out. I was over in a flash. She invited me to come inside, but not to the French brothel, only as far as one foot into the hallway, where she was the uncommunicative Leslie of old.

"To the Hilton," I told the driver. Warren was registered there. What I could not get from Leslie I might squeeze out of Warren. He was not in his room. I waited for him in the lobby after telephoning his press agent, Theo Cowan, to come over and help find him for me. Warren arrived first and I pretended it was pure coincidence I was there. "Let's have a drink downstairs at Trader Vic's," he said. When Theo appeared, Warren apologized to me. "I bet you think I phoned him to come, that I don't trust you." I kept a straight face, looking away from Theo, who said nothing, and who left soon after. This was Warren's favorite story until I finally told him that it was I who had asked Theo to come. He then punctured a story of which I had been ignorant. I had said to him, "I can't understand why Leslie gave me that wonderful interview about how much you loved each other and that you would be getting married, and afterward clammed up." "Did it ever occur to you," he replied, "that she was using you?" The guilty party who was going to marry again immediately after her divorce would get at least partial custody of her children. It was imperative for Leslie to have a reporter put the impending marriage into print.

Warren was miserable in England. He hated the weather, he hated having to stay in one place. He was publicly responsible for Leslie's predicament and, not being a cruel man, he stayed and suffered, making two films in England—after *Promise Her Anything, Kaleidoscope,* which was equally bad. If he had remained there to marry Leslie he would not have made *Bonnie and Clyde,* which changed the entire course of his career, but not his private life, which is still devoted to the ladies. He is popular with women of all ages, including me. I find him amusing. He brings out my motherly feelings. It's like watching an attractive little boy—I always think of him as little, although he is 6′ 1″—trying to be as outrageous as possible.

An interview at my Malibu beach house in California. Questions. Disjointed nonanswers. Warren restless. Standing. Sitting. Suddenly commanding, "Let's walk on the beach." Me with notebook and pencil, trotting alongside on the sand. Warren stopping abruptly, "Let's go back to the house and fuck," immobilizing my pencil in midsentence.

"Just how old are you?" I ask to change the subject.

"How old do you think?" surveying me, with his jaw jutting in masculine arrogance.

"Twenty-seven?"

"Yeah, twenty-seven."

Actually he was thirty. I could see we were not getting a printable interview. Back to the house. "I'm looking to rent a beach place for Leslie and her children." He was considering Peter Lawford's house in Santa Monica, he told me, but Peter wanted to sell it for $150,000 and that was too much. Besides, when he wanted to go to town several times a day it would be a lot of driving, but Leslie was coming soon and she expected to live at the beach. My assistant, Maye Maas, had a beautiful home a few doors away. Her husband had talked of renting it. Yes, Warren would like to see it.

"This is great," he enthused downstairs. Maye, Warren, and I went upstairs. In the master bedroom, with the ocean supplying the background music, Warren grabbed me, exclaiming dramatically, "Now that we're alone"—ignoring Maye—"we have a great opportunity," and attempted to throw me on the bed. It was so ridiculous I had to laugh.

"Why are you so rough on my girls?" Warren asked me during a recent lunch in the Bella Fontana Room at the Beverly Wilshire Hotel. He was half an hour late and his long hair was wild, his face unshaven, and no tie. The maître d', while I was waiting for Warren, confided, "He'll come in without a tie, but we can't turn him away." Errol Flynn, when he wore an open shirt, still looked elegant. Warren and today's young actors like Dustin Hoffman, whom I think of as the runt of the litter, look scruffy, unshaven, and not too clean.

"I'm not rough on your girls," I said, "I'm rough on you. What have you got against marriage?" turning the attack after Warren had taken in all the women in the restaurant, his eyes flickering for a few seconds on the pretty ones. But now he was giving me his complete attention, moving closer to indicate there was no other woman in the room.

"How's your son? How's your daughter?" The rapid questions were accompanied by restless movements of his long fingers—he had once fleetingly considered a concert-piano career but advanced no further than a Greenwich Village bar.

He tore the paper from a cube of sugar, twisted it, and stuck it up one of his nostrils, regarding me challengingly, head, nose, and chin up, eyes down. But he listened attentively while I gave him the latest news of my offspring.

"Are you a good mother?" I thought I was, but he seemed skeptical. Afterward I tried to put together what we had talked about, and as usual, it came out a noninterview except for some half sentences on his next vague film project.

"It's an original story," I was able to extract. I gathered he was writing it. "When I start a screen play [much clasping and unclasping of his hands, playfully jabbing me with a fork, putting on and taking off his eyeglasses, and looking trapped and uncomfortable] . . . do you really want to know? . . . I start with a basic concept . . . What are you doing for sex? . . . Then I break it down, then I go back and say it's no good . . . Why did you come in from the beach? I would have come out to see you there . . . You mean you came in all this way to see me?" The beach house would, in fact, have been easier for both of us because Warren at this particular time was living at Malibu with Miss Christie.

"What is the story about?" I asked. He unwrapped another cube of sugar, rolled the paper, stuck it up the other nostril. "Come on," I said, wanting something for the wait and the hour's drive to Beverly Hills.

"Well," and he did a semicircle with his neck, stood up, then down, "I'm writing something . . . *Natural State*—what's a state, what is not—some of the boundaries we've given ourselves are . . . It isn't prose . . . There's nowhere to go with prose . . . No use making a screen play a literary work . . . You write what's going on the screen . . . Have you been psychoanalyzed?" (I knew he had persuaded Leslie Caron, his "simple, quiet, straightforward woman," to undergo analysis.)

"Let's talk about MacLuhanism," I said, determined to get something. But I didn't.

"Oh," he said in what he deliberately made to sound like mock surprise, "she's intelligent!" Then, "Sure, I'll talk to you about MacLuhanism." But it was too late. His agent, Abe

Lastfogel, head of the William Morris office in Hollywood, came over and told him to hurry up. It was 2:00 P.M. and they were ready for the meeting. "There are five people waiting for me," said Warren, truly apologetic. "I have to go. I'll call you and we'll get together again and we'll talk about MacLuhanism, I promise." Warren never keeps Mr. Lastfogel waiting, and he hastily abandoned his lunch—one half of a grapefruit—removed the sugar papers from his nostrils, and departed with a backward what-can-I-do gesture.

I was first aware of Warren the Lover in 1960. Through Joan Collins. I was in Italy and visiting her on the set of a disastrous film rendering of *Esther and the King*. She talked only of Mr. Beatty. She had been A.W.O.L. from the picture three times, flying to New York from Rome to spend a mere few hours with the twenty-three-year-old actor who had made such a hit with the critics (but because of his open ambition, was detested by the cast) in the stage presentation of William Inge's *Loss of Roses*. Joan had divorced Maxwell Reed, a British actor, a few years previously, and she was ready to marry again. Warren did not break up anything in Joan's life, except her heart, ditching her for Natalie Wood, when he played her boyfriend in *Splendor in the Grass*. Joan's heart mended, stitched together by anger when she learned Warren had read one of her letters to him to the cast while lunching in an Italian restaurant on Third Avenue during the location of the film.

At the beginning of *Splendor in the Grass*, Warren seemed afraid of Natalie. She was a little girl—less than five feet tall —but a big star, and he was a beginner. It was his first film, but he overcame his shyness when he discovered Natalie to be feminine and clinging, and still traveled with her Teddy bear. Until she was twenty-one, Natalie, who started acting at the age of four as the daughter of Orson Welles in *Tomorrow Is Forever* (which also starred Claudette Colbert), had never written a check and didn't know how, had never bought a plane ticket or paid for a taxi. She went from babyhood to womanhood without a maturing process. The film was successful, and Warren was a hit with the critics and more so with Natalie, who was married to Robert Wagner at the time, but that made it all the more exciting for Mr. Beatty, who dearly loves a challenge. The more difficult the conquest, the greater the thrill.

It was more than a year before Natalie received her final divorce papers, and during this period I saw her often, in Hollywood and in New York where she studied at the Actors Studio, while Warren was more or less quartered at Delmonico's. Van Johnson kept a suite there, but Warren lets his go when he leaves town. He hates anything that smacks of permanency. The same is true for Hollywood. His penthouse at the Beverly Wilshire Hotel is rented when he leaves. During the Oscar period of *Bonnie and Clyde* some of his Bonnies were quartered on different floors of the hotel, and Warren, who has managed to remain friendly with them all, enjoyed the situation.

Natalie was not at the hotel—she has her own home in California—and has been engaged to at least three men since her divorce from Mr. Wagner and her abandonment by Warren. Her film career might have dipped through a succession of bad films, but she is a determined girl under the soft gentleness, and an adequate actress, and I expect to find her on top again one of these days. Unless she follows through with her promise to give it up for a man she can love and admire till divorce do them part. She longs to have a strong man who will take her by the hand and lead her around by her beautiful nose. She mistook the ruthlessness of Beatty's character for strength, and was shattered when he disappeared following her divorce. It shook her confidence as a woman, which is why she kept getting herself engaged. It was a gesture to prove she could get a man to marry her in spite of Warren, for whom she had divorced Mr. Wagner. I was at her home soon after she announced her engagement to the rich Arthur Loewe, Jr. She was prattling away about the house they had decided to buy that very day, and she showed me her big, brand-new engagement ring. Arthur went into another room for something and, listening to Natalie, I thought, she'll never marry him. She jumped to her feet in a rage, with no trace of the previous fake bliss, and shouted, "How dare you insult me in my own house!" I was full of apologies because she had every right to be angry. I had not intended to speak the thought while she was giving me the guff about the house and the ring. She had sounded different when she was in love with Wagner and with Warren, and I knew the difference. And so did she. I don't know whether she found her strong man in Richard Gregson, the successful British actors' agent who must have had problems getting a divorce from his British wife to marry Natalie. He was her agent for a while, but at last report, Natalie had returned to the William Morris Agency. In any case, Natalie is completely over her infatuation for Warren, who is not easy to get over.

One of his ladies (I will not be ungallant and mention her name) once explained what she believed was the real secret of Warren's success with women, and it makes sense. "He's the greatest roll in the hay. It was the best I ever had in my life." She has rolled with them all, and she knows, although you would never guess it looking at her innocent face.

If Warren had not made it as Clyde, the actor his close friends call "The Kid" might still have become a fine producer—as he proved with the film. Like Richard Burton before he met Elizabeth Taylor, Warren, before he played Clyde, did not have an overpowering personality on the screen. Now he can take his pick of the pictures and percentages that have already made him a millionaire: 40 per cent of *Bonnie and Clyde,* which he bought for $75,000, when he learned in Europe that Jean-Luc Godard was after it. Godard had been the idol of young filmgoers since he made *Breathless* with Jean-Paul Belmondo eight years ago. It was a new milestone in the realistic trail of the stark documentaries of Rossellini, and the digging into the subconscious by Fellini and Antonioni. If Godard wanted *Bonnie and Clyde*—François Truffaut was also interested—Warren knew he was on to a good thing, although previously it had been submitted to every studio in Hollywood and turned down. It was lucky for Warren that Jack Warner, the last of the autonomous Hollywood tycoons, was selling his studio to Seven Arts at this time and he needed pictures to push up the price. *Bonnie and Clyde* was budgeted at $2.8 million, which isn't much for an American-made film today. Mr. Warner thought so negatively of the prospects of the picture that he agreed to Abe Lastfogel's request that Warren would work for practically nothing, and instead receive 40 per cent of the gross after the picture had paid off its cost.

While Warren freezes with strangers—he was a total disaster on the *Today* and *Tonight* television shows, his little-boy face quite terrified—when he believes in a project as he believed in *Bonnie and Clyde,* he is completely straight-thinking and organized, and if he can express what he thinks in films of this caliber, his stumble-bumbling with words won't matter. The only sensible interview I have ever had with him was by accident. I was going into the Green Room Café at the Warners Studio. Warren was coming out. He had returned the day before from the Texas location for *Bonnie and Clyde*. He told me of meeting people who had known and admired Clyde Barrow and Bonnie Parker. He talked for half an hour without hesitation, without fidgeting, without making silly remarks. My pencil flew as his words flowed. He was as intelligent as his close friends always insist he is.

And yet he can drive producers and directors up the wall with his indecisiveness—should he or should he not play a scene this way or that way, or make this or that film. *What's New, Pussycat?* was written for him, but Warren refused to make it when Charlie Feldman, his best friend, wanted to give the girl's part to Capucine, and Warren wanted it for his girlfriend, Leslie. It finally went to Romy Schneider. While Warren is socially amusing—Princess Margaret had him on her right at the big film-star dinner for her in the Beverly Hills Bistro—on the set he is extremely nervous and erratic. Just before the camera turns, he is likely to say,

"Wait a minute. Is this scene really necessary? Why are we doing it?" He has to be nagged into it. Then he will bring up another point, and have it explained and say, "I see what you mean, you're right." The next day he'll say, "I'm not sure you're right . . ." at the same time trying to make every woman on the set. Except with women, he is cautious to an abnormal degree.

After his first three films (*Splendor in the Grass, The Roman Spring of Mrs. Stone,* and *All Fall Down*), he didn't work for two years. When he is offered a play or a film he asks, "Look, does the guy make out with the girl?" He insisted on one sex consummation with Faye Dunaway in *Bonnie and Clyde,* although according to report, Clyde was a homosexual. Robert Rossen, who has since died, fought to the end with Warren when he directed him in *Lilith.* Beatty gave him a hard time and, I was told, tried to take over the picture. "I was winning Oscars when that son of a bitch was a baby pissing in a pot," Robert growled on one occasion. The idea of playing an unbalanced young man had appealed to Warren, but perhaps because of the fights with the director, the picture was a failure.

Off the set Warren seems to be just a clown, but when the moment comes to be serious, he can be. He is remarkably intuitive and aware. And he is extremely kind. During Mr. Feldman's hospitalization for cancer, Warren took twelve-hour turns at his bedside with the French girl, Clotilde Barot, whom Charlie married when he knew he was dying. Warren just sat there reading, a friend when a friend was needed. When a writer in Hollywood who interviewed him for the *Saturday Evening Post* some years ago asked him to telephone his blind father when he was next in New York, Warren did more. He went to the Bronx to visit him.

He is friendlier now with his sister, Shirley MacLaine, than at the beginning of his career, when the sure way to silence him completely was to ask, "Why are you feuding with her?" Neither has ever explained it, but it might have been Warren's determination not to be swallowed up in his

sister's success. They still have some arguments. Shortly before the Academy Award presentations in April 1968, I
said to Shirley, "If Warren wins, he must say something
sensible. He can't just stand there with millions of people
watching and stutter. Why don't you tell him to prepare a
speech?" She looked at me skeptically, "Yeah, that's when we
start fighting." Shirley does not altogether approve of his
way of life although she was ready to welcome Leslie as a
sister-in-law—she never cared too much for Natalie and she
has never believed he would marry Julie—but there is a
family loyalty. Attack one and the other defends. When
brother and sister were not on good terms and a top critic
attacked Shirley's performance in *The Apartment*, Warren
saw him and methodically, not angrily, explained why he was
wrong and concluded, "I thought it was one of the most
brilliant performances I've seen, and not because she's my
sister."

They have only one feature in common—their eyes, and
they are both blind as bats. Warren has now come into the
open with big horn-rimmed glasses. Shirley wears contact
lenses. "We're two people who grew up with the same parents in the same tract house in Richmond, Virginia, and
we're quite different," Shirley reflected in her dressing room
at the Universal Studio where she was starring in *Sweet
Charity*. "My whole life has been a cliché, a middle-class
vanilla. But not Warren's. Father was an educator (turned
real-estater). He and my mother had eight years of college
between them. They believed in education, but neither my
brother nor I went to college, only high school," where
Shirley garnered straight A's. "It didn't mean anything. The
only thing I really learned was to type. I studied French for
four years, but didn't learn a thing."

Mrs. Beaty—Warren added a "T"; Shirley took her
mother's maiden name, Maclean, and spelled it differently—
gave drama lessons, and brother and sister played small roles
in a home version of *My Sister Eileen*. "My father was an
amateur musician, and I always was aware of music as a

catalyst to expression as I grew up. It was a happy childhood, although, on reflection, there were areas of frustration or why would my brother and I choose acting as a way of expressing ourselves?"

Warren, according to his sister who is three years older, was a late bloomer. "He was reluctant, very sensitive, not a tomboy. I was the tomboy, and was always protecting him. I left home when I was sixteen to dance in New York. When I saw the The Kid again on the other side of the world, I realized how far he had come. He had contended with his oversensitivity. He is very appealing. He has a passive personality, I'm active. I've always been able to cut right through to the heart of the matter. Warren was always wanting to wallow in the nuances of every situation." "With women too?" I asked, and Shirley doubled with laughter. She makes me tell her about the beach incident every time we meet, and she always gets hysterical.

Shirley has a reputation as a swinger herself—how true, I wouldn't know. It is true she is parted for long periods from her husband, Stephen Parker, who works as a film producer in Japan, and you know how they gossip in Hollywood. Shirley has assured me that the best way to stay married is for husband and wife to be parted most of the time. "I'm still married to Steve, aren't I?" she will say defiantly. While I am sure she loves their thirteen-year-old daughter, Sachi, she has not been too involved with her. Shirley believes that a child is better off without too much parent-in-person. Sachi, until the fall of 1968, attended school in Japan, although spending her vacations with her mother. She then elected to go to a girls' boarding school in England. "She wanted more freedom from her parents, and I thought I'd given her too much freedom."

I knew Sachi before she was born. Shirley and Steve, who lived together all the time before she was successful—it was spring 1956—were renting the beach apartment next to mine on the Old Malibu Road. They had recently arrived from New York, Shirley brought to Hollywood by Hal Wallis, who was in the audience when she substituted for the ailing Carol Haney in *Pajama Game*. She was large with child and her career in films was perforce postponed. They were a pleasant young couple, with two boxer dogs who were always getting her into trouble rampaging through the neighbors' yards, trampling flowers, and knocking down small children. She detested her first movie, *The Trouble with Harry*, although she told me on my daily television show she had been excited about Alfred Hitchcock directing her. The film was one of Hitchcock's few disasters. While *Around the World in 80 Days* was a smash hit for Mike Todd and some of the others, Shirley, as the Indian widow about to expire on the funeral pyre with her late husband, was dreadful—as wooden as the logs on the fire. "I'll always be grateful to Frankie [Sinatra] for giving me the break-through in my career"— the role of the tramp in *Some Came Running*, which won her an Academy Award nomination and started her on the road to her present $800,000–$1,000,000 per picture price. "But it's always a struggle," she sighed, "when you don't have enough, and when you have too much."

She is involved in many charities—principally involving orphans—and she has just resigned after serving two years as National Chairman of the Thomas A. Dooley Foundation. She is active in politics. She was a dedicated supporter of the late Robert Kennedy and was a delegate from California at the Democratic Convention in Chicago. She has been writing a book for the past three years about her experiences in Tibet where, she tells you mysteriously without going into details, she was almost murdered. In the book, I was told by someone who has read parts of it, Shirley keeps changing her age. Like Warren, she'd rather not look time in the face.

Brother and sister have one other thing in common. They both must win. The siblings walk a straight line to their objectives. They are both dedicated to their careers and themselves, although Shirley is less afraid, and Warren may lose his fears if he continues to be successful. Where Marlon Brando is motivated by guilt—"I don't deserve what I've got"—Warren believes "I don't have everything I deserve." He will drive himself relentlessly and others ruthlessly until he does. With actors so successful in politics, Warren could be President of the United States if he wanted to be. He could win with the votes of the ladies he has loved.

13)

Mama Mia

She was playing it cool, sitting quietly while the group
swirled around her. It was her first time in Hollywood and
there could be no mistakes. She wished for a fleeting moment
that she were back in Italy, but she banished the thought
immediately. This is what she had dreamed of all her life, to
be in Hollywood. And now all these people were here at the
famous Romanoff's Restaurant in Beverly Hills, just to see
her. She did not meet many of them—you never do at a
Hollywood cocktail party in your honor. She knew a few
words of English, but mostly when she was spoken to she
appealed to the Italian interpreter, who passed on the incon-
sequential, polite remarks. Her leading man, Alan Ladd, was
there. He knew a few words of Italian—about as much as
Sophia's English—but he patted her shoulder to reassure her
that everything was going well. It was a large turnout. Sophia
Loren had made an impression on Hollywood with the release of her film *The Gold of Naples*. The press and the
famous people of the screen were eager to see what the
tempestuous young Italian actress looked like in the flesh.
One reporter from a wire service with several drinks under
his tight belt took a good look and exclaimed admiringly,

"Mama mia!" Sophia smiled at him. Perhaps there would be others who spoke Italian.

Her hosts were 20th Century-Fox, for whom she had starred in *Boy on a Dolphin* with Mr. Ladd in Greece, on the island of Hydra. The party was almost over and Sophia was breathing more rhythmically, you could see her massive chest rising and falling. Some of the guests had left and she was wondering how soon it would be considered polite to follow suit, when there was a commotion at the door. Jayne Mansfield had arrived. She had seen Sophia's cleavage in *Gold of Naples* and she was not going to be up-cleavaged by any nonentity from abroad. The front of Jayne's gown was so low that when a Chicago newspaper printed a photograph of Jayne bending over to greet the quite startled Sophia, they put a big black band across Jayne's nipples with the word, CENSORED. Sophia, for all her own natural attributes, has never enjoyed nudity—in real life or on the screen . . . although in *Boy on a Dolphin* there was a classic shot of Sophia wearing a silk dress, and when she dripped out of the water, she was sexier than if she had been naked. She will always remember the party and the film, she told me— the party because of Miss Mansfield and because she thought her life as an international star was truly beginning—she did not know that Hollywood would do its best to ruin her career and that after two years, in 1959, she would flee to Italy to repair the damage. "I remember the film," she laughs, and says in perfect English, "because I was so much taller than Alan and during the love scenes I had to stand in a hole." For the fade-out clinch, standard practice for most of the films then, they had Sophia running on the deck of a ship with Alan tackling her and throwing her down, so that the embrace was horizontal. Sophia tucked up her legs to make Alan seem longer.

It is things like this that reveal the extent of Sophia's cooperation, and I had always thought she was very popular with the people she works with. I was surprised when one of her recent leading men told me, "Sophia never makes a move that isn't calculated. She's one of the smartest broads in the business. She is not easy to work with because she worries about everything—her image (the uninhibited authorized biography is still unpublished), her nose, the angle of the photograph, her hair, crows-feet—everything. The wheels," he continued, enjoying his massacre, "are going around all the time. She's the shrewdest self-publicist in films. She's cold, aloof. There's no kidding, no camaraderie. She's a tightwad. She has the first fifty lire she ever made; when they ask her to attend a premiere, she demands a complete wardrobe. She's not a sexy woman, would a sexpot marry Carlo Ponti, not only marry him, but she's actually jealous of him."

A sweeping indictment, and if some of it is true, you must consider what has happened in her life. The poor, illegitimate girl who became a picture princess through the magic wand of a short, bald, rather fat, aging Prince Charming. A beautiful peasant pinned together with the steel gossamer of her husband's press department and her own disciplined desperation to succeed. Of course she is calculating. How else could she have risen from the bleak ashes of her beginnings? How else can she be sure it won't all vanish with another wave of the wand? All the same, while her devotion to Carlo Ponti might have started as gratitude, if what she now feels for her benefactor is not the love it seems to be, it will do until another definition comes along. It couldn't be all calculated acting when she caresses him in public, holds hands with him at screenings—at one showing he removed her shoes and hugged her feet while she purred with satisfaction. It is true she is jealous of him—she is very possessive of everyone she loves—like all Neapolitans. "This is mine and no one can touch it." She was distraught when Carlo was bounced from his seat during a sharp drop of an Alitalia plane over Rome, almost severing his ear. She visited him at the hospital carrying an Italian magazine, whose reporters are obviously paid to hide under the beds of celebrities to garner the gossip. "What's this?" she demanded, opening to the page with a story about Ponti and another woman. He protested weakly, "You know these magazines—" "I believe you," Sophia replied crisply, "but if I ever find out it's true, I'll cut off the other ear." I was not under the bed so I cannot vouch for the accuracy of the story, although I have heard it in Rome from several of Sophia's friends.

Sophia has more contact with her husband than Shirley MacLaine has with hers. But not much more. Carlo is usually traveling, wheeling and dealing in films, and she is always working, one film after another, piling up the money. You can keep a lot of it in Italy, and in any case the Pontis have a residence and tax-free status in Switzerland, also a magnificent flat in Paris, another in Rome, and the fifty-room, sixteenth-century Villa Sophia near the Pope's summer palace eleven miles outside Rome. There she sometimes plays poker all night long—she loves to play but hates to lose even a penny, so unless she wins she plays until seven in the morning, washes her face, and goes to work. On pokerless nights she goes to bed at eight in a huge canopied bed and reads, mostly film magazines. Carlo has his own room and his own four-poster.

Two years ago Sophia conducted me on a tour of the villa, which cost $2 million to restore and untold millions to furnish the beautiful, enormous rooms. I thought at the time, This is a poor girl's dream of paradise, of how the rich live. It was all too splendid for me to remember it very well. But I have a jumbled memory of a kitchen bulging with bread—as a child, to buy bread was an event—huge sparkling chandeliers, glorious tapestries, painted ceilings, paneled walls, large glamorous settees, and gleaming silver everywhere—so many candelabra and candles—and one whole tableful of antique silver baby rattles that, Sophia told me, she had bought on London's famed Portobello Road market.

Baby rattles. In the past decade in Italy the most important topics of conversation were the floods and is Sophia pregnant. Her longing for a child was as much in the public domain as the birth of a royal child of old when the accouchement chamber was so jammed with members of the court that it was a wonder any of the princelings survived the suffocating atmosphere, and many did not. Sophia recently underwent an operation to make the safe delivery of a baby more possible. "The next time I will not miscarry," she promised me vehemently when I visited her on the set of *Once Upon a Time,* her 1967 film with Omar Sharif. "I was born to have children and I will have them." She is not content with the idea of only one. There will be more and they will all be legitimate, at least by French law. In Italy, Carlo is still legally married to Giuliana Piastri, the daughter of a general, and there can never be a divorce unless the Catholic Church agrees to an annulment, which is unlikely, or changes the divorce laws, which seems remote. "At one time a legal marriage in Italy would have meant something to me," Sophia confessed, "but not now." Her children will be French citizens. They will have a legal right to the name of Ponti. They will not be tormented as Sophia and her younger sister Maria were by kids who had fathers they could brag about. She has never hidden the fact or been ashamed as an adult that her father, Riccardo Scicolone, did not marry her mother. Ever since I have known her, she has worn this oversight like a majestic robe. Since she has been a star, no one has cast a stone. Everyone has been sympathetic, as indeed everyone should be.

In a more earthy way than Julie Andrews, Sophia is encased in a protective armor that only her close friends can penetrate. On the surface she is friendly. I have never found her to be anything but pleasant, but when you are an important ambitious star with so many people demanding your time, you must be ruthless and cut out what is not completely necessary or you will have no time for work. And her work is the most important fact in Sophia's life. It is the yardstick of her happiness, and when you understand this you understand Sophia. To be a highly paid star—her price is still close to $1 million a picture—comes before Mr. Ponti, although he made it possible. She has rarely stopped working since Ponti discovered her, an underfed, underpaid girl of sixteen working with her fiercely protective mother as extras, in Rome, in M-G-M's film *Quo Vadis,* which starred Robert Taylor and Deborah Kerr.

Sophia's early years were a crucifixion of poverty, and everything that motivates her today stems from the desire that the dread spectre will never be resurrected. She conserves her energy for what must be done to maintain her stardom status. Before starting a film she is given a list of the people who wish to interview her. Unerringly she picks those who write for important publications and tosses out the rest. In spite of needing help herself in the beginning, she has no feeling of getting others started. She does not have the time. I have a large syndicate and Sophia has always been happy to see me. She has invited me to stay at the Villa Sophia "when you need a rest." Is it because she likes me or because I am important to her career? I'd rather not find out.

Sophia idolizes her mother, who to feed her daughters went hungry during the German occupation of Italy after it crumbled with the downfall of Mussolini. Later Sophia's younger sister, Maria, was to marry Il Duce's youngest son, a jazz musician. It often happens that when children have been deprived through circumstances of the comforts and the necessities of life, they love their parents more than those who have been coddled in comfort, and when there is only one parent, they are even more grateful. When Sophia was a child in the slums of Naples, food, even with the sacrifices of her seamstress mother, was so scarce that to this day she suffers from a vitamin deficiency which causes her hair to break and fall out. She usually wears hair pieces or a wig for public appearances. She has not forgotten the hunger. The children of twenty families in Naples are eating the food paid for by Sophia.

She tried to bring her mother to live with her during the succession of disastrous films in Hollywood—*Desire Under the Elms* with Tony Perkins and *The Black Orchid* and *Heller in Pink Tights,* both with Anthony Quinn. Ponti had rented a big home for her in Beverly Hills. "But my mother won't leave Italy," Sophia told me sadly. "She's afraid of planes and afraid of boats. She's superstitious and believes something terrible will happen to her if she leaves Italy."

Sophia has inherited some of her mother's superstition. She would not come to Hollywood in 1961 when all the polls predicted she would win an Oscar for her brilliant portrayal of the young mother in *Two Women,* which had reactivated her career in Italy after the fiasco in Hollywood. "If I go I won't win," she explained. Instead she and Carlo jittered through the night in Rome, waiting for the result, and when Carlo received it by telephone from Hollywood at six-thirty in the morning and told her "You won," she wept. She wept again when producer Joe Levine brought the Oscar to her. She poured champagne over the gold-plated statuette and gave a Rolls-Royce to Joe, who had paid for the expensive advertising campaign. Like Cary Grant, with whom she made *Houseboat,* her only successful film in Hollywood, and who is also careful with his money, when Sophia gives a present, it's a costly one.

She stands for nothing less than complete dedication when she works. She is very professional, never keeps you waiting, although Carlo does. She expects everyone else to be on time and no nonsense on the set. One of the reasons for her dislike of Marlon Brando during *The Countess from Hong Kong* was because he sleepwalked through his role when he realized the mediocrity of Chaplin's script and direction. Sophia gave the best she could. She did not drag her talent in slow motion, as Marlon did, and was ready to work on the second of nine o'clock. One morning a driver was late to bring her to the studio. She bawled him out. The second time he was late, she had him fired. She would work twenty hours a day if they let her, and she cannot understand the people who ask her, "Why do you work so hard?" What else would she have to do—polish her jewels? She couldn't even do that. The big pieces, including the $400,000 diamond necklace she was given by Carlo after *Yesterday, Today and Tomorrow,* are kept in the vaults of the jeweler Bulgari on the Via Condotti. When she attends a function, Ponti trots to the shop to pick them up for her. Ponti replaced Sophia's entire jewelry collection, valued at $700,000 and stolen from her dressing room in England when she was making *The Millionairess* with Peter Sellers. The jewelry was not insured. Few companies will cover gems for actresses, or charge so much—5 per cent of the value every year—that stars do not insure their jewels; they keep them in vaults until they need them for fancy occasions.

I have never heard of Sophia being involved with any man except Carlo Ponti, who perhaps is a father image for her. Many of her leading men have fallen in love with her. Cary Grant has stated that he wanted to marry her, although I believe he said this to the press and not directly to Sophia, who was of course aware of his devotion. As usual with his leading-ladies-in-distress, Cary rushed to help when she was liable for arrest for her proxy marriage to Ponti in Mexico. Peter Sellers, always emotional, fell madly for his *Millionairess* costar, and afterward was on the telephone to her day and night. The cool knight, Sir Alex Guinness, found Sophia so enchanting he spent days, he told me, after their film *Fall of the Roman Empire* searching the Swiss mountains for a rare edelweiss to lay at her firm feet.

On the set, unlike Barbra Streisand, Sophia does not disappear into her dressing room. She sits in her chair watching the actors and being friendly to the people who pass. During *The Countess from Hong Kong* I found her in a dressing gown, hair in curlers, watching Chaplin convulsing himself while directing some of his children in the ballroom scene.

Sophia likes to see and be seen. She believes in the star system and all the hullabaloo that goes with it. The new stars of today are different. They never make an entrance in the grand manner. They creep into the theater and hope no one will bother them. The girls would just as soon turn up on the back of a motorbike. All they are concerned with is realism on the screen and being themselves in real life. If Sophia were starting her career today, she might have a difficult if not impossible time making it. By today's standards of the young filmgoers between the ages of sixteen and twenty-four who comprise 48 per cent of the audiences, Sophia is old-fashioned with her billowing breasts and her star attitudes. Her future will depend on how flexible she is in adapting to the different world of the cinema of the '60s. If she won't or can't, Miss Loren will not be around in the '70s.

Her favorite director, Vittorio De Sica, who gave her the chance for stardom in *The Gold of Naples* in 1954, is still directing films for her. His attitude is deferential, and he kisses her ecstatically after every scene. The failure of De Sica's picture with Shirley MacLaine, *Woman Times Seven*, was partially because it was made in English, and while he understands the language he cannot think in it. Sophia interprets for him with the visiting press. Mastroianni could not learn English, but Sophia with her scanty education could. And fluent French as well. Even though Hollywood nearly finished her, she would like to work in America again, she told me. She thought she would star at M-G-M in Irving Berlin's *Say It With Music*, but a more recent star, Julie Andrews, was signed instead. Even the slow-moving producers of Hollywood now believe that the day of the ponderous personality whose acting ability is incidental, is over.

The young stars of today are refreshingly frank with the press, compared to the falsity of the old campaigners. Sophia's disagreements with Brando were the talk of the film world in London, but when I asked her about it in Rome, she looked me straight in the eye and said, "I liked Marlon very much." Her denial made me wonder. She had always seemed so frank, so honest. I realized then that she thinks carefully before speaking, which is not a failing. In all the years I have known Sophia, she has not changed and I have never heard her say anything malicious. When Carl Foreman was trying to make a deal with her for *The Victors* and she was not interested, a story appeared in the newspapers that she had agreed to the project, then backed out leaving Carl stranded. She refused to refute the story or retaliate as it would have meant saying she had not liked the script.

The Dolly dress was never made for Sophia, but the miniskirt was. Her legs are beautiful and she walks magnificently, carrying an invisible basket on her head. She is a striking woman, but she is not pleased with her nose, which, like Barbra Streisand's, is too long for beauty. While their noses have not been their fortune, they have not hindered their success. A large proboscis did not hinder Jimmy Durante either, although he is very conscious of his own and other people's. Some years ago I was in Las Vegas to see the Durante show at the Desert Inn. Sophia and some friends were ringside. I was at the far side of the room and Jimmy kept interrupting his act to say, "I know Sheilah Graham is here somewhere. Stand up, Sheilah, so we can see you." I did not stand up, wondering when he would introduce the celebrity so near him. He did not. Afterward in his dressing room I said, "Why didn't you introduce Sophia?" "Where was she?" he demanded. I told him. "Oh," said Durante, "you mean de dame wid de long nose?" He had not recognized her.

Sophia, because of her nose, will not be photographed from a height or from a too-low angle. Except when she was very young and was called "The Stick," she always had an ample figure. The bra and girdle have not yet been made to contain it. To support her breasts and diaphragm, Sophia uses broad bands of adhesive tape.

She loves food but watches her weight. Like Marlene Dietrich, Sophia was plump when she first came to Hollywood. She is passionately fond of pasta and pasta fa zu, a favorite Italian soup; it has everything in it—beans, vermicelli, vegetables—everything except liquid. She takes her cook with her everywhere, but she does not need her, being an excellent cook herself. Food-loving stars pay a price for the fame and the money. Sophia is usually on a diet. But between films she loosens the adhesive and makes up for lost pasta.

She has a sense of humor. When she must appear in public, although she would rather stay home like a big cat, she shrugs and says, "Now I must put on my act, now watch me be a star," and, having made up her mind, she goes through the whole bit—haughty, regal, and removed. And while she says she does not like this part of her work, I think she enjoys looking and behaving like a queen.

Nothing is too much trouble for Sophia regarding her work. While she was in one film, she had to dub the English dialogue for another, and to do it she worked from six to eight every evening, between takes during the day, and sometimes at five in the morning. Even when the director was satisfied, Sophia would say, "No, I can do better. Let's do it again." This is the difference between a true star and a *nouveau* name like Mia Farrow who refused to come to Hollywood (after her futile attempt in Miami to reconcile with Frank Sinatra) for a two-hour dubbing session for *Rosemary's Baby*. It meant sending the director, Roman Polanski, all the way to London.

When Sophia made a three-city tour in four days—New York, Los Angeles, and San Francisco—to appear with her film *Yesterday, Today and Tomorrow,* the crowds in San Francisco were so large that the manager of the theater suggested, "Let's duck out the back way." In Italian, Sophia replied, "In a pig's eye, we will," and in English, "I'm here for the people to see. That's why I came all the way from Italy." And she left through the front lobby and shook all the outstretched hands and talked with fans in the bleachers. She has one fan who is always there. Once the man was on the same plane going to Los Angeles. "How did you get here?" Sophia asked him. "I read you'd be on it and I used my savings." Sophia kissed him warmly and did not destroy the gesture by offering to pay for the ticket.

Like most wives, Sophia hews to her husband's politics. In the last election in Italy the Communist Party was sure they had her—a woman with all her troubles, the early poverty, the illegitimacy, the nightmare of her childhood, the charges of living in sin with a married man (it took years for the bigamy case to be dropped). They believed this was the stuff on which good Communists cut their teeth. At the same time, Sophia had a bid from the Liberal Party to run as a Deputy in Naples. But when the Socialist Party held its first meeting in Rome, Sophia, Carlo and Vittorio De Sica were in the front row.

Sophia met Marilyn Monroe in Hollywood and was baffled by Marilyn's passion for nudity—although before she became an actress, before Ponti discovered and protected her, Sophia earned her living as a seminude model and in half-undressed quickie films. When Marilyn died, the Italian press called Miss Loren to get a statement from her. For a moment there was no sound, then they heard sobbing and a muffled, "That poor girl, that poor girl." Sophia was luckier than Marilyn. She had a Carlo Ponti to take good care of her. But for Carlo, this chapter might have been different.

14)

Actors, Not Stars

Paul Newman, Steve McQueen, and Rod Steiger are the solid core of today's Hollywood. They lead anonymous lives on the other side of the camera. They are actors, not stars. But like all actors they have some problems. McQueen will say "yes" to your face and "no" behind your back. Newman can never forget an injury. Rod Steiger is a compulsive eater. But they are real human beings, not inventions of a script writer. When they leave the studio, they shed the celluloid image and disappear into the obscurity of family life.

The only fight I ever had with McQueen was when I wrote something he did not like about the stability of his marriage. I was wrong and I printed a retraction. He was amazed that I would negate my own story.

Steve is not what he seems to be on the screen. Few of them are, and it isn't fair to judge them by the standards of the roles they portray. But of all the actors today who have scaled the heights on ability rather than flamboyant personality, Steve is the most unexpectedly different. We see him on the screen as a man who knows his own mind, calm and confident. We believe everything he does. His word is his bond. He is tough, but we must take him as he is. Well, some of it is true and some is quite the opposite. He has always been wary and suspicious of motives, the residue of an uneasy childhood, disrupted when his father, a Navy pilot during World War II, left his mother when Steve was a year old.

He lived with his grandparents on a farm in Missouri until he was eleven, when his mother, working in Los Angeles, sent for him. He would not go to school, and he was always in trouble. His restlessness and the lack of discipline at home landed him in the Boys' Republic in Chino, California. As a boy he was beaten up and had to fight to survive. He learned never to trust anyone. With his success in the *Wanted Dead or Alive* television series, *The Great Escape,* and *The Magnificent Seven,* he became more confident but not less mistrustful or cautious. He still considers every offer of a film as if it were a plot to put him out of business. He has become so dictatorial that Warner-Seven Arts, which had made a six-film deal with him starting after *Bullitt,* agreed that it would be better to cancel the contract, this in spite of the actor's top rating and popularity on the screen all over the world. They believed that Steve's demands added $1 million to the cost of the film. There was the swimming-pool incident in San Francisco. The mayor was extremely cooperative and Steve asked him "What can I do for *you?*" The mayor considered and then said, "Well, we could use a swimming pool in a poor section of the town." It would cost $250,000. "It's yours," replied Steve magnanimously. The Warner executives hit the sky. "We can't do it," they told McQueen. "But I gave my word," he stormed. When the clouds cleared the mayor graciously accepted $25,000 from the studio toward the cost of the pool for which the citizens of San Francisco were delighted to contribute.

An actor sometimes knows what is best for him, but more often not. In the days of Louis B. Mayer and Irving Thalberg actors were happy to leave the decisions to the men who paid them, and it usually worked. The actor is too close to the project to get a good perspective of the whole. "Steve is a self-made star, as Burt Lancaster is," said one of his directors. "They are both tough men, but the difference between the two is that Lancaster works from intelligence and Steve is all emotional reaction. He's as subjective as a woman. If you say it's a nice day, he'll growl, 'A nice day upsets me' or 'Is my tie straight?' " He has changed since the early days. With his first films he'd say simply, "I'll do it." Now, "I must read the script," which makes sense to me, because he has more to lose if he takes a bad film, as he did with *Nevada Smith* and *Soldier in the Rain* with Jackie Gleason.

"He's scared to death to be anything but appealing to people. He never makes anyone feel unwelcome to his face," said another of his directors. "He always says 'yes,' then takes steps to have the army of people who work for him change everything so he is still the good guy and they take the brunt of the blame." Everyone agrees that Steve is a loner. He is alone even in a crowd. He feels people are against him. He sees treachery in every corner. Perhaps this is why he tapes his messages. He is completely on the defensive. Away from the bosom of his family, he is a lonely man, also autocratic, self-centered, and sometimes unable to see the other man's problem. During the making of *The Thomas Crown Affair* the reporter for a top weekly magazine came to Hollywood to write a story that would break when the picture was released. Steve had agreed to see the man before he left New York. There were to be several interviews to get a story in depth. All went well until the day of the last session when Steve took off to visit the Indians in Arizona. The reporter needed another hour or two at the most to complete his story. He telephoned Steve, pleaded, but the actor was adamant. He wouldn't see him again. "What will you do?" I asked the writer. He wasn't sure. "I might be able to patch it up, but all I needed to complete the story was two lousy hours." He was bewildered by Steve's behavior, because, like most people, he had taken him at his screen image.

Don't misunderstand me, Steve *is* an honest man, which is the quality that comes across on the screen. He is loyal to the people in whom he believes. When a director was lacing into Robert Wise, a director Steve admires, he put up his fists and said, "You'd better not say that." And yet or because of his pugnaciousness, he is dreadfully insecure. The façade is hard, rough, unsophisticated, full of blue jeans and racing cars, a tough, inarticulate Bogart quality that can be endearing. But the quality of indecision has lost him some admirers. He will tell the press agents on his films that there is to be no mention of his family to reporters and that when his children visit him on the set there are to be no photographs. Then he allows them to be photographed and afterward starts everything in motion to stop publication of the photographs and it is sometimes too late and when the pictures reach the fan magazines, he screams bloody murder. The remedy was obvious—not to allow the photographs to be taken. If he wants pictures of his kids, it can be done at home.

Sometimes when Steve is offered a picture, he is excited and accepts. But before the start of a film, he might feel it is all wrong. At eleven o'clock at night he will call the director and he is worried and has to be reassured. He feels more secure once he has started the film, and the problems usually vanish as he goes along. Which is why the people who know him don't take his anguish too seriously.

Without a formal education—Steve left school when he was fifteen—he has invented his own vocabulary to express what he means. "Who's the head honcho?" he will ask, and you understand him. His "Let's get down to the nitty-gritty" has gone into the American language. There is a Nitty Gritty Dirt Band in Paramount's film version of *Paint Your Wagon*. He has his own definition of power. "Power," he says, "is forcing someone to give in to you." He enjoys his position of power and uses it to make bargains. He earns $750,000 against a percentage for each film, but he bargains like a Petticoat Lane peddler for every little and big thing. He will negotiate for anything—a tank of gas, a spare tire—to "hondle," he calls it. He bargains in the open marketplace. If he can get it for next to nothing, so much the better, otherwise he'll try to get it for less. Another word he uses for the same thing is "scamming." He'll scam for articles like cars, trucks, and pool tables.

He knows Mr. Ferrari and you can bet he did some hondling. In *The Thomas Crown Affair* he used his own wrist watch and sent the company a rental bill for $1,000. His clothes for the film cost $10,000. No one told me, but I'll bet they were scammed by Steve. It was Steve's idea, incidentally, to play Thomas Crown, a rich man. He wanted to get away from his tough-guy image on the screen. But while he was rich, he was still antisocial. In real life there are times when Steve likes to be with people and he will turn up unexpectedly at all sorts of parties. At other times he must be completely alone and he will drive off to the desert and take a two-week walk.

He has a great affection for machinery—when he was a moody struggling actor wearing sports gear and a leather jacket in the mid-50's, he had his souped-up jalopy. Now he has every kind of car—Maseratis, Ferraris, and trucks. It took a year for a Ferrari to be made to Steve's exact specifications. When it arrived, Steve took a trial run in it to the beach. It was a Sunday and Steve had stopped at a red light with the slow-moving traffic. Racing out of a side street, a Sunday driver smashed into Steve's Ferrari. A complete wreck. His wife wept when he called her to come and get him.

Steve is well known as a car racer and still dreams of making a film on the subject. He was set to go with *Day of the Champion* for his own company, Solar Productions, but *The Sand Pebbles* for 20th Century-Fox went six months overtime and he was too exhausted to start the film with John Sturges, who first made us aware of him on the screen in *Never So Few,* which starred Frank Sinatra. "But one day I'll do it," he assured me. The new title for his racing film—*Le Mans,* the annual and dangerous race in France. He will drive in some scenes, not all. He has had two bad accidents, and while he is still in his thirties and has won some races, he loves his family and his life too much to cause them further suffering, although according to famous racers Stirling Moss and Sir John Whitmore, Steve is capable of competing with the best. These drivers with death are strange people. Most of the men are married; some are like businessmen. The others are like mountain climbers, encased in aloneness.

Steve isn't quite that much alone. He will sometimes take people for rides on his motorbike. While he was making *The Sand Pebbles* at 20th Century-Fox, he spotted the portly Joe Levine outside his bungalow. "Hey, Joe," he shouted, "do'ya want a ride?" The two-hundred-pound producer eyed the machine suspiciously and asked, "How do you ride?" "You just get on here," indicating the back, "and make sure you go with the curves." "Oh, well, I'm insured," said Joe, who is a gambler by nature. He was scared stiff. "But I kept remembering my $3 million insurance policy." Steve might have been a mechanic instead of a film star. He put together a racing Jaguar which arrived in twenty boxes.

He has not forgotten his childhood or his time at Boys' Republic in Chino. He visits there frequently and talks to the boys, proving in person what they can become with hard work. His friends assure me that success has made him calmer. He has financial security for one thing, and when he sends a truck or other equipment to Chino, he explains, "I'm paying my dues." He is involved with helping the poor Indian— raising money, clothes, food, and medical supplies, which he drives to the reservations in his truck. He is also involved with the Youth Study Research Center.

Steve lives with his wife, the former Neile Adams, and their three small children in a house in Brentwood, which is not too grand and is normal except for the pool table in the center of the big living room. Neile, a Eurasian and a top dancer on Broadway, married Steve in 1956. They met when Mark Rydell was attending the Actors Studio. He brought Neile and a blind date for Steve to Downey's Restaurant near Broadway. The blind date was Joanne Woodward, who married Paul Newman. Now, Rydell, who directed *The Fox,* plans to direct McQueen in *The Man on a Nylon String—* about the lonely sport of mountain climbing.

Steve is perhaps the most popular film actor in France,

where they go for the tough, rugged type. He can't go out during the day in Paris without risk of being dismembered by his loving fans. "The last time was a nightmare," he told me. "I was a trapped animal in the hotel. I finally got hold of de Gaulle's make-up man for television, who put a beard on me, a black wig, a drooping mustache, and I could walk in the streets, go to restaurants, and no one knew me. One morning at 4 A.M. I took a walk without the disguise and went into Le Drug Store on the Champs Elysées to get some shaving cream. The woman who served me suddenly leaped over the counter and crushed me in a suffocating hug."

Steve's mother died a few years ago in San Francisco, where she was living, with Steve paying the bills for her comfortable home. When he was called with the news that his mother had suffered a cerebral hemorrhage, he flew there immediately and brought the body back for burial in Forest Lawn. He picked out a plot on a hillside with a tree—"I want it to be shady." It was the only time anyone ever saw him cry.

Paul Newman is probably the most sought-after film actor in the world today. And he tells the worst stories. Most of them are too barnyard to repeat. But what enjoyment he receives from the telling of them! This is one of the cleanest. Paul talking: "A guy goes to a dentist on Park Avenue to have his teeth fixed. It would cost him $3,000. 'Too much,' he said, and goes to a dentist on Forty-second Street, who wanted to charge $900. He goes to the Village, but $500 was still too much. Then he went to the Bowery and saw a dentist's sign over a butcher shop. It would be $27.50. 'How do I know you're any good?' he asked the dentist. 'Well, I took care of the butcher downstairs. Why don't you ask him? I fixed him up three years ago.' He went downstairs and asked the butcher, 'Can you recommend the dentist upstairs?' 'Let me put it this way,' said the butcher. 'Last Sunday I went rowing in Central Park. The oar slipped out of the oarlock. I reached for the oar and caught my balls in the oarlock and it's the first time in three years my teeth haven't hurt!' " And Paul throws back his head and splits his sides laughing. Paul puts as much effort into his bawdy anecdotes as he does into his acting and directing for stage and screen. He takes the punch line, tucks it into his head, and works backward. He is not a vulgar man, but his jokes are.

Paul's background was as solid as Steve McQueen's was insecure. His father had a prosperous sporting-goods store in Cleveland, and Paul attended the Yale School of Drama following his degree at Kenyon College in Ohio where he majored in drama and economics. Paul's original idea was to be a director, and he has now come full cycle. He recently directed successfully, *Rachel, Rachel,* in which his wife, Joanne Woodward, starred, and he told me he plans to give up acting, which he finds merely repetitious, and work behind the camera. To attain this dream, Paul had to agree to star in several films for Warner-Seven Arts, for whom he made a great deal of money with *Harper* and *Cool Hand Luke,* although he also made the worst film of his career, *The Silver Chalice,* for the same studio in 1955. He paid them $500,000 to get out of his contract.

Paul is not very shrewd or very articulate, but he is extremely pleasant. Joanne is the brains of the family, which she conceals under a soft femininity. But she does not fool Paul. He won't take a step without first consulting the blonde slender woman he married in 1957 after a protracted courtship of seven years.

His total of children today is six—three from his first wife, Jackie Witte, whom he met while a student at Kenyon College. The three daughters with Joanne are enchanting little blondes. And they don't have to curl their hair. Paul does it for them with the terrifying ghost stories he tells just before they go to bed.

Paul is not a vacillator like McQueen. He has a sort of arrogance that women find appealing and some associates do not appreciate. He has great ego, and on the set you'd better do it his way. At home Joanne wears the pants. She is a very secure person, a lady from Louisiana, from a well-off family—

her father was a book publisher. They complement each other, which creates a happy atmosphere. Joanne represents reality for Paul, who has never been known to glance at another woman—although in a recent magazine interview he told of whiling away an afternoon with Marty Balsam cataloguing "the various forms of fucking"—"for fun," "as medicine," etc. The one time I saw him really angry was when the late Mike Connolly gossiped in his column in the *Hollywood Reporter* that the Newman marriage was kaput. Paul avoids television, but he insisted on taping a show with a commentator, to say in forceful language what he thought of Mr. Connolly. "It was too strong to use," Paul told me regretfully.

He refuses to cooperate for anything suggestive in his films. It was all right to attempt to rape Pat Neal in *Hud*—his percentage made him a millionaire—and Claire Bloom in *The Outrage,* because in each case it was part of the story. But when it was suggested that in *The Hustler* he have a naked scene in bed with Piper Laurie, Paul said abruptly, "It's not necessary." The puritanical approach to his films could be why he is so bawdy in real life. When the Newmans were first married, they visited New Orleans and returned to their small town house in Greenwich Village with an enormous bed they had bought in a New Orleans brothel. It was so big they had to walk sideways to get into their bedroom. They told everyone of their treasure, which they proudly exhibited. When the late Edward Murrow did a *Person to Person* show at their home, they wanted to tell the story of how they had acquired the bed, but Mr. Murrow put his foot down.

This has nothing to do with the bed, or perhaps it has. Paul and Joanne's idea of a vacation is not to go to the South of France or Italy. It's to shack up in a hotel together with champagne and caviar, and they won't be heard from for several days. They own a $200,000 house in Beverly Hills four blocks from the Beverly Hills Hotel, but when they want a change, they stay at the hotel. They turn off the telephones, instructing the operator, "Don't call us, we'll call you." It gives them a change from family life—they can be alone at last. Also it gives Joanne a respite from cooking, which bores her, although she believes wives should do it now and then. She is a good cook, and when Paul was in Paris starring with Sophia Loren in *Lady L,* she learned some fancy dishes at the Cordon Bleu. Joanne is always learning something new. In Israel with Paul when he was starring in *Exodus* for Otto Preminger, she learned some Hebrew. In Paris she learned to speak some French. Wives of actors have a great opportunity to enlarge their education with pictures today made all over the world. Not all of them are as bright as Mrs. Newman, and they miss the opportunity to learn a language the easy way.

Joanne and Paul met in one of the strange accidents of fate that seem quite planned. Josh Logan was thrashing around trying to cast William Inge's play *Picnic* for Broadway. Paul was at the Yale Drama School, and an agent brought him to New York to meet Logan. While waiting for the audition, the agent took him to MCA where John Forman, another agent, sent him to CBS for a TV show for which he was signed on the spot. This was before color TV, but Paul's bright blue eyes sort of lit up every room he entered. It was the first job he ever went for and he got it. The agent told him, "You're handsome and talented, but you must get that chipped corner of your front tooth fixed." He did—but not until 1966. It was part of his crooked smile. Logan liked Paul, but did not believe he could carry the hero role—William Holden had it in the movie—and he gave Paul the part of the best friend.

Joanne had been earning money modeling nightgowns, negligees, and cosmetics to pay for lessons at the Neighborhood Playhouse. She had recently graduated from Louisiana State University. Like Paul, she had acted in high school. "In one play," she told me, "they put fifty-two curls on my head like Shirley Temple." At the Playhouse she appeared in Garcia Lorca's *Blood Wedding* in the secondary girl's role. Mr. Forman saw the play. "She was miscast, but marvelous. That night I signed her for MCA and sent her the next day to *Robert Montgomery Presents* TV show. (How long ago that seems, and where is Robert?) She got the job with a fee of

$300. "I can't believe there's all that money for me as an actress," she cried. Forman sent Joanne to Logan to read for a role in *Picnic*. He liked the reading, but said, "Unfortunately I've cast Kim Stanley for that part and Janice Rule for the pretty girl, but I'm looking for an actress to understudy both girls. You're good enough for Madge, but too pretty for Millie." "May I be excused?" said Joanne. She went to the ladies' room, removed her make-up, and put some on in the wrong places. "I looked really ugly." She returned and landed the job of understudying the two girls. Paul, in addition to playing the hero, Ralph Meeker's best friend, was understudying him.

One rainy Saturday midmorning in the winter, Mr. Forman received a call from them. "We're going on this afternoon," they told him. The star lovers were sick. "The single-bed preface of the stage version of *Picnic* was the sexiest I ever saw," Forman told me. It was obvious the understudies liked each other, and that was one reason they were so good. Joanne had been going out with other young actors as well, among them Marlon Brando. When Paul's divorce finally came through in January 1957—the year Joanne was to win the Oscar for *The Three Faces of Eve*—they married in Las Vegas. The ceremony at El Rancho was meant to be a secret, but the owner, Beldon Katleman, invited all the stars appearing on the Strip, and it was a rip-roaring affair. It was the last time the Newmans were in Las Vegas and the last big party they ever attended, except for the one they gave at L'Etoile in New York after the invitational showing of *Rachel, Rachel,* almost twelve years later.

Joanne has not made too many films because of her decision to work with or in the same city as her husband, as Elizabeth Taylor and Richard Burton have done. Joanne enjoyed being directed by Paul in *Rachel, Rachel.* He did not have to tell her what to do. He would put his hands on her face and neck, moving her around, and she knew what he wanted. "I might have to say one word." It isn't all as simple as it sounds. Joanne has no apparent complexes, but Paul has. He has a compulsion to prove he is not a Hollywood type, to be altruistic. He is sometimes frightened by his success. He can't believe that his baby blue eyes are getting him so much money a picture, now well over the million-dollar mark. He hates waste and in New York would rather take the subway than a taxi. He enjoys being on the worst-dressed actor list and never has more than two or three suits to his name. He wears dungarees and coveralls even in New York City. He used to race around Manhattan on a motorbike, but gave it up for a Volkswagen with a Porsche engine. He loves the look on the faces of drivers when he outraces them on the high-ways of New York and the freeways of California. Joanne and Paul have only the one small car between them.

When she needs a car, they rent or borrow. They live sim-ply in their three homes—they moved to a small apartment in New York from the big cooperative on East Sixty-seventh Street because they were rarely there. When they leave Holly-wood, they rent the house in Beverly Hills for which they say they have no affection. The books and antiques are in the 1732 Westport salt box with its eight tiny bedrooms. Joanne is a total balletomane and never misses the ballet in New York or Los Angeles. She keeps a framed Avedon photograph of Nureyev's foot in their Westport bathroom and Paul says, "No matter what I'm doing in the bathroom, I'm looking at Nureyev's foot."

Paul looks like Jack Armstrong, the all-American boy, but only on the surface. Beneath the confident ego, like all actors, he is uncertain, wondering "Will this be my last film? Why would anyone pay to see me? Am I getting repetitious?" If it were possible, he would rehearse but never open in a play. "The fascinating thing is everything up to opening night," he told me, "if only you could play without an audience." He and Joanne appeared free in *Baby Wanna Kiss*. The money they earned by the play went to the Actors Studio—which they attend when they are in New York. "With a film it would be marvelous to prepare everything, have a wrap-up party, and everybody goes home, and you don't make the film, and go on and on like that."

Paul's chief compulsion is to tell the truth and that in itself makes him unique in Hollywood. He was the first actor to come out for Eugene McCarthy. As far back as 1962, Paul was against Vietnam and McCarthy was his man as soon as he stated his platform for the Presidency of the United States. McCarthy was never as sharp and practical a politician as Bobby Kennedy and this appealed to Paul, who rang doorbells in New Hampshire to the delight of the housewives. He is a fervent believer in causes and when his son understood and agreed with him, Paul became emotional and said, "I'm so proud of you for seeing this." He was thrilled and almost wept. Like Brando, he wants to be known as a great humanitarian. They feel guilty earning all that money, and it can be frightening receiving $1 million for twelve weeks' work. Paul is a stanch supporter of the civil-rights program and gives financial aid and his time to the Center for the Study of Democratic Process near Santa Barbara. The Newmans practice the democratic way of life. Their colored cook has a young daughter, and when they brought them east to the house in Westport—a converted barn for which they paid $90,000 and put in another $100,000 with a tennis court and pool—they sent the girl to the same private school with the Newman children and paid for her to have ballet lessons. It wasn't always easy with six other kids around, but they managed.

Paul, now forty-four, will not allow his children to be interviewed although he has a son in college. A daughter said to him, "Papa, one of the kids at school said you were a movie star. Are you really a movie star?" "Don't you believe it," Paul replied, "I'm just an actor." Which is what I said at the beginning.

Rod Steiger is a year or two younger than Paul although he looks older because of his weight problem. Rod says it is not fair that while Paul puts away an incredible amount of beer—he is the definitive beer drinker—it does not show on Newman's trim 158-pound figure. He sweats it all off in his various sauna baths. There is one in the New York apartment, one in Westport and Hollywood, and a portable sauna for hotels and locations. The sweatbox also takes care of Paul's big intake of food. "I can't imagine," he told me once, "living anywhere where I can't get a corned-beef sandwich at three o'clock in the morning." Rod complains, "I'm younger than these guys—Paul, Marlon, Kirk, Greg—but until I won the Oscar for *In the Heat of the Night*, no one offered me lover roles." Rod did not look as fat to the producers after he walked away with the award, but he has only to look at food to gain weight and he does more than look, even when he is supposed to be dieting. He is the most disciplined actor of our day and the best on the screen, but when it comes to food, his will power is like water. Oh, the agonizing diets! He is always on—and off. The last one was the worst. He is a big man in all directions, but for the sake of the picture *The Illustrated Man*, in which he wore a skin-tight rubber suit under a total tattoo, he was existing on five hundred calories a day, which is starvation even for a child.

Unfortunately for Rod's shape, he had previously been working in Paris in *The Sergeant*—he is always working—but he finds French food irresistible, as who doesn't, and had added another twenty pounds to his already overstuffed frame. He had to lose 30 to 40 pounds in a hurry and he was gritting his teeth and weighing every bite and taking a daily shot of a pregnant woman's urine—he brought the vials to the studio and the nurse injected the daily dose, which some doctors believe gives the dieter strength to continue. Five hundred calories and Rod was working fourteen hours a day, five required for the ghastly make-up. In addition, he was playing strenuous tennis several times a week and sweating every day in a home sauna bath. How he did not drop dead is a mystery. Whenever I saw him at the studio or at an award function—he was winning everything in sight for his superb performance—I would ask, "How much?" and he knew I re-ferred to his weight. He shed 6 pounds in one day, 15 in a week, then he claimed a loss of 22 pounds and then 28 pounds. On weekends he would cheat with the food and suffer agonies of guilt. "I'm not a happy man when dieting." The last time I saw him he was off the diet. Up and down. Down and up. He loves wine—"You're talking to a man who has his own wine cellar."

He had a black Jaguar, on the small side. We had been lunching at the Beverly Hills Hotel. They brought the car to the front and Rod could not get into his own car. Smirks from the matinee women in gay print dresses and befeathered hats. Rod sheepishly maneuvering his bulk this way, that way. Finally, thank God, he's in, but why would a fat man want a small car? I hate to tell Rod this, because I like him as a person and have tremendous respect for him as an actor, but he will never be thin. He is a fat man and there is no thin man screaming to get out, and 20 to 30 pounds on or off makes little difference and his method of losing weight is dangerous. It reminds me of the skit played by Mike Nichols and Elaine May: "Have you heard about Piggy Trevelyan?" says Elaine. "No," says Mike. "What about Piggy Trevelyan?" "She's lost an enormous amount of weight." "Really, how does she look thin?" "Fat."

Rod rarely mentions his childhood and never talks about his father. Except recently, when I asked him point-blank, "Why do you never talk about him?" "Because I never knew him," he replied. "According to my mother he disappeared before I was a year old. I don't know if he's still alive, I wouldn't know him if he walked past me in the street." He was an only child.

Rod's mother died recently. She had married again and was living with her husband in New Jersey. Rod, making *The Sergeant,* was shattered and flew home to attend the funeral. He was fond of his mother and he liked his stepfather, who died last year. The only real fight he had with his mother was when he lied about his age and enlisted in the Navy when he was sixteen. She finally signed the papers, and Rod was in for four years. Under the G.I. Bill he had four free years of tuition coming to him and he chose acting as a profession, first with the New York School for Social Research, then two years with the American Theatre Wing, and the Actors Studio, which he swears by. Like Brando, Rod owes his career to Elia Kazan, who acted at the Studio and believed in The Method. Rod gets angry when the method is belittled. He played the homely butcher in *Marty* on television and his career was off and running.

On the Waterfront in 1954 with Brando, and directed by Kazan, was Steiger's second film. He had previously appeared in *Teresa* in 1951; he filled the gap with television and plays. No one imagined he could be a film star. He did not have the face or figure for it—in the years before the wholly realistic, usually homely people took over Hollywood. And Rod is partly responsible for the change. In the early '50s, you had to be beautiful like Marlon Brando, as you can see in his early films now on television. Rod is only forty-three years old, but he is the father image for all actors. His voice is paternal when he speaks of his coworkers. "It's a good profession," he assured me. "I've never met a good actor who doesn't make a good living. He may not be famous, but the important thing is he can feed his family." Food and family.

Rod was getting a divorce from his first wife when I met him during his third film, *Oklahoma,* directed by Fred Zinnemann. He had never sung or danced, but as Poor Jud, he hoofed and warbled with Gordon MacRae and Shirley Jones —Rod can do anything and be anyone. He *was* the cop in *In the Heat of the Night*—he's a man of a thousand roles and a thousand faces. I had heard he was difficult and I was prepared for anything, facing him across the table at the Beverly Hills Brown Derby, but I saw from his fidgeting and disjointed sentences that he was nervous. Actors were talking then of "my analyst," and Rod talked of his sessions and why he needed them. It was obvious that he needed reassurance from someone, but whoever was listening to his outpourings on a couch had not yet succeeded in helping his emotional malaise.

The next time I lunched with Rod, he had recently married Claire Bloom, the young British actress Chaplin had brought to Hollywood in 1952 to play the girl in *Limelight,* which was to be Charlie's last film in Hollywood. Claire and Rod had appeared together on the New York stage in *Rashomon.* He was a different man. The nervousness was gone. He was thinner and he was happy. Remembering our long discussion on psychoanalysis, I asked him if he was still undergoing treatment. "No," he boomed, "I don't need it any more. A happy marriage was the answer for me." He had been married before, but it had not worked out. Recently he told me, "One should go back to the psychiatrist every five years or so for a check-up. So far, I seem to be functioning well. I learned to know myself through psychoanalysis. Socrates said, 'Know thyself.' When you understand the processes of thought, you can interpret the thoughts of the person you are playing."

Unlike the Paul Newmans, with Joanne putting the marriage before her career, Claire Bloom is an ambitious actress and her career means as much, perhaps more, than her marriage. Rod understands this and has never interfered with his wife's work, although it has often meant they are parted for long periods while Claire is making a film in London and he is in Mississippi or Rome. At one time they were apart except for a week or two for two years, and Rod was not ecstatic about the situation. "But I'm not going to tell her she cannot work. She would be frustrated and in years to come, she would blame me. Acting is as much a part of her life as being married."

Claire, who is self-contained and gives an impression of coldness, slipped a curious remark when I said shortly before Rod won the Oscar, "If Rod wins, and I'm sure he will, it will mean a great deal of money for you both." "For Rod, not for me," she replied, disassociating herself from her husband's success. "Of course I'll be glad if he wins," she added as an afterthought. I was left with the feeling that her career was something entirely separate and that she would pursue it to the end, no matter how it might affect her marriage.

They have a daughter, Anna, born in 1961, and wherever Claire works, Anna goes with her, which means that Rod does not see his daughter as much as he would like. It's a restless life for a child, and Anna startled her mother last year by saying, "When I'm in London, I want to be in New York, and when I'm in New York, I want to be in Rome, and when I'm in Rome, I want to be in London." Sometimes Anna doesn't know where she wants to be. It could lead to some problems. Recently, for the first time since their marriage in 1959, they made two films together—*The Illustrated Man*, Rod playing a man in love with a fantasy, portrayed by Claire, and *Three into Two Won't Go*—in which they are husband and wife. "But," Claire insisted defensively, "it was only because the roles were right for me. It won't become a habit."

Rod is considerate of Claire's love of city life. Before the marriage he bought a house at Malibu, and it is full of Rod's collection of paintings. It is right on the beach with a swimming pool in the back yard. This is Rod's idea of paradise, but it isn't Claire's. To please her, he rented out the beach house and compromised with a house in Brooklyn Heights. He is a big man and likes a house to move around in, but even Brooklyn was too far from Manhattan for Claire. "I'd rather live in one room in the city than a palace in the country," she told me. Rod resisted for several years, and then they moved to an apartment on Park Avenue. "Partly," he explained tactfully, "because Claire told me three men had followed her while she was riding on the subway to Brooklyn, although one ran into her later and apologized." He left the decorating of the apartment to his wife. "Except for one room. My friends call me Caesar, and I asked the designer to provide me with a Caesar room. It has an antique gold ceiling, marbleized rooms and Roman rings. One room in any house should always be absolutely insane, a sort of decompression chamber. It usually becomes the favorite room in the house." But he would rather be in the Malibu home.

"Although fundamentally I like Europe better, the lazy way of life, the privacy. Basically, while Hollywood has always been good to me, I don't care where I live. Artists must seek different environments. You can't sit in one place or you start drinking or only reckoning the profits. I don't love Hollywood any more than I dislike New York, but I'm too much of a loner to connect myself with any one place. Any way, it all depends on whom you are with." He added, a bit wistfully, I thought, "For an unmarried man Hollywood is a gold mine of beautiful women."

When they are together, and they have been more together this last year than at any time since they married, they have a good time. "We like to do the same things," Claire confided, "we like to be alone. We like to walk down Madison Avenue and look in the art galleries." She confessed that she did not dislike California as much as she used to. "I've accepted the fact that it is really a resort and clothes must be hideously bright and casual." When film work takes them to Hollywood, they live in the heart of town at the Chateau Marmont, while the house at Malibu continues to be rented.

They are both rather hung up about their ages. Rod will keep mentioning that he is forty-two or forty-three as he is now, and every other sentence of Claire's includes, "Of course I was a child then," when she appeared in such and such a play or a film. Rod is extremely conscious of time. "With the bombs, no one believes any more in a sixty-year guarantee." He prefers the young people of today to his own age group. "It's the most rapidly informed generation ever. It is fed the news of the world instantly. It doesn't believe in voluntary death. The rebellion was started by the English against the establishment. The young generation today wants reality, not the crap that mine was fed. The values have changed for the better. The beautiful new people. The new moderns. I'm for anything that's easy, enjoyable, and exciting as long as it is not psychologically and mentally detrimental." I wondered if the fame and financial rewards were corroding to the character. "It depends on the rate of arrival," said Rod. "The fast arrival doesn't mean too much—one year you're in fashion, the next you're out. It took me twenty-one years." He agreed with me that his Oscar-winning film *In the Heat of the Night* was his best performance, but *The Pawnbroker* was pretty close. He was nominated for an Oscar for *The Pawnbroker*, and it won awards all over the world.

Rod comes on strong. His characters are sometimes larger than life. Like Olivier, Steiger is the pure actor. You don't see Steiger, you see acting. He is generous in crediting Sidney Poitier for his success in their film. "Our friendship goes back to when we first began as actors. We knew each other back in the Village. We had a great relationship. He underplayed and made me look good. I have a great love for Sidney. Why are American men so afraid of showing love for each other? This country is crazy in two areas—the youth cult and the virility thing. Men spoil the women and are ashamed to show love for another man."

Rod is a Renaissance man. He can paint and sculpt and write poetry. He has also written three screenplays. It's a treat to find an actor as articulate and erudite. Rod can talk intelligently on almost any subject—art, history, books, and philosophy. He is a highly educated man, but he doesn't tell it that way. "I wasn't born to be an intelligent, hard-working, egomaniac actor," he assured me. "I was born to be a beach bum, in a warm country, painting bad pictures." But he can dress up when he has to—he has two wardrobes, one elegant (the suits made by an English tailor), the other loose and comfortable (for the fat times). Today Rod has the world by the tail, but when he was asked recently on a television show, "What impels you, what motivates you?" he replied, "Fear, undiluted fear."

15)

The Terrible-Tempered Twins: Burt and Kirk

I always think of them as twins. Burt Lancaster and Kirk Douglas. Their careers in Hollywood were born at the same time, fathered by Hal Wallis. Hal, in his actor-buying years, peopled the Hollywood scene with a large family of successful offspring—Charlton Heston, Jerry Lewis, Dean Martin, Elvis Presley, Shirley MacLaine. And Burt and Kirk, who not only arrived in Hollywood together, but became important stars within a few years of each other. Burt immediately, in *The Killers,* and Kirk in *Champion,* after some floundering in *The Strange Love of Martha Ivers, I Walk Alone,* and the mournful *Mourning Becomes Electra* with Rosalind Russell, which almost finished them both. Burt was autocratic almost from the start. Kirk waited three years and seven films before he dared be himself.

When Burt and Kirk hit Hollywood in 1946 after serving their respective terms in the armed forces, World War II had not been over very long. Things were still pretty quiet on the home front. The tourist trade was only just picking up—gasoline rationing had forced Ray Milland, Humphrey Bogart, Dick Powell, and Allan Jones to ride to work on motorcycles. Food rationing had killed the big parties, but Sonia Henie was emerging as an extravagant hostess. At a gathering for two hundred at her Bel Air estate with the tent breezing atop the boarded-over swimming pool and sculptured ice dripping all over the place, the dinner announcement, with Hoagy Carmichael at the piano, was growled in rhyme by the ex-ice-queen in her excruciating accent. An old-timer at the party talked about the good old days of Pickfair parties in Hollywood, and Jack Warner reprimanded, "My boy, *these* are the good old days." And they were for the studios. Every trashy film was swallowed by the entertainment-starved U.S. public. It was a time of unprecedented prosperity—the happy lull before the dark storm of television and the hatred and suspicion of Hollywood films and actors created by the zealots and bigots behind the House Un-American Activities Committee. Larry Parks was blissfully posing for Jergens Lotion ads. Betty Grable was the pin-up girl the G.I.'s "wanted to see most." Films like *Mission to Moscow, North Star,* and *Song of Russia* made in 1943 with the laudable intent of aiding the war effort would soon be called on the Washington carpet and condemned as subversive. Virginia Mayo was advertising Drene Shampoo and my colleague, Louella Parsons, was shattering the airwaves with "My first eggsgloosive . . ."

This was Hollywood when the boyish, blond, wavy-haired Burt costarred with another unknown, Ava Gardner, at Universal in columnist Mark Hellinger's first film, *The Killers,* a low-budgeted story of a gangster. I met Burt on the set and masculinity was oozing from every pore. "Hmmmm, Lancaster," I said, playing for time to catch my breath. "Are you related to the Lancasters of the Wars of the Roses?" I hadn't been educated by Scott Fitzgerald for nothing. He grinned and thought perhaps he was, although he had been born, he told me, in New York City, where he had his share of being chased by cops on East 106th Street between Second and Third Avenues. He was thirty-two, but looked twenty-two, and what a physique. I could see the muscles rippling up and down beneath his open shirt. It's a pleasure to be with a future star at the beginning. He is always so friendly, so eager to please. He makes a hit and it is a different man. The symptoms appeared during Burt's second film, *Brute Force,* when he was already telling Jules Dassin, the director, how to direct, although a few months previously in *The Killers* he had been so unsure that the director, Robert Siodmak, sometimes made fifteen takes of one small scene and Burt was embarrassed and apologized humbly. Burt was loaned to Universal for both films by the astute Mr. Wallis, who does not make many movies himself but did handsomely with his stable of contractees, receiving large sums of money for their services and paying them low salaries for which they had been delighted to sign. They fought for their freedom when they realized the discrepancy between what they got and what Wallis was paid.

I had lunch with Burt during *Brute Force* and was discomfited to be seated at the community table for the cast and some of the crew. Oh, well, I will ignore them, I thought, and concentrate on my questions to Burt, but he had decided to have some fun with me. I'd ask a straight question, he'd pick it up and announce it to the others and his reply was intended to and did embarrass me. I didn't know why he was doing it, but pretty soon I felt a choking sensation, a mixture of rage and tears, and made an excuse and left.

Over the years I have learned that Burt enjoys taking his temper out on people who work for him and are usually not in a position to retaliate. He was using me as a test pattern, to see how far he could go, to prove he was an independent man who could make fun of a columnist and to hell with the consequences. I cannot bear to be humiliated in front of others—this is one of *my* failings—and I dug my claws into every one of Burt's bad performances. My typewriter zinged merrily when he played the wooden Sicilian prince in *The Leopard,* perhaps the worst thing he ever did. It followed *Judgment at Nuremberg,* in which he was a Nazi judge on trial for war atrocities. Burt's conception of the role was to be waxily immobile. He won the Oscar for *Elmer Gantry,* and I recorded this fact. In *The Rose Tattoo* with Anna Magnani he was good, I thought, and very good in all his Westerns—

excellent in *Gunfight at the O.K. Corral* and more recently in *The Professionals,* and I said so in my column. Love and work are two areas where you must be honest or you have nothing. But good or bad, Burt the man had lost me as an admirer during *Brute Force,* a good title for this very physical film star. He delights in a display of force and you never know when it is coming. He was lunching with Ernest Lehman, who wrote the script for *Sweet Smell of Success.* Things were going along pleasantly when Lancaster growled, "I've got a good mind to beat you up." "Why?" asked the astonished Ernest. "I think you could have written some of the scenes better," Burt shouted angrily. "Go ahead, beat me up," replied the amazed author, "I'd like to get my hands on some of your money."

Lancaster is a rich man. Everything he touched turned into money. After the first two films he made a new deal with Wallis which enabled him to go into independent production with Harold Hecht, who was a literary agent when he undertook the task of furthering the acting career of the ex-circus-acrobat. Later, without bothering to consult Harold, another partner, Jim Hill, one of Rita Hayworth's husbands, was added. The first film, *Kiss the Blood Off My Hands,* was a moderate success. The big money came with *The Crimson Pirate* in 1951, directed by Mr. Siodmak, who had only good memories of Burt from *The Killers.* He was quite startled when Burt shouted at him in front of the crew and cast, "You silly old has-been—this isn't the way the camera should be." He was also quarreling with Nick Cravat, his partner in his circus days and now his trainer. Burt, off and running, told his press agent, "Don't bother me with any of these creepy newspaper people." Kirk Douglas on the other hand was being charming to the press. One time when I asked him, "Why are you so interested in publicity?" He replied, "I don't want to wake up one morning and hear someone say, 'Who is Kirk Douglas?' " It can happen. I once heard a sixteen-year-old girl say, "Who is Garbo?"

The money piled up for Burt with his swashbucklers and

Westerns, and ten years after his Hollywood entry his company won several Oscars for *Marty,* which starred Ernest Borgnine as the shy homely butcher. Later Ernie had to buy his way out of Lancaster's company. I was shocked that an actor would make another actor pay for his freedom. But Burt is a tough hombre.

Harold Hecht is a little man—Burt called him "The Mole" or Lord Mole. "Here comes Lord Mole and his [now ex] wife Lady Bird Legs," Burt would shout. (The former Mrs. Hecht has very slender legs.) Lancaster's terrible temper is well known in Hollywood. He can restrain himself for the screen, and this held-back anger is very effective in his films. But in real life when he is annoyed, his eruptions are alarming. At a party Mr. Hecht gave to show off his expensively decorated home, Burt was invited but did not want to attend. He isn't much for parties, but he was convinced he should go. It would look bad if he stayed away. He had a drink or two—he is too careful of his superb physique to get drunk ever—but those who knew him could see he was in a black mood. Those who did not were startled when Burt asked in a loud voice, "Where is the can?" Horrified silence. "How do you like this?" enjoying his bombshell. "He builds this dump with my money and I don't even know where the can is. His host made haste to show him. Fifteen minutes later Burt was laughing and joking as though nothing unusual hand happened.

Almost anything can set him off. On one occasion when Burt was returning by train to Hollywood, Hecht had arranged to have a photographer at the station. This was enough for a torrential outburst. It was over in twenty minutes, but while it lasted everyone was drenched. Burt is a good bridge player, but casual friends who used to play with him don't usually go back because he abuses them outrageously. He was one of the founders of the Savoy Bridge Club but hasn't played there much since the night he had a fight with a prominent lady member. He called her a shocking name. She threw the cards in his face. Now he plays mostly at home, with two tables; when he gets into an argument at one, he switches to the other. All bridge players, it seems to me, are furious if a partner makes a wrong bid, but Burt's anger is alarming. And he's so strong no one wants to challenge him to a fight. Strangely I haven't heard of any fist fights—who would deliberately run into a steel wall? It might be good if someone took him on. Burt, I believe, would laugh like a jovial giant holding a struggling pygmy.

One of his worst exhibitions of temper occurred when he was showing a film in the projection room of his new home in Bel Air, which can best be described as plastic modern, built on the ashes of the house that burned to the ground in the big fire of 1961. His wife Norma was present, another couple—the man works for him—and a woman friend of mine who was invited by Mrs. Lancaster. Near the end of the movie Burt suddenly shouted a stream of profanity at the wife of his employee. Before the film, she and Burt had discussed whether a young woman should have premarital relations with a man. Burt thought "yes," the woman thought not. Her opposition had burned a hole in our hero, who could contain himself no longer. He ordered them out of the house and followed the couple to their car. "Don't ever come back," he yelled, kicking the car as they took off. I know they have been invited back because Burt's rages die almost as fast as they arise. The woman who told me this story thought that he might have been drinking and asked Norma, "Is he drunk?" "He hasn't had a drop," she replied.

She was not too embarrassed. She had learned to ride with the storms. I understand that the association which began in a USO canteen during the war in Italy and culminated in marriage in 1946 and five children and some grandchildren has run its course. During the filming of *The Swimmer* in the rich pools of Connecticut, Burt's new lady, a former hairdresser, was very much present. Jackie knows how to keep him in order. They have some fierce fights. During his film

Castle Keep in Yugoslavia, one of them threw a bottle, and one of them landed in a hospital. According to report, it wasn't Jackie.

I wonder, would Burt have been different if Mr. Wallis had not steered him into stardom? He might have been, although with his looks, physique, and character he would always have been a personality, always resourceful and physically arrogant. Burt was flying to Boston after his film *Trapeze* in 1955 accompanied by some of his executives. They had a few drinks on the plane, and Burt decided to stage a phony fight in the aisle. He did a back flip and landed on the lap of a passenger who screamed, "My hands, my hands!" It was Artur Schnabel, the famous pianist. When they arrived in Boston with the usual fanfare for a visiting movie star, Burt espied a ten-foot fence, hurdled it magnificently, and disappeared. He used to give Hal Wallis near heart failure by standing upside down on one hand on the ten-inch ledge outside his third-floor office at Paramount.

Both Burt and Kirk had many fights with Mr. Wallis while they were under contract to him. But when Hal asked them to come back and costar for him in *Gunfight at the O.K. Corral,* they returned—for a hundred times what he had paid them before. This time they were in the driver's seat and they made sure Wallis knew it. When Hal was interested in signing Charlton Heston from Broadway, he was described to him as "another Burt Lancaster." The producer paused and said, "Yes, but do we need another Burt Lancaster?" He obviously did because Charlton was signed and became successful right away in *The Greatest Show on Earth,* a Wallis loan-out to the late Cecil B. de Mille, followed by the Biblical pictures— *The Ten Commandments, Ben Hur.* Wallis became a millionaire, but Chuck had to wait until his percentage from *El Cid,* by which time he had worked out his term with Wallis, who was better at picking pictures for his stars than they were themselves.

To digress. As soon as the serious, somber Charlton was free, he decided to make a comedy, *The Pigeon That Took*

Rome. It was the pigeon that took Charlton. What a horrible film. I remember it well because I visited him on the set near Rome, and we ate outside in the hot sun at a long table—delicious pasta with meat and the sour bread of the country-side. It was very friendly and I was in a happy mood flying back to London. The same night I was awakened at four in the morning with the telephone ringing. I was half asleep and looking for the light switch and broke a glassful of water at my bedside. "Hello," I said. Charlton screaming with rage: "You have kept me awake all night and now it's your turn." "What? How?" I was drenched with water. "You wrote in your column," an inflamed hiss in my ear, "that I was having an affair with the script girl," his disembodied voice was like a steel rapier. "I did?" I was surprised. While I don't usually remember every column, I would have remembered a tidbit like that. "What did I say?" I asked, searching my mind. "You said," he repeated, "that I was having an affair with the script girl. I have never had an affair with a script girl and I never will." His voice was now a scream again. "You have made a mistake," I said, trying to placate him. For the life of me, I could not remember the item. "Two people telephoned me from Hollywood about it. I demand a retraction," he shouted, and hung up.

I was now wide awake. What had I written? I went to my desk and found the copy of the column. It was a harmless paragraph about the devotion of the script girl to her job. Of how she had flown from Rome to Hollywood for two days because Billy Wilder needed her for some retakes on his *One, Two, Three* film and that afterward she had flown back to the film with Charlton. Now *I* was raging. I called Mr. Heston in Rome, angrily read the paragraph. "There's nothing wrong with that," he said uncertainly. "You bet there isn't," I shouted. "How dared you wake me up when I was tired from seeing a bastard like you in Rome? Before I ever forgive you, you'll have to crawl to me on your hands and knees," and I slammed the receiver down. He wrote me a letter of apology which I tore up. The pompous ass. Who did he think he was?

Six weeks later I was at a preview in Hollywood at the Directors Guild Theater. Charlton was there. He came over. Apologized. On his feet. And I said, "Okay." He was too tall to crawl anyway, and the real culprits were the people who had called him from Hollywood.

This is the difference between Heston and Lancaster. I can't imagine Burt apologizing, no matter how much he is in the wrong. "Don't ever take him on in an argument," his father once said. "One Sunday when he was a youngster his brother Jim did. Burt conked him on the noggin with a baseball bat. That taught Jim never to argue with his brother again. He has never outgrown his love of arguing." He once tossed a reporter for a national magazine out of his hotel suite in New York because he objected to one of the questions. The same magazine asked its Hollywood office for a story on Burt with photographs at the *Gunfight at the O.K. Corral* location. The time was set and the reporter and photographer made the long journey. Burt greeted them, "You guys are assholes. You ask people to do things and you do nothing in return. You waste our time and there is no guarantee that the story will appear. I can go into a market and buy a can of beans and I pay for it. That's good business. But you guys . . ."

Burt was taking expensive ads in the publication the reporter was representing. The frustrated writer said, "You're spending all this money in the magazine. Wouldn't it be a good investment to give us thirty minutes of your time and you'd have several pages of publicity free?" "Absolutely not. You guys are assholes," Burt insisted. "I don't care what you do," he concluded before walking away. "You can take pictures of me picking my nose or scratching my ass, but I won't give you any of my time." To the credit of the two bewildered men, they managed a story without undue maliciousness. I would not have behaved as well.

At Sam Goldwyn's Studio in Hollywood, Mr. Lancaster maintains an office and a staff in what was a large warehouse for keeping props. Burt imagined it as a big barn and wanted to paint it a bright red. Goldwyn said, "No, it would ruin the look of my studio," which is in a soft sand color. This is one time Burt lost. When Sam makes a decision, you can include everyone else out. However, yielding to Burt's impassioned plea, he allowed him to put up red shutters.

Burt's splendid physical shape is the result of careful exercise and diet. He took up golf and practices in his office. When anyone opens the door, Burt will shout, "Fore!" and take a swing. Nick Cravat has been on his payroll since the old days in the circus. He works out with the fifty-five-year-old Lancaster every day and runs with him around the UCLA track every morning. They play bridge together and Burt always finds a role for Nick in his films. He does not fight too much with him, perhaps afraid he would leave if he did. He needs him for his alter ego.

The most violent arguments are reserved for Burt's directors, but like all actors and all people in this business, the quarrel is forgotten when one needs the other. Burt had some violent battles with Sidney Pollack while they were making *The Scalphunters,* but Pollack returned for more punishment in *Castle Keep,* which took longer to make because of the verbal fisticuffs at the beginning between the director and the star. The young actress in the film decided it was too much to take and she was at the airport before they discovered her absence and persuaded her to return.

There was an English director on Burt's pet film project, *Bird Man of Alcatraz.* He stood the abuse for a couple of days before he was replaced by John Frankenheimer. Arthur Penn, who directed Warren Beatty in *Mickey One* and *Bonnie and Clyde,* lasted four days as the driver for *The Train.* Burt did not agree with Penn's methods and decided to replace him even though the idea for the story was Penn's. It was a bit sticky, and he had his producer call the lawyer in New York to say, "We have to fire Arthur." "Where is he?" he asked. "Across the hall." "You mean," stuttered the attorney, "neither you nor Burt have the nerve to fire him yourselves?" The answer was clearly "no."

For all his unreasonable rages, even the victims of his anger concede that Burt knows a great deal about film production. He is expert in every department: editing, advertising, lighting, writing, make-up. One very good thing about Burt—he has no personal vanity. He couldn't have, not the way he dresses. I once saw him leaving the Essex House in New York wearing an electric blue suit, white shirt, bright canary yellow tie, and his perennial heavy brown shoes. He is one of the few stars who does not care how he looks in the dozens of still photographs taken every day on every set. When he shaved his head for *Bird Man of Alcatraz* he did not object to candid photographs, and his bald pate was showing when he attended industry functions. He *is* vain about his professional integrity. He knows his lines. He is always there. He is not emotional in spite of the angry outbursts that seem to come from outside of him, not from within. When he is not working (and often when he is) he is a contained man. When his brother Jim, a retired policeman who was an assistant director on *Bird Man*, dropped dead on the set after lunch, the body was removed and Burt continued working. They thought he would abandon work for the day, but whatever he was feeling, he managed to conceal.

Burt has a cold personality, but he is a leader and people follow him. He is a tough guy but he keeps his word and he can think objectively. In Mexico with *The Scalphunters* he was walking across a field after some hard exercise—he was playing a mountain man chasing thieving Indians before the Civil War—and he was slightly out of breath. He talked about aging. "I think," he said, "that getting older means a diminishing of curiosity. As long as you are curious, you defeat age." Burt is curious about most things. On the Mexican location he learned Spanish; he had lessons every evening. He also learned about the music and the culture of Mexico. They were having a Gian-Carlo Menotti Festival in Durango and he attended every performance. He is an omniverous reader—everything—the classics as well as modern books with an eye to filming. In 1961 he read *Zorba the Greek* and predicted, "It's going to make a helluva picture." He wanted to do Aldous Huxley's *Brave New World*.

He is interested not only in films. Recently he sat with the top brains of the Rand Corporation in Santa Monica wanting to know what it would be like in the twenty-first century, and was able to talk intelligently with them. His friends include doctors, businessmen, attorneys. People from every profession except acting come to his home. He has courage and follows through with projects he believes in. He was among the first actors to go into independent production. Recently he has said that he is tired of acting, that he would like to direct and produce only; when he is in a dull picture, he usually talks of retiring. I think he means it now because, like Paul Newman, while he still enjoys the preliminaries of acting, once the cameras start turning it's all been done as far as he is concerned and he is not interested again until the cameras stop and he is involved with postproduction. When Burt gives up acting, he will be surrendering $1 million against a percentage for each film.

Meanwhile he is a busy man sharing his time and energy between his career, his children, his cultural pursuits, and his social conscience. He can be sadistic to those near him, but, like Dr. Martin Luther King, he has a dream—to help the poor, to promote civil rights. He flew back from Europe for one day to walk in the great March on Washington, then flew back to his film. He lends his home for fund-raising to promote constitutional rights. He has a monolithic personality. He is a giant single. He is made of steel but he listens to the far-off cries for help, and gives it. Nothing is too much trouble, and he will knock himself out for a cause. He is a great salesman, can talk you in and out of anything, an idea, a property, how to play a scene, money for a good cause. He has tremendous ego and he is very opinionated, but perhaps he is entitled to it. The trapeze swinger, once called "Mr.

Teeth and Muscles" and earning $3.00 a week in a third-rate circus, has come a long, long way.

No one quite knows why Hal Wallis signed Kirk Douglas. Every play in which he had appeared on Broadway had failed. But the astute producer saw more than the dimpled chin of the blue-eyed, blond actor. He bought him at a bargain price of $500 a week. Kirk never ever made it on Broadway. In 1963 when he was a well-known star and starring in New York in *One Flew Over the Cuckoo's Nest,* his film-star reputation was not enough to save a bad play, although Lucille Ball's fame in television had made a success of her mediocre musical *Wildcat.*

When I first saw Kirk in Hollywood on the set of his first film, he was shy, modest, and almost inaudible. He smiled sweetly and listened anxiously to my questions and answered them carefully. He was a "B" actor in an "A" picture and it showed. When I knew him better—I can still see his eager delight at my approach—he told me his father in Amsterdam, New York, where he was born, "was a peddler" and that he had worked as a soda jerk at Schrafft's and how when he walked home across the park he would look up at the expensive Hampshire House Hotel on Central Park South and promise himself, "One day I will stay there." He told me of his wife, his first, Diana Douglas, when she was wearing a Tartan skirt to match her name, and a knowledgeable Scotsman said to them, "Oh, you're from the clan Douglas." "I laughed," said Kirk, and told him, "I'm from the clan Issur Danielovitch Demsky."

Alas, it all changed with *Champion.* We were chatting when an associate said, "Well, Champ, it's time to go." A month before, Kirk would have laughed, "What's with the 'champ' bit?" but now he pushed out his chin and you could see he liked it. He wallowed in the new deferential attitude toward him. It isn't always the star who changes so much with success, it's the people around him. But Kirk not only believed everything that was written about him, he added more.

He had a press agent who told him every day, "You're the greatest actor in the world."

It might never have happened for Kirk but for *Champion,* which he made reluctantly in 1949. He had been signed for the low-budgeted film written by Carl Foreman with Mark Robson directing. Robert Siodmak, because of *The Killers* and other successful films at Universal, was in great demand, and was at M-G-M preparing an expensive picture, *The Great Sinner,* for Gregory Peck and Ava Gardner. There was a good male secondary role which Kirk coveted. His agents tried to get him out of *Champion* and into *The Great Sinner.* Mr. Robson heard of the unethical sleight of hand and called Siodmak. "I understand you are signing my actor Kirk Douglas." "Oh, really," said Siodmak. "Yes," said Mark, "his agents are trying to put him in your picture." Siodmak swore on a stack of Hollywood Bibles that he had known nothing of what Mark told him, and after a slight pause, said, "I don't want *Kirk* Douglas. I want *Melvyn* Douglas," adding, "What do you want him in *Champion* for?" Mark was beginning to wonder himself. But a deal had been made and he intended, legally if necessary, for Kirk to honor it. Siodmak called Robson that night, "Rest easy, I've made sure he won't be in the picture." Melvyn Douglas had the part. *The Great Sinner* was a great failure. If Kirk had made it instead of *Champion,* it could have finished him in films and he might have had to jerk sodas again at Schrafft's.

After *Champion* the new Kirk emerged. Overnight success rolled away the protective layer of humility. "He's a tough shit," said one of his best friends to me the other day, "but a shit with style. Don't quote me, I don't want to lose him as a friend." A typical Hollywood remark.

The year is 1950. I can see Kirk on my Beverly Hills living room floor in front of the fire, drawing imaginary diagrams on the carpet of how he was planning his new film *Young Man With a Horn* for Warners. Charlie Feldman had a special showing of *Champion* for Jack Warner and Jack had signed Kirk on the spot. It was his first important film as a star. I had a radio show and featured rather sharp profiles of the film celebrities: "What are the stars really like, with their make-up off and their hair down?" I would give my honest opinion. Soon after Kirk started his film, I concluded my profile of him with "He is now starring in *Young Man With a Horn*. It should be a cinch; he never stops blowing it."

The post-*Champion* Kirk was boastful, egotistical, resentful of criticism—if anyone dared give it. Kirk has rarely been successful on the screen as a nice guy. (The same is true for Laurence Harvey.) Kirk is at his best in a *Champion*-type role. As a hero he is colorless. In *Young Man With a Horn* he portrayed a fictionalized version of Bix Beiderbecke, the famed trumpet player. He was too nice to be true. Ten scripts were turned down before the starting date. Jerry Wald, the producer, promised Kirk, "Don't worry, you're going to be wonderful. We're getting you a famous stage director." Then suddenly the famous stage director was not doing the film. It seemed that when Kirk was a struggling stage actor, he was up for a play with this director, who turned him down. Now that he was a star, Kirk would not accept him.

Kirk for all his tremendous success in *Champion* and his drive to succeed was perhaps, and still is, nervous about his career. He is more afraid than most actors to associate with people who can hurt his future. He was in London in 1952, on the popular tax dodge. If you stayed away from the United States for eighteen months, you did not have to pay any income tax during that period. The law was amended later to a ceiling of $25,000 free before income tax, but not before Kirk, Gene Kelly, and David Niven had made a fortune.

During Kirk's eighteen-month tax vacation in Europe, he ran amuck with the pretty young starlets. By this time he was separated from Diana, part of the Hollywood pattern; when the husband or wife becomes a star, they invariably drop the partner they married when they were poor and struggling. Kirk had a compulsion to prove he was a champion in all departments, and he was picking up women and dropping them like acorns. At least Warren Beatty contrives to like his loves, but loyalty to a lady was not in Kirk's lexicon in that wild time of his success. After a few years he simmered down and accepted his triumph more calmly and has been happily married since May 1954 to French Anne Buydens, who worked as a press agent on one of his European pictures. They have two sons—there were two sons from the marriage with Diana —but Kirk has not lost the habit of titillating the girls, although it is more of a reflex action today. Not long ago a young girl reporter interviewed him at New York's Sardi's East. All during lunch he sounded as if it were the dearest hope of his life to have sex with her. From her reaction she seemed flattered. When Kirk said he would walk down Park Avenue to his hotel, she said, "I'm going the same way. Let's walk together." Kirk immediately stepped back to his press agent and whispered dramatically, "For God's sake, get rid of her."

Like Lancaster, Kirk's body is very important to him. He looks at his muscles and he feels strong, and in many respects he is. At St. Lawrence University in Canton, New York, he was undefeated intercollegiate wrestling champion for three years. He is an excellent tennis player and plays daily at his court in Beverly Hills and in Palm Springs where he has another home. And he swims every day in one of his two pools. It's a good life. Because of his muscular body, Kirk seems taller than he is. When he stands up, you realize that his legs are rather short. He is proud of his hair and combs it with his hand all the time, regardless of where he is.

On the set he demands perfection. Mistakes are punished immediately if the film is for his own company, Bryna Productions, which he founded in 1955 and named for his mother. The company has made him rich with films like *The Vikings* and *Spartacus*. He keeps his production people on their toes with slogans—"Anticipate," "Be Organized," "Be Ready." But he is not always ready himself. During the filming of *The Vikings,* Kirk was late to the set on several occasions and when the director remonstrated, "Maybe you shouldn't go out at night so much," Kirk replied sharply,

"Look, you take care of the directing, I'll take care of the —" Kirk, next to criticism, most dislikes interference by a leading lady. He was unhappy making *Strangers When We Meet* with Kim Novak, who was engaged to the director, Richard Quine. Like Rod Steiger, he is wary of situations where the actress, between embraces, can persuade the director to slant the script her way.

Kirk is not a natural actor. He has to work himself into a lather before the scene to get into the mood. Some actors can chat with you to the second before the call for "action," but not Kirk. He will stall and complain before the scene. Away from the set he insists on his rights as a star. If a car is late to pick him up, he raises holy hell, also if another actor receives more attention at a function. "Why are they all crowding around Rock Hudson?" he beefed at one premiere. It wasn't that he was jealous of Rock's popularity, but he felt it was a reflection on his status as a star. He is a Grade-A complainer where his career is concerned.

But when he is not working or on parade, and not under stress, he can be charming. Kirk is a man of taste, as you can see with the paintings and statuary in his homes. He gives the most exclusive parties today in Hollywood. His wife, who is always on the best-dressed lists and who dominates her husband socially, is a tremendous plus. She is calm, efficient, and an excellent hostess. He prefers to give parties in honor of such politicians as California's former governor, Pat Brown. Senator Javits was another guest of honor. Where the Gary Coopers would entertain royalty and famous people from all over the world regardless of political affiliations, Kirk and Gregory Peck to a lesser extent are concerned with being nice to the important men in politics. The stars have money. The status could be raised with an ambassadorship to one of the South American countries. Issur Danielovitch Demsky, the Honorable Ambassador to Bolivia. It sounds great. While waiting to accomplish the impossible dream, Kirk travels to some of the backward countries to promote Americanism. Apart from his genuine desire to help the unfortunate, his travels for the government keep him in the Washington spectrum. Kirk has an almost maniacal drive to be the best. When he was courting Anne, they took a trip to Switzerland in the winter. She could ski, but he could not. "But I'm going to," he said grimly. The first day on the slopes, he grabbed the instructor by his jacket and said, "Make me ski well."

Kirk sets up appointments and sometimes breaks them without notice. While he was starring in *Town Without Pity* in Rome, he went to Paris for the premiere of *Spartacus* without letting anyone know where he was. They learned of his whereabouts in the newspapers. Burt Lancaster could never do that, although Mr. Brando and Mr. Sinatra could and have. It was tense when he returned to Rome, but from the way Kirk hollered and argued, you would have assumed everyone else was wrong and Kirk the injured party. His co-producer Edward Lewis had an arrangement with Kirk that he was not allowed to yell at him. They got into a screaming argument and Kirk shouted, "Eddie, if you don't agree with me, I'll lose all respect for you."

Kirk can rationalize himself out of any situation. With his millionaire friend Ralph Stolkin he had rented a house in Grenoble, France, for the February Olympics as part of his public-service image—he is the unpaid press-relations director of the U.S. Olympics Committee. I was dining with Ralph one night and he was worried. He had heard, he told me, that Grenoble was not a fun town. I was not too surprised to hear later that Kirk had canceled Grenoble because, he said, the President of the United States had asked all Americans to stay home in the name of patriotic conservation of the dollar. Instead, Kirk went to Acapulco with Ralph and had a delicious time aboard the Stolkin yacht. It was all right for him to go to Mexico, his press agent explained meticulously. "President Johnson said nothing against traveling in this hemisphere."

While Kirk was costarring with Richard Harris in *The Heroes of Telemark*, the two men almost came to blows. After one argument Richard dared Kirk to show up at a designated place and he would knock his block off. Kirk with his gift of rationalization allowed himself to be talked out of it on the grounds that injury might result and hold up the film.

Tony Mann directed *Telemark* and he did not want a repetition of *Spartacus,* when Kirk had him fired and brought in Stanley Kubrick, giving him his first big chance to direct. Mr. Mann and Kirk had differed on the concept of Spartacus, on the motivation of the character. "But, Kirk," Tony pleaded, "if you see him as a Mongoloid idiot, a Neanderthal ape, how do you expect the audience to believe the slaves would follow you to the death?" "What d'ya mean?" "Well, play him with a spark of decency, of humanity." "No," said Kirk, setting his dimple obstinately, "I'll do it my way, *now* like an ape, *later* like a human being." The next day Mann's agent at MCA called to tell him, "Kirk wants you off the picture." By treading delicately Tony remained with *The Heroes of Telemark* until the end. He was not as lucky with *A Dandy in Aspic.* Tony died a few days before the film with Laurence Harvey and Mia Farrow was finished. Mr. Harvey completed the film, which Tony's friends insist is why it was such a disaster.

Kirk is a positive man and gambles on films he believes in, even when his associates assure him they are not commercial. He believed in *Ulysses,* the earlier version, and *Act of Love;* both lost the investment. He believed strongly in a story called *The Lonesome Country,* retitled *Lonely Are the Brave,* which received great reviews but fell on its box-office face. Film buffs revere this great film.

Kirk has a restless, intelligent, probing mind. He could have been a fine actor in the Burton-Olivier class, if he had done more in the theater and studied his craft. He knows everything that happens on the set—whether the lights are right, if the dialogue is O.K.—and like Burt, he has interests outside of film making. He speaks French and Italian fluently. He thinks, a rare attribute in an actor—another quality he shares with Mr. Lancaster. But where Burt could give up acting without regret, Kirk will hang on for the whole ride. I am sure he would not be happy without the sweet sound of applause—and the money. As recently as *In Harm's Way* in 1964, Kirk was paid $400,000 for the picture. I don't know how much it is today. I would guess it is less, but it is still a fortune for the actor whose parents came to this country as refugees from the pogroms of Russia.

16)

The Fondas: The Papa,
The Mamas, and The Kids

Henry Fonda has a reputation as a good actor and a bad father. One assumption is correct, the other is wrong. Henry's children, Jane and Peter, are always running off at the mouth about what a terrible childhood they had and how he was never around when they needed him. "No one told me, man," said Peter, referring to the suicide of his mother in 1950. "Years later I was in a barber's chair and read in a magazine that my mother had slashed her throat with a razor." He was a boy of ten when his mother died, and it was hardly likely that even the worst father in the world would explain the details. But he must have heard something because soon after his mother's death Peter put a bullet, point-blank, into his stomach from a .22-caliber rifle, which did not quite manage to kill him. Jane has complained during interviews that her father sent her to one school after another, that she did not see much of him because he was always getting married; and while she never talks of her mother's terrible death, you know she is blaming her father.

I have known all the Fondas very well in my long time in Hollywood, including four of Henry's five wives. Of all the Fondas, the one who stands a mile above the rest as a decent human being is the sixty-three-year-old Henry. Jane and Peter are not a patch on the old man, in any department. He suffers when the kids destroy him in print, but he does not turn away from them. He dislikes Jane's nudity on and off the screen—did you ever see that naked shot on the beach for a national magazine? He has detested his son's boastful bouts with LSD and marijuana, but when the boy with the longest adolescence of this generation was hauled into court, his father was there as a shield between Peter's usual reckless remarks and the press. Hank, an expert fielder of treacherous questions, answered for his son, who soon after gave a long interview murdering his father all over again. So it's the rebellion of today's youth against their parents. But Peter was twenty-seven, man, and by that time you are supposed to realize that your father was shaped and is just as much a victim as you are of the mores and morals of his generation— that he worked hard, and fought in a war, while all you went through was affluence.

Jane, born in 1937, two years before Peter, ought to know better. And I believe a bit of daylight is dawning. That at the ripe age of thirty-two, she is beginning to realize that her father is not as bad a parent as she thought. She even telephones him now and then, although she is still skeptical and satirical about his marriage record. A year or so ago Jane was conducting her husband, Roger Vadim, around her father's beautiful town house in the East 70's in New York. Like most children of all ages, the junior Fondas feel that papa must allow them the run of his home even when they are publicly lambasting him. She took Vadim to a well-lived-in love seat. She lifted up the top covering and said, "This is Shirlee my father's fifth wife." The material below was Afdera, his fourth, she explained. The one below that was Susan (the socialite Miss Blanchard), the mother of his youngest daughter, Amy. Underneath Susan, was "my mother"—Frances Seymour Brokaw. The last loose covering—I've been in the house without noticing anything unusual about this marital heirloom—represented Fonda's first wife, Margaret Sullavan —the late actress who committed suicide two marriages and three children later. One of Miss Sullavan's daughters,

Bridget, also committed suicide. Suicide is catching—young Fonda tried three times. When I first met him about seven years ago when he was starting his acting career in Hollywood, he told me matter of factly that he had tried to end it all when he was seventeen by swimming out to sea from a Greek island. He must have kept one eye looking back, because a boat soon came and rescued him. But for his son to blame Henry for their mother's death is unfair. She was in a mental institution and chose a punishing time for her fatal act—when Hank was on his honeymoon with Susan. It certainly was not meant to help his new marriage. But of course she was unbalanced, and this must have been apparent during her marriage to Henry, which caused her erratic behavior and resulted in the divorce.

A tactless woman, the actress wife of a producer, asked Henry at one time, "What was it like to be married to all those women and two of them committed suicide?" Fonda can be an angry man and an impatient one, but he had obviously thought a great deal about the subject, wondering if he were to blame. "Well," he answered quietly, "I loved them all—in a way I still do. I could not have saved one of them and they could not save me. Everyone has to save himself."

Mr. Fonda had been in Hollywood a year when I met him at 20th Century-Fox in 1936 on the set of *The Farmer Takes a Wife*. He had starred in the play on Broadway, which I had seen when I first came from England. He had America of the Midwest all over his face and tall lanky frame. I was invited to dine with Henry and two other bachelors, Jimmy Stewart and Josh Logan, who shared the house in the Hollywood Hills. The three had met in summer stock in New England, and Jimmy and Henry had shared an apartment in New York before *Murder Man* on the stage had brought Stewart to M-G-M at almost the same time. I was rather dishy in those days, and Hank and Jimmy have both told me in recent years—when it was too late to do anything about it— that they had leched after me. I had no suspicion during the dinner but bloomed with the attention. Afterward Jimmy said enthusiastically in his cathedral-roof-to-his-mouth way of talking, "Let's go into the hills and shoot bobcats." The men armed themselves with rifles. It seemed exhilaratingly dangerous. We didn't see any wild cats, but it was fun and we were good friends until I wrote something about Hank in my column that made him angry. He remained annoyed with me all during the war, I learned from a friend with him in the Pacific fleet. "He said he doesn't like you," I was told. When I found myself in 1948 sitting at the same table with him at an Associated Press Editors dinner, I thought, "Oh, Lord, it's going to be a rough night." But he was absolutely charming to me, and I could see then why women loved him. He was still married to Frances—she was with him—and I liked them both very much. He was a quiet man then and now, but he is warmer now, although the talking still seems an effort and controlled.

Henry came to a Hollywood that was recovering from the grim years of the Depression of the early '30s. Shirley Temple was the Number One queen of the box office and had her own bungalow and school on the Fox lot. Darryl Zanuck had not long before taken over as head of production for the newly formed 20th Century-Fox with Joe Schenck as president. Alice Faye was the top musical-comedy star, starring in *She Learned About Sailors;* Garbo, Gable, and Norma Shearer reigned supreme at M-G-M; and Errol Flynn had been discovered for Warners by Michael Curtiz in *Captain Blood.* Unions were having a hard time, and neither the Screen Writers Guild nor Screen Actors Guild were on firm ground. It was a time of major labor upheaval, and while his best friend Jimmy Stewart veered to the right, Hank, a devout Democrat, was active in the liberal causes; in the late '40s, "liberal" was to become a dirty word.

"My father was a rebel in the forties," his son Peter told me with a certain relish. "Now he is a conservative pillar of the Democratic Club." Men usually get more conservative as they get older. Even Peter in the last year has taken a quieter turn, although he still berates his father for being absent so much when he was a child. "He just wasn't there very often." Peter was three years old when his father enlisted in the Navy. His friend, Jimmy Stewart, enlisted as a G.I. in the Air Force and became a colonel. They were both giving up lucrative film careers to serve their country, but Henry's children saw it only as desertion from the family hearth. Peter swears he remembers his father in uniform reciting a poem to him before leaving for his ship. "My doggie's name is Guess, my doggie's name is Guess. He shakes his head for 'no' and wags his tail for 'yes.' " "It was his way of saying good-by," Peter concedes. "When the war was over and he came back, Jane and I were waiting at the top of the stairs in the Tigertail Road home [in Brentwood] with a photograph in our hands to know what he looked like."

The Fonda children knew he was a film star when they saw him grow a mustache and a beard and he explained it was for a film. "The first time I saw my father on the screen," Peter told me in one of his rare loquacious moods—he can be very uncommunicative—"I was four. He played this character Chad Hanna. I saw him get in a cage with a lion and I was terrified. I went up to the screen to touch it and I ran out screaming. When he was on leave, he came to see us at the Brentwood Town and Country School. I ran away from him shouting, 'That's Chad Hanna!' " Peter resents having been sent away to school when he was six, but with his father working all the time and a mother who was showing signs of incompetence, a boarding school was perhaps the best solution at the time. Peter obviously does not think so, and he says he will never send his own children away. With such a mixed-up father, it will be interesting to see how *his* kids turn out. Well, I hope, and the prospects for them are better, because Peter in his twenty-eighth year decided some of the fun and games were over and accepted the responsibility of independent film production with two friends—Dennis Hopper and Bill Leland Hayward. "It's confusing, man, all the relationships. Dennis, who is the director, is married to Brooke Hayward, whose mother Margaret Sullavan was my father's first wife. I was in love with Bridget Hayward, who committed suicide. Bill's father, Leland Hayward, was my father's agent."

The first of Peter's independent pictures is titled *Easy Ride,* which the Fonda kids have had—born in the silk-stocking district of East Sixty-third Street and Madison Avenue in New York City, to a father who was earning a star salary before they were born, a Social Register mother who left them $60,000 each, and an entry into an acting career with the respected name of Fonda. Of course it helps to have a famous parent in the business. How many talented kids never get a chance? There must be thousands of them. If you don't have talent, nothing helps, as Bing Crosby's brood learned the easy way.

"How not with it can a man be, man?" Peter ran his nervous fingers through his long hair. "My sister Jane was at Malibu with Vadim and my father had a house nearby. But because my father felt he should set an example for Jane, every night he drove Shirlee back to her home. Crazy, man, crazy." And yet when Peter married his Susan, it was very posh and very square in St. Bartholomew's Church on Park Avenue in New York. "They wouldn't let me wear my jeans and cowboy boots and I only had one pair of shoes, so there I was kneeling at the altar, man, and everyone in the church could see the big hole in the sole of my shoe. Vadim and my father," he continued, "don't seem alike, but they are. Vadim is quiet and reserved when he doesn't know people, and so is my father. It's a great effort for Vadim to be sociable. Like my father, he is not a man who reaffirms his affection. He expects you to take it for granted."

Henry might have married Shirlee before Malibu, but the next marriage, he told me, must be the last. In the spring of 1966 I had bumped into them in the gift shop at the Kahala Hilton in Honolulu, and he introduced me to the blonde, pretty, airline hostess—she was on leave from her job—but for the first time in the thirty-odd years I have known Hank, he seemed tranquil. Later in Hollywood I asked him, "Are you going to marry her?"

"I want to," he replied seriously—at one time he would have frowned at such a personal question. He waited six more months to be sure.

"I like Shirlee fine," Peter told me. It would be hard not to. She is a pleasant, intelligent woman with the quiet know-how of a good nurse or a good secretary, or a good airline stewardess. Shirlee is helping the two generations to bridge the years of antagonism and rebellion. Peter assured me he is through with LSD after eleven "trips." He described the first. He tried to make it sound thrilling, but it was terrifying. "I can only equate it with four years with a good psychiatrist if it could all be done in one session. You see it all at once. You know what it's all about. I witnessed death. I felt and believed I was dying. I experienced panic—this thing called ego-death. I burst through the balloon. I was on the other side. It was a helluva trip. I saw my childhood when I was never told the basic problems in life—as a child when you don't see anything else, you think what is happening is the normal. Marriage and love and mother and father were something different for me. Merely words. I knew I loved my dog and I had great affection for the planet. When you are in the experience, you don't know it will change until it comes back to normal. I saw me, the me that approaches me. The me that lies. The me that is religious. The me, the agnostic. The Tibetans do it without the drug by fasting." He apologized for speaking so much. As we both knew, he could be silent. "Part of my gig as an actor," he continued, "is to be able to speak out. When I came back from the trip, in choosing myself, I chose what I was going to be. I chose the personality I wanted. I gave birth to myself. I became my father and my mother. I became a living, breathing organism. I am part of the universe."

Jane worries a great deal about her brother; she is very emotional about him. She was delighted with his success in *Wild Angels* about today's problem kids, which cost $300,000 and earned $5 million, and *The Trip*, about LSD, which followed and was also very successful. They love each other and enjoy being together. They also enjoy hurting each other—

the quarrels are rather Freudian. "How did Jane feel about the LSD?" I asked Peter. He smiled, "Jane and I are Army buddies. When we meet, we say, 'Here we are together again. My God, what we have gone through together.' I feel super, super now," he assured me, "well off, because unlike my father, I don't hide anything from my children. They know everything and"—jumping away from LSD, marijuana, divorce, suicide—"that's why we're going to live away from Los Angeles, away from the phonies. And I don't want them to die of lung cancer in the smog. I want to live near the San Francisco peaks where we can see the planet. We are the revolution. My entire generation is involved. After my arrest, kids would come up to me and say, 'That was me up there, man.' After my bust I became a numero one in the country. I was cheered in the streets driving to court. I was discovered by the groupies, the hang-around rock and rollers, the kids yelling 'Sock it to 'em, man.'" Peter, quite obviously still mixed up, believes he is some sort of hero when he is merely the product of too much, too young. Most of the LSD takers, the beatniks, the hippies, the scruffy people come from comfortable homes.

Jane told me she had not wanted to be an actress. After a brief brush with higher education at Vassar, she tried art and languages in Paris with Pop of course footing the bills. (How often do these independent kids refuse to accept the money?) Children of famous actors usually gravitate toward the same career, and Jane had already appeared with her father during her summer vacations from the exclusive Emma Willard School in New York State—in *The Country Girl* in Omaha, where he was raised, and in *The Male Animal* in Denver. Hank had starred in the film version of the latter in 1942 before he went to the war. When she decided to make a career of acting, Josh Logan, who had known her all her life, tested her with Warren Beatty for *Parrish,* which didn't come off for either of them. But Jane landed in Logan's *Tall Story* with Tony Perkins. Whether she would have made it but for her father's friendship with the director is open to question.

Logan had directed Henry in the film and stage version of *Mister Roberts,* a smash success in both mediums, and Jane had a right to relax—her career was in good hands. The picture was not a hit, but Jane, looking from the screen with her father's eyes, was launched.

She studied at the Actors Studio in New York. Once she had chosen the career that would yield her a harvest of $400,000 a picture, she was going to be the best. She is not her father's daughter for nothing. She was a chubby adolescent, but she dieted and exercised and the glamorous figure we see so much of today was born. We have seen nearly all of Jane's epidermis since she met Mr. Vadim, the famed stripper of his women. Vadim ordered the brunette Miss Fonda to dye her hair bright yellow, to wear it straight and long, and transformed her into a country-club Brigitte Bardot, whom he had married and undressed in *And God Created Woman.* It wasn't God, it was Vadim. Previously she had been a happy little brunette playing kittenish maids in films like *Helen of Troy.* If Brigitte had not bounced into Vadim's view, I believe she would have had a happier life. I doubt whether she would have tried to commit suicide—the last escape from pressure—when she was in her mid-twenties.

For the sake of Jane's father as much as for her, I hope the pressures will not be too much for Jane. She is more sensible than her brother, and having a baby has calmed her down.

I would not want to see her again as she was on the last day of filming *Any Wednesday.* She was like a tornado the day I lunched with her at Warners. Between bites of a meager lunch she was frantically trying to learn where Vadim expected to meet her the next morning. First it was Paris, which meant flying to New York, then overnight to France, and she hadn't packed yet; then it was to be Mexico, then not Mexico. It would be New York. She had been on the phone to Paris six times that morning between takes on the set, and she excused herself twice during our lunch to talk to Paris again. With every call she asked to have her whole chain of reservations changed, and I thought she would have a nervous breakdown. At the very last minute when she was leaving for the airport, Vadim called to say, "Stay where you are, I'm flying to Los Angeles."

She was calmer when I saw her in Rome during *Barbarella,* with Vadim directing Jane, after a lazy layoff from work when he announced that he would do some writing while his wife worked for them both—he might have been kidding, but I don't think so. She was as undressed as she had been in *The Game Is Over (La Curee).* Her long legs were bare almost to the waist and her arms were uncovered, but the rest of her, except for her head, was encased in armor. Somehow, she managed to look nude even to the steel belly button over her navel. In *The Game Is Over,* with Peter McEnery, who gave Hayley Mills her first grownup kiss, they had a rip-roaring naked time in their bathroom and bedroom with Jane, nude, straddling McEnery's boyish shoulders while they whooped it up around the room and later consummated the whipped-up sex with grunts and groans. I was not amazed when she went insane at the end of the film. In the Vadim farmhouse near Paris, where Jane lives with her husband, the bathroom is divided from the bedroom by a clear wall of glass, so they always know what the other is doing. The game is definitely *not* over.

Before Vadim in Jane's love life, there was Andreas Voutsinas. I met him many times with Jane and he seemed pleasant enough. He has not done too much since their breakup. When I last heard of him he was directing something minor in Yugoslavia or Hungary. Andreas took charge of Jane's career with Svengali intensity. They were together all the time—he was always on the set coaching her and directors hated it. She insisted on Voutsinas to direct her Broadway play *The Fun Couple,* which featured another young pretty lady, Dyan Cannon, who was to be Mrs. Cary Grant. Cary was around during rehearsals. I did not see him on the opening night, which alas, was also the closing night. It was lucky for Jane that she had already established herself in films. Even in the play she showed as much of herself as possible, without being arrested, in a gasp-making bikini. "Why are you always undressing?" I asked Jane in Rome, and "Why does Vadim always undress his women?" She protested, "It isn't true. I've only been nude in three films." Why does it seem like three hundred?

Whenever I saw Jane with Voutsinas, I'd ask, "Are you getting married?" Voutsinas was willing, but not Jane. "Marriage is a serious thing," she would say somberly. "I don't want to be married as many times as my father. I'm in no hurry." Andreas would shrug and look unhappily at me. Jane's father did not like him, and I used to think this was the reason why Jane continued the association for so long—it lasted several years. Andreas was often brutally rude to Jane, who is the slave-girl type. One time during the *Fun Couple* rehearsals, Voutsinas shouted at the woman he loved before everyone, "You have no talent!" She took it meekly.

Jane is a woman who gives everything to her man no matter what he withholds from her. Vadim will state, "I want a drink—*now,* and if you don't hurry," with only half a smile, "I'll hit you across the mouth." It's a game between them, I am sure, and it's all in French which gives it a softer sound. Jane asked Vadim to give her a baby. Kids who believe they have been abused in their childhood like to try their theories on their own children. I was surprised when she told me casually that her husband had said, "I'll give give you a baby if you give me a red Ferrari car." She was amused and rather touched by his request. He got his Ferrari from Jane—a blue one, a girl has to show *some* independence—and she got her baby. If she is the bright girl I know her to be, she will continue with her career. Vadim would be bored with a housewife who is not gathering grapes in the film vineyards. Beautiful actresses can lose their glamour for certain men when they retire. It happened to Rita Hayworth when she gave it all up to be the Princess Aly Khan. You would have thought being a princess would be glamor enough, but without the movie-star label, Rita was just a dull girl unable to keep up in the fast world of her husband. Jane is not dull. She is outspoken and that is always interesting, as when she gave me her opinion of Laurence Harvey when they made *Walk on the Wild Side* at Columbia. She detested him. Her comments caused a flutter in the weekly news magazines, one of which has kept the vendetta going with Larry. To be fair to Mr. Harvey, Jane playing a southern, illiterate prostitute in the film and Capucine as an aristocratic prostitute with a hilarious death scene were unbelievably bad. Cap had to die and did not know how. In the end Harvey strangled her—figuratively speaking.

Jane is vitally interested in people and in the artistic world. She might learn something if she would take the time to get close to her father. Henry has excellent taste in paintings and *objets d'art,* and he is the best actor-painter around. When the pressure of film and stage acting is too much, Henry goes upstairs to his studio and paints. The walls of his homes in New York and Bel Air are covered with his water colors and oils—in the style of Andrew Wyeth. He takes his painting paraphernalia wherever he goes. In Rome last year for *Once Upon a Time in the West,* he told me he had placed a bowl of fruit on the ledge of his balcony that morning at the Hassler Hotel and painted it against the whole city of Rome with St. Peter's in the background. When he was making *The Cincinnati Kid* at M-G-M, I told Henry that I had recently returned from Madrid. "I hope you also went to Toledo to see the El Grecos," he said. No, I had not. I never have time on the travels for my column to take side trips. Henry lost his funereal solemnity as he launched into a fascinating description of the El Grecos. The next time I was in Madrid, I made a point of going to nearby Toledo to see them. I must confess it was easier for me to find the time for El Greco because El Cordobes was fighting the bulls in the Toledo ring at 6 P.M. on the same day. I am an *aficionado* since Hank Werba of *Variety,* who used to live in Madrid, explained the art of bullfighting. He came with me to the El Grecos and I went with him to the bullfights.

"Henry was not always so grave," Jimmy Stewart (who is three years younger than his friend) assured me. "He used to be the funniest guy. He was tremendous. It was out-and-out slapstick humor—Laurel and Hardy. Hank and I were sitting around listening to records after we came back from the service," Jimmy continued. "He was married to Frances Brokaw, I was still chasing pretty ladies. [Jimmy married Mrs. Gloria McLean of the McLean diamond family when he was forty, and they have twin teen-age daughters. Gloria's two sons by the previous marriage are in their twenties.] MCA was handling both of us. They were always taking us out to lunch and Hank decided we should give them a party at the Beverly Hills Club. It would be a spoof. After cocktails we went in for dinner and there was nothing on the table except place cards. Hank got into a prearranged argument with the waiter and said, 'Let's go somewhere else.' The thirty-five MCA agents were starving, and Jules Stein, who heads the company, said meekly, 'No, let's give them a couple of dollars.' 'No,' said Hank, 'we're not wanted here. Let's go.' There was a bus waiting outside. 'Ah, ha,' said the hungry agents, 'that was a good joke. Where are we having dinner?' Dinner was to be at Romanoff's, to be interrupted by a phony fight, but there was a real fight and we ended in the upstairs room at Chasen's. By this time everyone was loaded and they were breaking plates on each other's heads and squirting seltzer. We've never had so much fun."

I simply cannot imagine this sort of joke in today's Hollywood. For one thing, the all-important business managers would not disgorge the money for it. The new people all have at least five advisers and one astrologer telling them which films to make and how to conserve their cash. Jack Warner told me one of the reasons he sold his studio was because of the large entourage behind every star. "In the old days you called the actor and made the deal with him. Now they bring an army." Perhaps because the stakes are so much higher and the amount that can be saved after taxes is so much less. Fonda made his fortune in the days of low taxation. He is scrupulously careful of his money. There is a joke that if you make a telephone call at Henry's home, he will charge you the ten cents plus tax. But he has not been frugal in the spending for his children, and, in their respective ways, they have cost him a great deal.

17)

A Mixed Bag

At one time names like Anthony Quinn, Gregory Peck, and Ava Gardner would have been strong enough to carry a film to success. Today and for a decade past, it's the film, not the name. But the glamour still lingers around the old-time stars, and Gregory Peck can still be paid $750,000 and a percentage, although some of the others are glad to walk away for 50 per cent less.

Anthony Quinn has become more positive and more virile in the years I have known him. He was in Hollywood before I arrived. I can see him now at Warner Brothers in a "B" picture—slinky, sleek, his black hair painted on his skull in the fashion of Rudolph Valentino. Cary Grant was still styling his hair this way—the bushy mop of the early Eddie Fisher was still lock-moons away, and today's long hair for men had not been dreamed of in this century. Tony was a great dancer, he told me, thrusting his dark face close to mine, and would I like to go to a place where they really danced? I would. He took me to an unlit cave where all the men were young Negroes or dark Spaniards—a kaleidoscope of flying faces and marvelous dancing feet. I danced until I could not dance any more. It was the best time I ever had. He would call me now and then, but as a columnist for a responsible syndicate, I thought I'd better not go to the cave again. I knew he wasn't using me to get his name in the column, but he might be too much to handle. He was like an uncontrollable bull—except when he danced and was light, graceful, amazing.

I was in Paris when he was costarring with Gregory Peck in Fred Zinnemann's film *Behold a Pale Horse,* one of Fred's few failures. Tony had recently become an extramarital father with a pleasant-looking Italian girl, Jolanda Addolori, who had looked after his wardrobe in his Biblical film, *Barabbas.* They had spent some idyllic hours together in Rome and Tony had proudly proclaimed his fatherhood to the world. The boy was only three or four months old when I learned from a mutual friend that Jolanda was pregnant again. My source was unimpeachable and I used the item in my column. As it was so soon after the first baby and as Tony had made no move to divorce Katherine de Mille, the adopted daughter of Cecil B. de Mille, who had maliciously allowed his son-in-law to direct as well as star in *The Buccaneer,* I timed the item to appear in my column on Tuesday, the day after I was visiting Tony on the set.

When I came in, he was dashing out. "Where are you going, Tony?" I called after him. "Hi, Sheilah"—we had been good friends over the years despite my declining his dancing invitations—"I'm going to kill a rumor," he said pleasantly. Could it be my baby item? But this was Monday and my story was for Tuesday. Nonetheless, I was slightly apprehensive. Could the syndicate have switched the columns? I was soon to know. Tony roared back on the set like a bull in the last extremity and screamed, "Get her off the set, *NOW!*" Obviously, the baby. Had my source been wrong? What to do? I wanted to run, but it would seem as if I had been thrown off. It was very awkward. "Would you," I said to one of the press agents on the set, "tell Tony that if my item is wrong, I will make a retraction?" He came back from the actor, who was still screaming with anger and pain, and said, "He'll talk to you, *only* on the basis of a retraction."

The scene was a hospital ward and Tony was sitting on a

bed. He did not get up or ask me to sit down, but I did anyway. "How could you do this to me?" he yelled for all to hear. Hear? The entire action of the film had stopped and everyone was straining to see how the fight between the bull and the bitch would come out. "You're not going to be a father again?" I asked cautiously. "No!" he bellowed, and again demanded, "How could you do this to me?" "If I'm wrong, I'll be glad to make a retraction." "Of course you're wrong and I demand a retraction. Look," he said in a softer tone, thank goodness, "you've known me all these years. You know I tell you everything, even when I have an orgasm." (Well, not really.) But his tone was more conciliatory so I said, "On the basis that you tell me everything, even when you have an orgasm, how are you managing *not* to have a baby?" I knew Jolanda was living with him in the villa he had rented in a suburb of Paris. "We sleep in separate rooms." I knew he was lying even though his voice was tearful. "I am trying to get a divorce," he whimpered, "and a story like this could ruin everything." "Oh, a divorce," I said, my reporter's mind clicking. This was the first indication of a divorce. "Yes, I want to marry Yolanda and then I'll have a million kids." I was busily writing. "What are you putting down?" he demanded suspiciously. "That you're getting a divorce." "How will you put the retraction?" "I'll do it in your own words," I said magnanimously. The divorce was a news story. I could afford to be generous. I made the retraction.

Two months later—it was January—I was in the Los Angeles airport in the TWA Ambassadors Lounge waiting for my plane to be called for New York. A blonde woman came in and greeted me effusively while I wondered, who is she? "We just flew in from Rome," she said. Ah, now I knew. She was the wife of Tony's agent. Her husband came in and was delighted to see me. Yes, he had been with Tony in Rome. "When is the baby coming?" I asked casually. "In April," he replied, smiling. "What does Tony want, a boy or a girl?" I continued with deceptive nonchalance. "A girl—they've even got a name for her—Alexandra." My plane was called. I smiled sweetly and left. I wrote my story 37,000 feet high in the sky above America. This time there would be no retraction, and with the baby coming in less than four months, the cat would soon be out of the bag anyway. I enjoyed writing that story telling it from the start in Paris. All I left out was the part about the orgasm.

Tony was right; I knew a great deal about his sex life. I have often been there when it is happening. I was at Lake Arrowhead when my children were quite small, and I met Tony coming into the lobby of the hotel with a tennis racket in one hand and a well-known blonde film actress in the other. It was obvious they were staying at the hotel together and I did not embarrass them further by lingering, but every time Tony saw me in Hollywood after that he would roar loudly, making the sound he uses for laughter—it's an OOO-AH-AH-HA. He wanted a child by this actress. He asked his press agent, "What will happen to my career if I have a baby with her?" This was in 1956 when people did not go around so much having children out of wedlock, and he was told, "Forget it."

Tony never knew much about his Irish father, Frank Quinn. Some of Tony's studio biographies say he died when Tony was nine. Others put it at thirteen. He was an only child and imbued with the idea of re-creating himself, peopling the world with his children and giving them his features if not always his name. His mother was Mexican, and Tony is pure Mexican although bigger and taller than any one I have seen of his race.

When he was starring in a play on Broadway, he was having a love-hate affair with a leading lady. His behavior with her was the talk of New York. He took out his grievances on the hapless lady, who had never experienced such virility. She did not know that Tony was servicing three other women as well as his wife at the same time. It would have made no difference if she had. She was in love with him. Tony is always amazed when they are not. There is a difference in Tony's and Warren Beatty's approach to sex. They are two bulls, one older, one younger. Junior will say, "Oh, look at that field of lovely cows. Let's go down there and have them all." The old bull yawns and says, "Let's wait until they come up."

I saw Tony in Rome last year when he was playing the Pope in *The Shoes of the Fisherman*. He had forgotten my retraction of his retraction and was full of the violence in America. "I'm coming back to live there to help the situation," he boomed. He had a year of films to make in Europe first, but he was bursting with the patriotism of being an American who wanted to do his share to help his country in distress. He always believes what he says—at the moment. I think he really believed that Jolanda was not pregnant that time because that is what he wanted to believe. His ego is something you must see to believe. I think he would come back and work on the civil-rights crusade if he could be an alive Dr. Martin Luther King and win the Nobel prize. If Quinn were not so obviously sane, you might think he was a schizophrenic, one day obsessed with material possessions, the next day saying, "If a man is not free to walk away from what he has, that man is corrupt." He'll tell you that the real pleasure is to walk barefoot in the surf and see the sunrise come up, and then he turns around and buys an expensive villa in Rome and spends half a million dollars furnishing it with a library of five thousand books, paintings by Rouault, Renoir, Degas and Gauguin, whom he portrayed on the screen in *Lust for Life*. He still bemoans the fact that he sold his interest in *La Strada* for $15,000 and sometimes refers to its director, Federico Fellini, as a son of a bitch. Heaven knows why, because it was Tony's idea to sell. If he had hung on, he would have made a million dollars.

Tony, as you can see from some of his screen roles, especially in *Zorba the Greek,* is highly emotional, with a great capacity to learn. He's a people-user. He is friendly when he needs them, but when he feels he can do it all himself, he pays them scant attention. In the old days he treated some of his associates as his father and his mother. Now he treats them as his rightful slaves and mostly uses them to get him out of the deals he makes on the spur of the wildly enthusiastic moment. An Italian woman who spoke English worked for weeks on a script for him. He tired of the project as he often does, and when last heard from she was trying to collect her money, which I am sure he will eventually pay, if he has not already. He was going to build a big house in Ojai in the mountains near Santa Barbara and tired of it before it was finished. He was going to found an art colony on the Greek island of Rhodes—the king himself had given him the land. He used the excuse of the troubles in Greece to keep from starting the project. With his acting he is always professional, if sometimes overwrought. He was rehearsing the play *Let Me Hear the Melody* and the atmosphere was tense. Tony imagined that Morris Carnovsky was upstaging him and he wanted to hit someone—at fourteen, he was boxing in the cheaper rings of outer Los Angeles—and suddenly he picked up a chair and flung it far out front, crashing into the seats. Rehearsals were over for that day. He apologized after cooling off.

Tony can be enormously warm and kind and generous, but he is terribly insecure, which is why he bellows so much. He's like a shrewd child, easily hurt, easily offended, a mass of contradictions. He's a character. You always know when he is around, with his abundant vitality. In the three and a half decades of his career, he has played everything—priests, saints, sinners, painters, punch-drunk fighters—he was brilliant in *Requiem for a Heavyweight,* his favorite film. When I told him in Rome recently how much I had liked him, he went into the tough, adenoidal speech he used in the film, then roared with laughter. He has played Indians, rebels, the Brando role in *Streetcar Named Desire,* an Eskimo, a Greek gorilla, Becket, a sheik in *Lawrence of Arabia.* But the part he plays best is Anthony Quinn. A lover of paintings, of music, and of women. A student of many languages. A man of many dimensions. Solid-looking in this flimsy-whimsy world of the cinema—even though he is not so solid as he seems. But which actor is?

You might think that Gregory Peck is as free from anxiety as he looks—stern, secure, capable. Shall I shatter another myth or leave you with your illusions? Mr. Peck came to Hollywood from Broadway via his native town of La Jolla in very southern California, where you can see Mexico on a clear day (they have fog but no smog). I swooned for him immediately after meeting him on the set of his first film, *Days of Glory.* In his second, *Keys of the Kingdom,* he played a priest, but it made no difference to the flutter in my not too girlish breast. This was the lover all women desire—calm, efficient, and strong, yet kind and gentle. But he can also be very peevish. He is not entirely what he seems to be on the screen. He is sometimes mistrustful, wondering whether other actors and most producers and directors, also script writers, are trying to drag him down from the Hollywood mountain he scaled in one jump with his first film.

My awareness of this quirk in Peck's thinking came when he was cast as the late F. Scott Fitzgerald in the film version of *Beloved Infidel.* He was right not to want to do it, as he was completely wrong for the role. When I had suggested Richard Basehart, whom I had admired as the poetic fool in *La Strada,* producer Jerry Wald had sloughed it off, saying, "Oh, no, we'll have someone much more important." Mr. Peck owed the studio a film on an old contract—those old contracts for what seems a fortune at the time of signing—and he was dragged into the film while protesting he did not want the part because it was a woman's story. He was right, as Deborah Kerr knew when she called her agents and implored them, "Get me *Beloved Infidel.*" They did, to her regret. "I thought I was going to play the cockney girl leaving the orphanage and then being presented at Court and all that," Deborah told me recently in London during lunch at the Aretusa Club on the Kings Road. But even if Greg had not insisted on his friend, Sy Bartlett, rewriting the script—in the original he did not appear for thirty pages—Deborah would still have been wrong for the role. She is not as straight-laced as she appears, but too controlled, too proper and ladylike to be credible as Sheilah Graham—Queen Victoria playing Lily Sheil.

Peck was a pain, to put it mildly. Deborah, being so nice and all, could only fight him through a layer of charm and by bringing in her own writer, Ivan Moffatt, and by appealing to Mr. Wald. He was so dazed by his determination to bring America's top writers—Hemingway, Faulkner, and Fitzgerald—to the screen that he changed the whole concept of the book and made it a man's story. Knowing what can happen when a book becomes a film, I decided not to stick around and have a nervous breakdown. I went to Europe and covered film production there. I returned a scene too soon. They were still working and I thought, I may as well see what they're doing. Why should I boycott my own story?

Greg was in his dressing-room trailer outside the sound stage. "Hi, Sheilo," he said, using Scott's greeting. I felt somewhat embarrassed, although ever since I had met Mr. Peck, I had thought I would faint if he ever said "I love you"—which he had to do in the film. "What are you doing?" I asked him. It was the scene in the Los Angeles airport when the girl (I always refer to myself in the third person when discussing *Beloved Infidel*) discovers that Fitzgerald has fallen off the wagon, that the clear liquid in his glass is not water but gin. "Perhaps," I said diffidently, "you'd like to know exactly how it was." I gave the true account—that I had realized the flush on Scott's face was not caused by the excitement of accompanying me to Chicago where I would battle with my radio sponsor who wished to replace me, but that for the first time in the three months I had known him, he was drunk. "When I tried to take the drink away, Scott, whom I'd known as a kind, gentle man, grabbed my arm and flung it viciously away." "Oh, no," said Greg, "I don't see it like that. I will say something pleasant and smile." The true scene would have created a much-needed change of pace—it might have made the audience sit up and take notice instead of yawning all the way through.

What I did not know then was that Greg is a slow thinker and mover. He finds it hard to change action in midstream. If you expect an immediate answer from him, you won't get it. He plays for time. If you say, "The sun is shining," he is likely to ask, "Why did you say the sun is shining?" He has to know ahead what he must do, and he finds it almost impossible to change what he has planned. He was making a film in Europe. In the story—I must let you guess the title—the players were close friends, but a situation had come up. Tony Quinn's wife and child had been killed by one of the enemy. The traitor in their midst, a good-looking girl, had been discovered. It was decided she would have to be killed, which would mean a change in the script. This was two weeks before the scene was to be shot. But it threw Greg. His voice went up four octaves as he shouted at the producer, "I've been waiting for something like this. I thought you were too good to be true. You've been trying to throw the script to Tony Quinn since we began. Unless we go back to the original, I won't report tomorrow." The producer was at a loss. "It wasn't true," he assured me, "and it was a minor change, but Greg got to the director and enlisted him on his side. That evening I had a call from the director. 'I think the scene was good the way it was.' 'You've been talking to Greg,' I said, getting angry. 'Oh, no, but what if he doesn't report tomorrow?' 'We'll keep shooting around him,' I said grimly. 'How long for?' 'Until I can start a lawsuit against him for three million dollars.' Greg was on the set the next morning, but we did not talk to each other until the film was over." You would have thought that would be the end of their working relationship. Not at all. Greg has already made one movie for the same producer and is discussing another.

But Mr. Peck has integrity even while he is sometimes scared after one of his films fail. If he gives his word, he'll keep it, although he might say, "I think this is wrong, but I gave my word." In some respects he is like Gary Cooper, but more limited. He is very conscious of being a star and zealously guards his position and the prerequisites that go with the title. In between set-ups most actors will sit or walk around, but not Mr. Peck. During *McKenna's Gold* Greg was asked, "How come you never sit with the others?" "I can't," he replied, "I'm the star." There were some other big names in the film—Omar Sharif, Edward G. Robinson, and Raymond Massey. But while Peck is pompous, he is also honest, and when Robinson went flawlessly through three pages of dialogue without a single fluff, Greg applauded with the rest and told him, "You're the greatest of them all. I hope I'm as good as you."

He has no sense of humor and takes everything very seriously. As a tax advantage Greg coproduced *The Big Country* with Willie Wyler directing. As in most of these deals, Greg's coproducership was more of an honorary title, although he was consulted on preproduction matters. Peck and Wyler were good friends until they made the film. As everyone in Hollywood knows from Sam Goldwyn to Barbra Streisand and George C. Scott, whom Wyler fired the first day when he reported at 4 P.M. instead of 9 A.M. to the set of *How to Steal a Million,* he will not take interference from anyone. There was a closeup and Greg wanted it one way and Wyler wanted it his way. After some arguing the star drew himself up to his over six feet and said, "I'm the producer." "Shit," replied Wyler. They didn't speak to each other for years.

Greg is not a method actor. His acting ability was always a bit in doubt until he won the Oscar for the phlegmatic lawyer in *To Kill a Mockingbird.* But he is very methodical. He writes notes on his scripts and asks himself questions. He does his best to understand the character, but it usually comes out Peck, Peck, and Peck. Even when he struck Miss Kerr in *Beloved Infidel* and made like an angry man, it was Peck pretending. He would like to be a good actor and some years ago risked his reputation by appearing in the La Jolla Playhouse, which he financed with David Selznick, Joseph Cotten, and other top stars. For his pains he was murdered by the critics. I don't remember his taking another chance.

He is very active in politics and in the motion-picture industry. He has been president of the Academy of Motion Picture Arts and Sciences since 1967 and has raised a great deal of money for the Motion Picture Relief Fund. He has been Chairman of the Building and Endowment campaign for three years and collected close to $10 million. In past years about 50 per cent of the Oscar nominees were conspicuous by their absence, but Greg took the trouble to make sure the spoiled darlings would show up. Paul Newman was busy in New York and he was not coming. Greg telephoned him and he came. Estelle Parsons was in a David Merrick play and Merrick was not giving her the time off to be in Hollywood. After Greg pleaded with him, David, a bargainer from 'way back, told him, "You can have her on one condition—that you appear as a presenter on the Tony Award show in New York." Estelle won the Oscar for her supporting role in *Bonnie and Clyde* and Greg kept his part of the bargain.

There very nearly was no award show at all, if you remember. Dr. Martin Luther King had been assassinated on the Thursday before Monday, April 8, the night of the awards. All the colored presenters, including Sammy Davis, Jr., and Sidney Poitier, decided they could not attend and most of the others thought they should not. Greg made the decision at an eleven o'clock meeting on Friday night to postpone the awards until after the funeral—the first time this had ever happened in the history of the Academy. He had to convince NBC, the sponsor (Eastman Kodak Company), and all the performers who had come from all parts of the world to stay with it for another two days.

About nine years ago Greg started making speeches for various cultural programs and for Adlai Stevenson and Lyndon Johnson and all the causes for the Democrats. I asked him once if he would ever be a candidate for political office himself. The answer was an emphatic no. Perhaps he realizes he is not emotionally equipped for the hurly-burly name calling of a campaign. He is too dignified in any case for that sort of thing and not fast enough on his feet.

Today he is not as big a star as he was in those early years. Some of his expensive pictures were failures, but to use one of his favorite phrases, "He has a good track record." And he is still paid between $500,000 and $800,000 against 10 per cent of the gross and he is still popular with the exhibitors, although even they are beginning to realize that a name is only as good as the film and will accept unknowns if the advance word on the movie is good.

Regardless of who will or will not want him for their films, Greg has one clause in all his contracts—that he must leave the studio by 6 P.M. so he can spend time with his children before they go to bed. He has three grown sons from his first marriage to the former Greta Konen, whom he met while she was Katharine Cornell's hairdresser, during his tour with Miss Cornell in Shaw's play *The Doctor's Dilemma*. Because he is reserved and secretive about his private life I never questioned him, even when the marriage broke up. It was one of those unexpected bombshells that used to happen in Hollywood all the time.

He has two small children, a girl and a boy, by his second wife, Veronique Passani, who was a reporter for a French magazine when she interviewed him in Paris. He asked her to dine with him that night. (Why didn't something like this happen to me? No one I have ever interviewed, except Quinn, asked me to dine so fast—always excepting Errol Flynn.) Veronique, attractive and chic—she is always on the best-dressed lists—did not fall immediately into Peck's lap. As she told me the story, she made him wait a few days—and perhaps this is the secret of how to capture an eligible, sought-after, man. Mrs. Peck does not henpeck her husband, but she, like Mrs. Paul Newman and Mrs. Kirk Douglas, is numero one in the marriage. The Pecks seem very happy. He has always been a devoted father—I used to see him at all the events in the school our children attended when they were small. I don't believe they will ever think they have cause to lambaste him in print. I will always like him, although I am not sure he will like me after reading this chapter. Perhaps one should not tamper with one's idol. You find out too much when you dig beneath the surface.

Ava Gardner was being interviewed at the quietly elegant Claridge's Hotel in London by a quietly elegant British woman journalist. Ava was in a relaxed mood and in reply to questions revealed that she was not interested in any man at the moment and was leading a quiet and proper life. Ava does not like to be interviewed, especially by women, but it was going smoothly. The journalist had her story and was picking up her handbag and gloves when Ava said, "Don't get me wrong, honey, I think fucking is a great sport. It's all the fucking talk you have to listen to from the man before." There was one of those sudden silences, and it was heard all over Claridge's.

This is the Ava Gardner of today. It is not the simple, soft-spoken shy girl I first met at the M-G-M commissary. I had left Hollywood in the late spring of 1941 after the death of Scott Fitzgerald. I returned in the early winter of 1942. In the interim I had covered World War II in England for my syndicate, married, and given birth to a daughter. I had been gone for less than two years, but the change in Hollywood was tremendous. Many of the stars were in the war, some fighting, some doing their share on the home front selling war bonds. In the spring of 1942 Carole Lombard had crashed to her death in the plane carrying her on a bond-selling tour. Some of the old stars had disappeared and young newcomers were riding the crest of the almost frantic production in the Hollywood studios, to fill the demand for escapist films preferred by Americans packing the movie houses.

Mickey Rooney, an adolescent actor when I started my column in 1936, was now in his twenties and a top star at M-G-M where his Andy Hardy films were making a new fortune for the studio. "See that girl over there?" said the executive who was paying for my lunch. "That's Ava Gardner, the girl who married Mickey Rooney in January. Would you like to meet her?" He brought her over and, surveying the tall, slender brunette, I thought, she obviously married him for his money. Such a tall girl and such a little man. He was very difficult then, as they usually are when they're on top. I had found him quite obnoxious the time I had met him on the *National Velvet* set with Elizabeth Taylor. But he must have had something, because Judy Garland and later Jane Powell were in love with him and Elizabeth had liked him.

I was wrong about Ava. In the twenty-six years that I have known her, she has never done anything that was not honest or spontaneous or that she did not believe in. She is loyal to her three former husbands. When Rooney was broke she loaned him money. She has never said a word against Artie Shaw, although he gave her a bad time when she was so vulnerable, eagerly exposing her mind to his knowledge of books, music, and paintings. She bought Sinatra's ticket to Hollywood from Africa when he was visiting her, for him to test for *From Here to Eternity*. He was in debt at the time and the role started him on the road up again, where he has remained. Frankie has repaid Ava over and over again. She can use his jets, his homes—and his advice is at her disposal any time she needs it. She was in the hospital recently for an operation and it was Frankie's jet that brought her to town. On Frank's piano in Palm Springs there is an enormous photograph of Ava. She is somewhat of a hypochondriac and is in and out of hospitals for various reasons. "I'm not afraid of death," she told me. "I wear it on my bosom like a carnation. But I am afraid of being scarred." Even when the scar on her cheek, caused when she fell trying to do Rejonear—bullfighting from a horse—had disappeared, she still believed it showed and ultimately had plastic surgery again to remove the imaginary blemish.

She no longer plays the bulls or the men. But she has fun. She can afford to live any way she pleases. A friend of mine was with her on the Gardner Day of Independence. She was living in Madrid then, which was as far as she could go from Hollywood and still be in an interesting world (she had a penthouse in the same building as Juan Perón, former dictator of Argentina). When she hung up after the call from Hollywood from her business manager, she whooped for joy. She had saved her first million dollars. "Now I don't have to make any more fucking films," she crowed. She did of course.

But for a long while she did not work, enjoying herself in her fashion—drinking vodka (a sip from ten glasses), dancing flamenco until dawn with the gypsies and the bullfighters she invited to her home, weeping ("the music makes me cry"), sleeping all day, with breakfast at six in the evening, then repeating the routine. She was hoping she would marry again and have children and was disappointed when bull-fighter Luis Dominguin married someone else. Then along came the good-looking Italian actor Walter Chiari. But he was a dead duck after giving out a statement that they were engaged when they had not quite reached that point, and he was too indiscreet about their relationship.

He did not know that Ava carried a prudent hangover from her years of poverty in North Carolina where her father, Jonas Gardner, was barely able to support his wife and their five children with what he earned on a tenant farm picking cotton and vegetables. As a child she ran around barefoot because they were too poor for shoes except for special occasions. Ava still prefers to walk barefoot. But that is the only bare part of her. She does not approve of nudity on the screen or in real life except in the privacy of her bedroom. She still has a good figure, although years ago it was glorious. An M-G-M executive once walked into her dressing room without knocking and she was naked from the waist up. He had never in his life, he said, seen anything so beautiful. She had told him off in the choice language she was beginning to acquire.

Ava has never worn a mini-skirt and has never flaunted a romance for publicity or for personal ego. One of her close male friends was a guest in her house while she filmed *The Barefoot Contessa* in Rome in 1954, where the papparazzi were buzzing around her without cessation or sleep. She was living near the Spanish Steps, and she allotted her friend a room on the ground floor of the four-story building. In the morning as she entered the elevator near the stairs on the top floor where her bedroom was located, Mr. Chiari suddenly appeared. She slapped him across the mouth and said angrily, "There have been enough innuendoes, you don't have to prove they were right!" It would have made no difference to the man in the room downstairs to know that Chiari had spent the night there, but it made a difference to Ava that he knew. In North Carolina when a girl was in love it was discreet. You did not parade it.

Ava has always avoided the spotlight when she can, although when she was recognized recently by a middle-aged lady at the Royal Opera House, Covent Garden, in London, she was rather pleased. She dresses well for occasions like the opera, but not in flamboyant fashion. Her friends are not famous people. The person closest to her, except her sister Bea, is her hairdresser, Sidney Guillaroff. Stars often let their hair down with the men who put it up, and Mr. Guillaroff's view of his still world-famous client differs sharply from the New York writer who destroyed her in his piece. "She is genuinely unaffected by glamour and prestige," he assured me in the bar at the Sherry Netherland Hotel where he was quartered during the New York location for Shirley MacLaine and her *Sweet Charity* film. Sidney had recently returned from Europe where Ava is still regarded as one of the great stars of the screen. He dressed her elaborate coiffure for her role of Empress to James Mason's Emperor Franz Josef and the mother of Crown Prince Omar Sharif in *Mayerling*. Reporters came from all over Europe to interview her. She would not see many, but every one said how beautiful she was. "This girl has built-in sexual glamour without having to undress."

"I made it as a star dressed," Ava once told me, "if I

haven't got it dressed, I don't want it." She is secure in most areas of herself and always has been. She is completely her own woman with full knowledge of what she is, but not always of what she wants. She is as restless as Warren Beatty. She can be talking to you in Madrid telling you she will be staying for months, and five minutes later she is on her way to London or California. She travels more than Jackie Onassis or Mrs. Eleanor Roosevelt in the old days when Ava was emerging as a star. Perhaps she was always restless, but now she has the money to go where her whims take her. She has no obligations to anyone and she can leave at a moment's notice.

Her home base is the apartment in London overlooking Hyde Park, which belonged to her good friend, the late writer Robert Ruark. She seems happy in London where no one bothers her, but every once in a while she flies to Spain for some sun. Never to Italy—she has sworn she will never return because of the papparazzi. She catches cold in "the goddam climate" of England. A doctor in London told me, after I said I was a Hollywood columnist, of this middle-aged lady who came to see him and gave the name Miss Ava Gardner. And when he looked blank, she grabbed his hands and said with a joyful incredulity, "You mean you don't know who I am?" whereupon she told him and he still looked blank. Someone had sent him a bottle of vintage liquor and it was on his desk. They celebrated her anonymity by drinking all of it between them. He was a good doctor, a Harley Street specialist. All the same, I am glad my appointment was not on the same afternoon.

Ava is kind to her own sex—as long as they are not interviewing her. I have never heard her say anything that could make another woman feel too uncomfortable although she herself might be. But if any member of a group casually asks a question that she considers unwarranted, she will snap, "Mind your goddam business," and rush off to the Caribbean or Timbuktu. Ever since a trusted friend wrote a series of articles about her for a London newspaper, she has suspected anyone who asks a question.

Ava has no vanity at all. During *55 Days at Peking*, filmed in Madrid, I saw her stop on the set to look at herself in a long mirror. She was wearing a turn-of-the-century costume. "Oh," she said in surprise, "I look as pretty as my mother. I wish she were alive to see me." At forty-seven it is unlikely that she will have children—unless she were to adopt a child, and at this late hour that too is unlikely. But she is not unhappy about it any more. For a long time she carried an Olympic-size torch for Sinatra, but that has also gone. She still has her moods when she wants to paint the town red and she will down a lot of liquor although she does not like the taste. But the occasions are fewer. She has sworn a mighty oath that from now on she will live her life as she wants it, see only the people she loves and trusts; the circle is small and includes her secretary and her servants, all of whom are on a first-name basis. And make love when she wants to, which she has always done. She has always chosen the man, always been the aggressor. She will only work now when she feels like it, play, listen to music, especially jazz and Sinatra records. She reads a great deal. She is interested in what is going on in the world today. All things considered, it is not a bad life, and it might have been worse if she had not discovered what she really wanted after first going through the Hollywood human-grinder.

18)

Ronald Reagan-Progress Is His Least Important Product

It was early spring of 1965. I was chatting with Ronald Reagan, his wife Nancy, and the Robert Taylors at the Golden Globe Awards at the Cocoanut Grove. It was still several months before the Republican Party would select their man to run against Governor Brown, who had grown fat in office and had alienated the young Democrat voters by coming out strongly for President Johnson's position on Vietnam.

Ever since his brilliant speech for Senator Barry Goldwater the night before the Presidential election in November 1964, there had been talk from the Republicans about Reagan for Governor. "Do you plan to run?" I asked him while his wife turned a keen ear in our direction. "Of course not, no one has asked me." He laughed boyishly. "But if they did?" I persisted. "I'm an actor," he replied, "and I intend to keep on acting." He seemed amused. "Why don't you ask *me?*" interrupted Robert Taylor, and then, mercifully, we all went in to dinner.

A month later, sitting with Ronnie in the dimly lit bar of the Oak Room in the Beverly Wilshire Hotel, I asked him the same question and received a different answer. "If the people want me, I will run." He was confident, sure. *"Do* they want you?" I pressed him. I was getting a good story. "Quite a lot seem to." He smiled his good-guy smile. "I have been surprised at all the letters and requests from people and groups who want me to run." He mentioned some of them. He talked passionately of what was happening in the country, that we now had a one-party system, a dictatorship, and it was the duty of the patriots to save the nation. "The federal government is moving into every area," he said. "Does this mean you will run for Governor?" I asked again. "If I am convinced the people want me, yes." I could see he was convinced. I headlined my story, "Ronald Reagan Will Run for Governor of California." It was the first definite announcement of Ronnie's plans. With anyone else, I would have been taking a chance, but I knew from the set of his mouth that he had decided to rescue the people of California.

In the twenty-eight years I had known him I had not wasted much time with Ronnie. He did not make many films, and he was too verbose, a nice guy but dull. "Ask him the time," Jane Wyman confided during her marriage with Ronnie, "and he will tell you how the watch is made." Ann Sheridan was often a guest in their home in the Hollywood Hills. "I'd go there," the late actress (who starred with Reagan in *Kings Row*), told me, "because Jane was such a good cook. On one occasion Ronnie, a baseball nut, had heard a game on radio and he gave us a play-by-play account. After the fourth inning, Jane said, 'Ronnie, please stop, Annie doesn't care about baseball.' But he went on for all nine innings." Jane once remarked that her husband was such a talker, he was making speeches in his sleep.

He was always a good speaker, and after the war, which he spent making films for the war effort at the Hal Roach Studios—they called it Fort Roach—a few miles from his home, he became very active in the Screen Actors Guild, where his mellifluous voice was always available for battles and causes. Jane was a busy campaigner for the Guild in her early years in Hollywood, and Ronnie caught her enthusiasm after their marriage following a cross-country tour in 1938 with Louella Parsons, who was paid to present the young hopefuls of Hollywood at various theaters. Neither Ronnie nor Jane thought of refusing, or *hopeful* would have become *hopeless*. "Button-nose," Ronnie called Jane. (He calls his second wife "Mommy" and she calls him "Daddy," although he was nicknamed "Dutch" by his father.) They were a pleasant happy couple. By the end of the war, Jane was an important star, while Ronnie resumed his roles in mediocre films, except for *Kings Row* and *Knute Rockne,* in which he earned some critical praise. But Jane was the star of the family and he was her good-looking, talkative husband. "They'd call him at all hours to make speeches," Jane complained. She was getting bored listening to the playback at home. She became peevish. "Go away," she said to her husband. "Go get the world straightened out. Don't bother me." This was near the end of the marriage.

As early as late 1946, Ronnie was regarded as a man with a national future. Articles were written stating that with the help of his wife, there was no knowing how far he would go. The words were prophetic. He would go far with the help of his wife, but it was a different wife, the former Chicago debutante Nancy Davis, and for a different political party. Ronnie refers to his years as a Democrat, as his "bleeding heart" period, meaning, I suppose, that he bled for the poor and unfortunate. I must confess I liked him better when his heart bled for the poor, when he was as devout a liberal as he is now a reactionary Republican. It is incredible today to believe that in 1950, Reagan was a stanch supporter of Democrat Helen Gahagan Douglas when she was fighting to retain her seat in Congress which she lost to Richard Nixon because he more than hinted she was a Communist fellow traveler—this when the mere suspicion of being a Commie was enough to destroy the career of actor and politician alike. Only two years later, after Ronnie married Nancy with William Holden as best man and Mrs. Holden as matron of honor, he switched political allegiance.

While still officially a Democrat, he supported the Presidential candidacy of General Eisenhower. Naturally this delighted his fiercely Republican bride, whose family friends included Barry Goldwater. Ronnie insists it was his own decision, but his record indicates he is susceptible to the brainwashing of people he admires. Nancy's father, Dr. Loyal Davis, a well-known neurosurgeon in Chicago, has a winter home in Arizona next door to Goldwater, who dangled Nancy on his knee when she was a baby. Her strong chin is a clue to her character. She is the boss, but she is loyal, devoted in all respects to her man. She was bitter about Ronnie not getting good picture offers during their marriage. "Marlon Brando gets everything," she complained, implying that Ronnie's rightist politics was the reason.

After Ronnie was nominated for Governor, I had tea with Nancy in their beautiful, completely electrified—courtesy of General Electric—home in Pacific Palisades. I warned her that I was a Democrat and didn't think I would vote for Ronnie; I had reestablished my California residence solely to vote against him. I had met Governor Brown with John Kennedy, who was then a senator, at a campaign fund-raising dinner in Los Angeles. There was certainly no foreboding then that Reagan, whom I had known merely as a "B" actor in mediocre films, could ever boot Edmund G. "Pat" Brown out of the gubernatorial mansion in Sacramento. And he might not have, if Brown had played up his respected father image, a man with a good record in government and all he accomplished for California. Instead, he sloughed Reagan off as a bad actor and went on a diet trying to match his opponent's trim figure. He could not grow his hair back or make it as black as Ronnie's, which had been a deep chestnut color when I first knew the ex-radio sports announcer from Iowa in 1937, after he signed a contract at Warner Brothers at $200 a week, all the money in the world for him at that time. When Ronnie's barber at Paramount—even after he was elected he took his hair problems to the studio—landed a job in Sacramento, I thought how very convenient for the

Governor. The vibrant, unlined make-up for his numerous television appearances is applied in the privacy of his home. In the last decade he has worn contact lenses for private and public appearances which give his eyes an extra sparkle. He and Nancy were lunching upstairs at Sardi's Restaurant in New York a few years ago, and I was rather startled when, after the main course, Ronnie took out his contacts, put them in his mouth, sucked them for a few seconds, and put them back in his eyes before the dessert.

I had always found Nancy a pleasant girl during her brief career in minor pictures at M-G-M, but during our tea party with her public-relations expert in attendance, she was tense and cautious. A friend of mine not long before had bumped into Nancy at the Saks Fifth Avenue store on Wilshire Boulevard, and called to tell me, "He's running, she was nice to me." Nancy's laugh was strained when I wondered, "If Ronnie wins the governorship, will he try for the presidency?" "All we are thinking of now," she said with controlled irritation, "is running for governor." Ha! "Is it true," I asked her, "that you caused Ronnie to switch from a Democrat to a Republican?" For a moment she lost her cool and glared at me. She swallowed, managed an almost-smile. "Ronnie is too clever to take advice from me," she cooed, "and I'm not clever enough to give it." The fact remains, he *does* consult on everything with Nancy, the power behind the pants, a lady who learned her politics from her father and his conservative friends. Her family was so sure that Reagan would be governor that months before the election and the inauguration which took place one minute after midnight on January 1, 1967, they booked hotel reservations in Sacramento for the uncles, aunts, and cousins.

Ronnie sounds emphatic in his opinions, which is why he was a good salesman for the General Electric Company. Their slogan, "Progress Is Our Most Important Product," was delivered with happy conviction by Reagan every Sunday night for eight years. There was a joke about someone listening to Ronnie's spiel for the G.E. nuclear submarine and remarking, "I didn't really need a submarine, but I've got one now." He believes what he says and he says what he believes he should say. But he can compromise. He can change from the strongest of his stands. I remember a meeting of the Screen Actors Guild, of which Reagan was president for eight years, when he exhorted the members, "I don't want to see any of you going over to the enemy"—meaning television. The last time I talked with Ann Sheridan, we discussed this meeting, and she said, "When I came back to Hollywood after living in New York, I turned on my seven-inch set and there was the son of a bitch on television," the medium that transformed Ronnie from an actor into a politician. His speeches to the thousands of G.E. employees around the country gave him the style and ease which proved so effective in his political career. He would tour for a few days, then return to Hollywood and do the show. He described one of the trips with "When I was speaking before the great unwashed Americans . . ." a significant indication of Reagan the politician's attitude toward the unaffluent people.

I appeared with Ronnie in one of the General Electric Theater segments. I played his aunt. I don't know whose idea it was to give me the role, but it could have been the Governor's, who understands the power of the press. He needed us more when he was an actor. Before he signed to be the host of the series in 1954, his film career was slipping to the point of having to work in Las Vegas. When I visited the set, I was warned never to bring up politics. The slightest question was enough to set him off. After John Kennedy was elected President in 1960, despite Reagan's campaigning for Goldwater, the actor was like a man possessed, ranting about the mistakes being made in Washington. He had a fixation that the Democrats were ruining the country. I listened between takes while Ronnie stated, "Federal aid to education means Big Brother in education. It's a form of creeping socialism."

There was a telephone call for him. Ronnie excused himself. He was smiling when he returned. "A very silly thing

just happened," he said. "A group of Republicans asked me
if I'd be interested in running for governor." I too thought
it was silly and did not bother to write about it. It had to be
a joke. I remember someone kidding, "Of course you'll run."
"Of course not," Ronnie grinned, "but it's a wild notion, isn't
it?" And he was off and running about how the newly elected
Democrats were "leading us to ruin with too much power
concentrated in Washington." He quoted statistics that none
of us were able to challenge, and my feeling was that he
invented them as he went along. I had the same thought
when I was on the *Mike Douglas Show* and Governor Wal-
lace of Alabama was another guest. To hear him rattle off
figures and facts you'd have thought he was the best friend
the Negroes ever had. Ronnie became such a bore with his
dire prophecies on the sets of G.E. Theater and *Death Valley
Days* (for which he signed in 1964 at the same salary of
$125,000 a year) that he was finally ordered to stop discussing
politics. It was like asking the waves to stop breaking.

Ronnie's chief phobia was about big government spending. He was always referring to the way things were managed
on a small budget in Eureka, Illinois—population under
3,000—where he attended college and made speeches for the
students who were striking against the old-fashioned over-
strict rules. It was mostly because of Reagan's campaigning
that the president of Eureka College resigned and the rules
were liberalized. But there was nothing liberal on his program when he became governor—the proposed cuts in the
state budget, in education, his talk of sending more troops to
Vietnam, his fight to retain capital punishment, his support
of everything reactionary, everything and more espoused by
Goldwater. The students of California are not among his
admirers. Neither are the professors. There is talk that
Chancellor Franklyn D. Murphy, who resigned as President
of U.C.L.A. after Reagan suggested that students in the state
pay a tuition fee, and who is now Chairman of the Board
and Chief Executive of *The Los Angeles Times,* will oppose
Ronnie for governor in 1970. With the support of *The Los*

Angeles Times and the disillusioned Democrats who elected Ronnie to the office with the overwhelming majority of a million votes, Murphy could succeed. In any case I doubt whether I will have to reregister in California the next time.

On the well-put-together surface, Reagan looks like a Senior Boy Scout at peace with the world, but when he purses up his lips, watch out. It means his temper is seething underneath the forced smile. Even if he is not elected for another four years, or if the signature writers ever succeed in having him recalled—it takes only 750,000 signatures—he is now totally dedicated to politics, and he will stay with it in one form or another regardless of mistakes or unpopularity because of his aptitude for changing his spots. One time on the road for G.E. he attacked the government for the money it was spending on the Tennessee Valley Authority and forgot or was unaware that the biggest contractor on the project was General Electric. When this was explained to him by his boss, he did not mention it again, which was being sensible. The boss, fortunately, was a good friend of his and there was never ever serious trouble. But when *Bonanza* took the ratings away from Ronnie, the show was dropped. Friendship is one thing, but how can "Progress Is Our Most Important Product" be effective when the people have switched allegiance to another show? Ronnie was not complaining. The years with General Electric had made him rich. He was upset only when a local columnist questioned his duties after the company made him an executive. When the reporter asked, "Do you plan any changes in your new position?" Reagan was genially vague and explained that it had something to do with his tax situation. When the story appeared with the added comment, "We don't have to worry, Ronald Reagan is going to save the country," the future governor was on the telephone, complaining, "You double-crossed me. Our conversation was off the record." "That was never mentioned," the writer protested. "But you put your pencil and paper aside," Ronnie wailed. Reporters sometimes do this to let the person talk freely without getting the request we detest, "This is off the record." Ronnie was foolish to have talked to a reporter this way.

He is more careful now. He is primed by the people back of him for at least an hour before every public appearance and he won't see any of the press in private. But he slipped an interesting remark after the Hollywood premiere of *Dr. Dolittle*. At the supper party afterward he stopped to talk to a former television associate. When the governor reminisced of "the old days," he was asked, "How would you compare working in television with working in Sacramento?" "It's really the same," replied Ronnie, "the only difference, in Sacramento"—wryly—"they change scripts on me every day."

He is not exactly bright, but he has a great memory. He can remember what his backers tell him. He is also competent. I was assured by Charlton Heston, a strong Democrat, "He did a good job when he was President of the Guild [as Charlton is now]. Ronnie led us through the 1960 strike and he did it with great energy and resourcefulness. Those who think he is a fool, are making a mistake." Another member of the Screen Actors Guild was less complimentary. "His one effort during his tenure as president was to get the actors a very small residual from their films shown on television." Someone I know who was paid $2,000 for three days' work in *College Confidential*, which starred Steve Allen, receives something like $1.85 when the film appears on TV. It costs almost more for the postage to the bank.

Reagan has been called a bigot. If he is, it is something new. He never was in all the years I knew him as an actor. There was the incident in the late '30s at the Lakeside Country Club in North Hollywood. It was founded by actors, cameramen, and directors. It had a reputation for anti-Semitism. The Gentiles in the business joined Lakeside. The Jewish golfers were members of Hillside in West Los Angeles, opposite the 20th Century-Fox Studio. Jack Warner, whose studio was within hailing distance of Lakeside, applied for membership. He was blackballed. When Ronnie, a member, who was under contract, heard of it, he asked, "Is this true?" It was. "You're anti-Semitic," he stormed to a club member. "You're damn right we're anti-Semitic," was the reply. He resigned. Actually Lakeside did and does have Jewish members—not many, but some. And the chief reason Warner was blackballed was because some of the members worked for him, "And we don't want him looking over our shoulder and saying the next day, 'Why weren't you at work?'" Jack was delighted to learn of Ronnie's action, and who knows, it might have kept him under contract a bit longer. Also at that period, he was a Democrat and a dedicated fighter for the minorities—not that you could ever describe Jack Warner as a minority.

I have been assured by Democrats that Ronnie's easygoing manner and amiability is calculated and contrived, that underneath the outer crust of charm, he is emotional, erratic, and insecure like all actors, that it is all a façade. During some tight moments as governor he has lost his temper, usually when he is asked questions after debarking from a plane. Ronnie was always frightened of flying. Half of the General Electric business is in plane parts, but when he traveled for them he went by train. The governorship was too juicy a plum to lose by yielding to his fears and presenting the image of a timid man. During the campaign and since he has traveled everywhere by plane. He was more afraid of losing the governorship than of losing his life. You can't be more dedicated than that.

19)

Caine and Connery

British actors have always been popular in Hollywood. From the earliest days they migrated to what used to be the center of film making for the world—Chaplin, George Arliss, Leslie Howard, Ronald Colman, C. Aubrey Smith and his cricket team, Merle Oberon, Laurence Olivier, Vivien Leigh, Deborah Kerr, David Niven, Greer Garson, Audrey Hepburn, Rex Harrison, Charles Laughton, James Mason. The British were always coming.

But in the past decade something new happened. Hollywood went to the British. The Oscars were stamped "Made in England." Swinging London filled the screens of America, which surrendered without a fight: Vanessa Redgrave in *Morgan!*, Albert Finney in *Tom Jones,* Richard Harris in *This Sporting Life,* Peter Sellers in *Lolita,* Sir Alex Guinness in *Kind Hearts and Coronets,* Terence Stamp in *Billy Budd,* Peter O'Toole in *Lawrence of Arabia,* Julie Christie in *Darling* and *Dr. Zhivago,* David Hemmings in *Blow-Up,* and the Beatles in *A Hard Day's Night.* The most unexpectedly popular and profitable British players for the American companies were the rugged Sean Connery as James Bond, super-sleuth 007, and Michael Caine, a tall, pinkish man with horn-rimmed spectacles, as the nondescript secret agent, Harry Palmer.

It was interesting finding them both at the same party in Montagu Square in London: Mr. Caine unobtrusive in a corner, his pale eyes behind the spectacles bulging at the celebrities; Mr. Connery talking to his new boss, Harry Saltzman (Sean was then still on good terms with the man who was to make him a millionaire). Michael had been hanging around for twelve years in British television and small parts in British films, never dreaming he could ever be a star. I had seen him in a featured role in *Zulu.* Sean had become successful instantly as Bond. Harry beckoned Michael to come over to be introduced to Sean. Within a few years he would make as big an impact on the screen in *The Ipcress File* and in *Alfie* as Sean had in *Dr. No* and *From Russia With Love.* It sometimes takes only one or two films to put you on easy street and to effect a character change. Michael has struggled to remain the man he was before he became a star. He has tried to keep the image of a friendly man with his feet on the ground. Sean is indifferent about his image—his few intimate friends know him for what he is and like him. He doesn't give a damn about the rest.

When Sean was starring in his last film as the always triumphant 007, I wrote a piece about him in my column titled "Has Success Spoiled Sean Connery?". I was kind to him and stated, "No, but it has spoiled the people who work for him." I was wrong. Success *did* spoil Mr. Connery. He actually believes that Mr. Saltzman and his partner, Cubby Broccoli, held back his career. He also believes they should have paid him more because he feels he alone is responsible for his success. And yet, before he played Bond, Sean was almost unknown as an actor, certainly in America. Recently on television I saw *Another Time, Another Place,* the film he made in London with Lana Turner in 1957. He was very good-looking then with his own hair, but he was noticed mostly because of his romance with Miss Turner, who at the time was considered the special property of gangster Johnny Stompanato, a romance which was terminated with a kitchen knife by Lana's teen-age daughter, Cheryl. Sean was told by the "boys" to lay off Lana, and he did not need a second warning. He was so unknown that when he signed for *Dr. No* his leading lady, Ursula Andress, demanded, "Who is this Sean Connery?" and she had to be persuaded to play opposite him. The Ian Fleming books were knocking around for years without any takers until the late Gregory Ratoff paid 6,000 pounds for the disastrous *Casino Royale.* Later Broccoli and Saltzman had a difficult time raising the cash to buy the rest.

I had met Sean before the Montagu Square party. The producers asked me to have a drink with him in the bar of the Connaught Hotel in London shortly before *Dr. No* would be released. Sean was eager to make a good impression. He told me he was grateful to Cubby and Harry for giving him the break in the picture and left shortly for rehearsals of a play which proved unsuccessful.

Sean, with his thick Scottish accent and stolid shyness, was not my idea of James Bond, which proves how wrong I can be. He was uncouth and uncomfortable. I had read all the Bond stories written to that time, and I thought a young Cary Grant would have been better. The unsuave Connery was the antithesis of Fleming's Bond, but he brought an important ingredient to the role—sex. "There was never any trouble getting girls," I heard him say once. "But it's big trouble getting rid of them." The virility he possesses in real life came through on the screen. There was always at least one woman in his life. (Naturally I am discussing the time before his marriage to Diane Cilento.) Sean was somewhere in the South of France and he had arranged to be interviewed and photographed at eleven in the morning. The press agent, with the reporter and photographer in tow, knocked at the door of his hotel room and, receiving no answer, opened it. Sean was in bed with a girl. "Oh," he said without a trace of embarrassment, "I'll be ready in ten minutes." Sean worships his wife, with whom he had a child either just immediately before or just immediately after the legal ceremony. Diane told me during a lunch in Rome, "We've been married two years and our child is three." She had been married and had to get a divorce.

If the Connerys ever have a final parting, it will be Diane who wants it. Like so many actors who are tough on the screen, Sean is a mild man at home. I believe he would have been content with the Bond pictures and continued with them forever, but for Diane. She always considered them rather trashy and was sick of hearing about them and of being asked, "What is it like to be the wife of James Bond?" Diane is a better actress than Sean is an actor, and she was better known than her husband before the Bond pictures. She despised the physical derring-do and the gadgets. It was dead-pan nonacting. She told her husband, "Look, when there's Lear and Macbeth, why do this?" Except for the money, he began to wonder why indeed. She was bugging him all the time with "And for Christ's sake stop acting like a star." When she was abruptly relegated to the little woman in the background, she hated it. No one was asking about her career, only about her husband. When a tactless reporter suggested that she should make a film with Sean, she yelled, "Never!" During the height of the Bond furor she would not be interviewed with him, and only then with the proviso her husband's career would not be discussed. This was somewhat understandable but rather silly, I thought, for a woman as intelligent as Diane. She is much brighter than Sean, who is a simple man.

His family in Glasgow was poor, and when Sean left school he worked as a coffin polisher. The physique we admired in the Bond films was developed during his years as a weight lifter. He was on a Scottish weight-lifting team that came to London, where he answered an advertisement for muscle men to play the sailors in the stage production of *South Pacific*. He remained in the chorus for eighteen months, then went on tour with the show; and as people dropped out he took over small roles which grew larger with the tour. He did some television in London, appearing in *Requiem for a*

Heavyweight, and was put under contract by 20th Century-Fox, who dropped him soon after. As a chorus boy in *South Pacific* he was paid $50 a week, which was more than he received as a coffin polisher. He earned about the same as an extra in films.

Herbert Wilcox, the British film producer, was having a shave and haircut at an exclusive men's hairdressing establishment in Mayfair recently and was talking to the man in the chair next to him. As he was leaving, the man said, "Mr. Wilcox, please give my regards to your wife." "I certainly will. What name shall I say?" Herbert asked. He did not recognize the bald, drooping-mustachioed man. "Sean Connery," was the reply. "Oh," said Herbert, "I didn't know you knew Anna." "I was a chorus boy in her film *The Glorious Years"*—which Wilcox directed. Some actors object to having the early years of struggle mentioned when they are famous, but not Sean, who in many respects is the same ordinary man with a passion for football that he was before he left Glasgow to try his luck in London. Whenever the Scottish football team is playing, he flies north for the game. When he became rich he took up golf, also ping-pong.

For Sean everything is black or white. He either likes you or he hates you. And he hates Mr. Saltzman in particular and has sworn he will never work for him again. Harry was never able to penetrate Sean's suspicion and hostility. After suffering temporary paralysis on one side of his face, Harry visited the location of *You Only Live Twice* in Japan. An executive on the film pleaded with Sean, "Be nice to him. Remember he was paralyzed on one side of his face." "Good," said Sean, "I'll be glad when it happens to the other side." He was just blowing off. He is a dour man, not cruel.

His quite atrocious behavior toward the man who made him a millionaire (in pounds) was caused, I have learned, from an early disagreement over money, a commodity of which Sean is very fond. *Dr. No* was budgeted at around $700,000. Sean's salary for the entire film was $12,000 on today's devalued pound (it was closer to $15,000 before the drop). Because of the low payment, Sean's agent succeeded in getting an extra $200 a week for Sean as expense money on locations abroad and in England. When the film ended, he claimed he had been docked the $200 for each of the ten weeks. He stormed into Saltzman's office, "Look, the $200 was on top of the price." "No, I did not promise that." "How can you say that," angrily, "when my agent was there?" Harry paid off, but Sean never forgot or forgave him. That $200 a week cost the company much more. In the subsequent Bond films Sean played it his way. He would go off and golf of an afternoon if he felt like it. He was difficult about publicity and when he did see reporters, he gave horrendous interviews, butchering his producers, mostly Harry. "He's a big pig," he told me emphatically on the set of *Thunderball*. Ultimately they were afraid to let him talk to any member of the press, and this was fine with him.

Lewis Gilbert, who directed Sean's last Bond film, *You Only Live Twice*, invited me to visit the set, any time I liked. I called the British press agent and said I was coming for lunch and I hoped Sean would be available. He would relay the message. The press agent met me in the paneled dining room at Pinewood Studio. He was sorry, but Sean was too tired to see me. It was during the World's Cup football finals and Sean had met the English team that morning, and furthermore, about thirty reporters and cameramen had been invited to visit the incredible set complete with realistic imitation nuclear bomb and a moveable lake above. It was a complete town and had cost $2 million to build, twice as much as the first two Bond pictures put together. "Where is Sean now?" I was furious. "He's in his dressing room and you cannot disturb him." While he spoke, Sean came into the dining room. I left the press agent with his sentence unfinished and went to Sean, who had stopped to talk to some people at a table. He was friendly and asked me to walk with him to the set where we talked long enough for me to get a story.

I was not in Spain when Sean was starring with Brigitte Bardot in their western, *Shalako*, but I read some of the many interviews he gave. This picture was for his own company, and that usually makes a difference. I was amused at all the stories on the set about a romance between Brigitte Bardot and Stephen Boyd. If she had a romance with anybody it would have been Sean. They acted like two hounds in heat when they met, before the film started, to take photographs for publicity. If this was acting, they should both win an Oscar. Sean was panting after her, straddling over her on a bed, at the same time taking pictures of her while she lay back breathing seductively on the pillows while professional photographers recorded the scene.

Sean has no sense of humor—this is one of the big differences between Sean and Caine. As long as Sean is watching a game or playing one, he is completely happy, but otherwise he doesn't have much to say and he loathes the fame (if not the money) which came with the Bond package. He was unhappy when his son Jason came home from school and when he asked him, "How was it today?" the boy replied, "Wonderful, Daddy, none of the boys spat at me." Diane has convinced him that he can do better as an actor, and yet most of the films he has made away from Bond have been box-office failures. Perhaps as a Western star he will do better.

If there is ever new trouble between the Connerys—they separated briefly a few years ago—it could be that except for acting and sex, they have very little in common. Diane was raised in an intellectual atmosphere. Her father, Sir Raphael Cilento, was a famous doctor in Australia and Diane was expensively educated. Sean is a man of the people—he is anti-establishment but close to those he works with; the crew love him. He is a radical who helps the unemployed dockhands in Glasgow and has made some documentaries on their behalf. He is a good man. He lives modestly and saves his money. Michael Caine will sometimes buy a round of drinks or pick up the dinner tab. But Sean is more cautious. You don't often see him in an expensive restaurant unless he is a guest. He won't waste money on fashionable clothes as Caine will do—Michael has a huge wardrobe. I had a bet of a pound ($2.40) with Sean that Lyndon Johnson would win the presidency by a landslide. "What is your definition of a landslide?" he asked me suspiciously. "If *The New York Times* says it is, will that prove it?" I said. He thought a minute, then, "All right." I waited for my pound for several weeks, then sent him *The New York Times'* headline, "Johnson Wins by a Landslide." I got my pound. He was asked recently, "Why did you play a secondary role to Richard Harris in *The Molly McGuires?*" "They paid me a million dollars for it," he replied, "and for that kind of money, they can put a mule ahead of me."

"I never met a star who was used to success," said Michael Caine. We were dining at Alvaro's, then his favorite restaurant on the Kings Road in Chelsea. "You're amazed when it comes, amazed when it continues, and amazed when it ends." His philosophical soliloquy ended sharply as he glanced at the next table. "Camilla!" It was a gasp. A few days before, the London newspapers had detailed the parting of Michael and Camilla Sparv, the exquisite Swedish actress. She had divorced her rich film-executive husband Robert Evans to marry Michael, but the romance had foundered on an old rock—*she* wanted to get married, *he* did not. The day before my dinner with Mike, I had casually mentioned the date to Camilla during tea at the Connaught Hotel. She was not interested. "I have finished with him. What he does is no concern of mine."

And here she was almost within touching distance and having an animated conversation with the three other people at her table. "She looks beautiful," breathed Mike, waving his hand to attract her attention. She had to be blind not to see it. "What a coincidence," he sighed ecstatically. "I thought it was all over," I said. "It is," he said, "but," he giggled, "if I look at her much longer it will be on again." For all the attention he was paying me, I might have been a napkin on the table. "You're still in love with her," I said. "Yes, I am," the myopic eyes through his glasses suctioning the blonde beauty. "Why doesn't she look up and see me?" he asked, with the naïveté of men that always amazes me. "Do you think," turning his face away from Camilla, "do you think she knew I was here and that's why she came? It's our favorite restaurant, you know." "Of course she knew," I told him somewhat testily. There was a time I would not have been the onlooker. "Look," I said, "why don't you send her a note by the waiter?" He could have reached over and given it himself but that might have seemed too eager. "And make a date to see her later." "Oh, she might snub me," he said. After all, it was he who had not wanted to marry her. "She wouldn't be here if she didn't want to see you. Go on, write her a note and ask her to have supper with you." Caine and Sparv together again—it would give me a good story.

I tore a piece of paper from my notebook and loaned him my pen. "Look away while I'm writing," he said, "or she'll think we're laughing at her." I attacked my lasagna. The note was delivered. Loud giggles from the next table. The waiter brought a note back. Mike's pink face reddened with rage. "What is it?" I felt guilty because I had made him send the note. He uncreased the tight ball of paper and read quietly, " 'O.K., but who will we talk about—you or me?' " Actors *do* talk about themselves and this was a nasty slap. He was miserable through the rest of the meal. But this dog never stopped pointing. He watched every bite she took, strained to hear everything she said. Her group was leaving. Mike straightened up. If she passed him without speaking, everyone in the intimate restaurant would know that Michael Caine had been snubbed by a bird.

"Phone me," she flicked as she passed. "You're not going to," I said, now as angry with her as he was. "I will," he replied grimly. "If you want to get her back, you shouldn't," I said. "I have to find out two things," he replied. "Did she know I was coming here, and did she see me before I sent the note?" How can men be so stupid? I saw him a week later and they had resumed. He told me he loved her more than ever. "Will you now marry her?" I asked. "I wouldn't be surprised," he replied. *I* will be when and if he marries anyone. I have seen him in love before—with the pretty French model-actress Elizabeth Ercy and before that with the British actress Edana Ronay. Edana lasted three years, Elizabeth two. Camilla ruled the Caine heart for a year. Then the Nicaraguan beauty called Bianca. Then?

If you had to sum Mike up in one word, it would be "uncommitted." If he will ever commit himself to a woman or to life, he would be a complete person. Oh, he's a good actor, although in the last couple of years he has made some stinkers, but that was not all his fault. Harry Saltzman owns his contract, and before starring him in *The Ipcress File* he had signed a deal for ten pictures and Saltzman approves all the loan-outs he makes for other producers. His price today is $750,000 against a percentage, an impressive raise from the $6,000 he was paid for all of *The Ipcress File*. Harry gives him everything he makes, and Caine, unlike Connery, is grateful to the man who gave him the big break. Perhaps this is why the producer has torn up his contract four times with an ascending salary boost.

Michael seems gregarious, but he is not. He has a phobia against the telephone. "I'll call you," he will say, but he seldom does. He promises to have lunch and he is not there when you arrive. It is as though he is paying everyone back for the years of waiting and mounting anger. He has these moods when he simply cannot face people, and he flies off or shuts himself up until the gloom is gone. Then he is the friendliest man you could hope to meet. He is faithful to his girls for as long as it lasts. His months in Hollywood for *Gambit* were the exception. He was wildly unfaithful to Elizabeth Ercy, who perhaps should have accompanied him. They believed it would be better for his career if she stayed in France. "Let's face it," Mike told me, "the Hollywood birds phoned me. I didn't phone them." And by the time he had promised to join Elizabeth, he had met and fallen in love with Camilla Sparv.

He loves women and wants the relationship to last just

this side of marriage. "I expect to marry again," he assured me, but didn't say when. He was in love with Faye Dunaway during *Hurry, Sundown*. He flew to Miami every weekend where Faye was making *It's a Happening* with Anthony Quinn. He was breaking his contract, which forbids flying when filming. "But," he rationalized, "you can get killed just as easy on the freeway." More easily. The rumors had something with Anna Karina during *The Magus* in Spain. This followed Miss Sparv's revenge and abandonment of Mike. He inevitably gets dropped by the tall lovely model type. A man who knew him well told me, "He's a Pisces. Pisces men are selfish with women." The only female he has completely loved is his daughter, Dominique, a slim, blonde, lovely twelve-year-old from his first marriage in his early twenties to Patricia Haines. They starved together until Mike went off to Paris to starve alone.

While Caine is more generous than Mr. Connery, he does not waste money needlessly. We know all about his poverty as a child in the Elephant and Castle district in London with his brother and his mum (who supported them by working as a charwoman, cleaning other people's homes) and that his real name is Maurice Micklewhaite. He gave nonstop interviews about his humble beginnings—the old cockney days and good old mum. You can overdo the hearts and flowers. But it was all fresh to me when I lunched with Mike at the Caprice Restaurant the week after the premiere of *Zulu* in London. I had been amazed to learn he was a cockney. His upper-class accent, as the thickheaded supercilious officer, had fooled me completely. Watching the film at the Plaza Theater, I had thought a trifle bitterly, "These Etonians, who do they think they are?" He had tested originally to play the cockney soldier, but Stanley Baker, who had seen him in a BBC television show, had the courage to give him the bigger role. Mike received good reviews, but he was still a supporting player who had been acting for a long time and would never be a star.

Jimmy Woolf was lunching in another part of the restaurant, and as we left he whispered in my ear, "What are you wasting your time on him for?" He had known Mike for some years, he told me later. "He shared a flat with Terence Stamp and when he was starving, Terry would bring him over and I gave him food and loaned him money." After Mike was successful, Jimmy fumed to me, "He still hasn't paid me back. He says he can't get at his money. He says it's tied up in Switzerland." When Jimmy died of a heart attack at the Beverly Hills Hotel while reading *Valley of the Dolls*—and who can blame him?—his estate called on Caine to repay the loan. "I don't owe it," he protested. "But to save a fuss I'll pay it."

Mike is a good actor, but his quest for money has led him to make too many bad pictures. He was the hottest actor on the screen after *Alfie* and he loved his new affluence. "I'd stand opposite Bloomingdale's for hours and watch the long line opposite at the Coronet. All those people waiting to see me." He took me to Bloomingdale's after lunch at the Plaza to see the line again and to buy the latest in stereo radios to take home. In spite of *Alfie* the salesgirl did not recognize him and I wanted to tell her who he was, to make him feel good—or perhaps to make myself important. (As I wanted to tell the doorman of my New York apartment that it was Marlene Dietrich when she walked back with me from an interview at the nearby Sign of the Dove.) "I was in the underground at Charing Cross Station," he told me reflectively, "and a fat woman who must have been sixty came in lugging a huge parcel. There was something familiar about her face and I suddenly thought, 'Blimey, it's Jessie Matthews," [whom I understudied when I was A Cochran Young Lady] "and I knew this could happen to me one day."

Mike must make some good pictures to wipe out his recent mistakes. You can have a bad one after two hits and nothing happens to your career. Not every film Clark Gable made was successful, but he had good ones in between which is why he lasted as a glamorous star for thirty years. No one became such a big star as fast as Caine once he had made it. After *Zulu* he went from picture to picture without a day off. When Lewis Gilbert signed him for *Alfie*, the director suggested to Mr. Saltzman, "It's not an expensive picture, why not let him have a percentage?" The message was relayed and Michael replied, "I would rather have the $75,000"—then his film price. He could have made $2 million.

Mike almost didn't do *Alfie*. Terence Stamp turned it down to make *The Collector* for Willie Wyler at Columbia. It won some awards but did nothing for Terry's career. Previously Jimmy Woolf had wanted *Alfie*, which was a hit on the London stage, for his protégé, Laurence Harvey. But the deal stated that whoever did the film must first do it on the Broadway stage. I was staying in Jimmy's spare bedroom in his apartment in Grosvenor House and he asked me to read *Alfie* to see if it would be good for Larry. I thought it would be smashing for Larry. Larry refused *Alfie*. "He did not want to be on Broadway at the same time as Richard Burton," said Jimmy. Burton was coming in for *Hamlet*. "There's room for them both," I insisted, "and how can you compare the two plays?"

Mr. Stamp was wild to do the play in New York. "I'm so keen to do it," he said, "I'll do it for nothing, just give me 15 per cent of the show." I was there with Mr. Woolf on opening night. At the party upstairs at Sardi's, he asked me what did I really think. "Terry isn't strong enough, but Larry would have been." The play lasted a few performances. After this disaster Stamp lost his nerve and turned down the film, opening the way for his best friend and former roommate to come and get it.

Shelley Winters, who worked with Mike in *Alfie*, giggled. "He's the sexiest, funniest man I've ever met. Remember that scene on the floor where I'm seducing him? I'm supposed to be on top of him, then he rolls over and he's on top of me with his weight on his elbows. He slipped and I'm black and blue all over for days. Englishmen are so hard and bony. Except for the bruises it was a ball. Usually I'm not good at love scenes—in *Lolita* James Mason had to get me drunk before I could function." Miss Dunaway, who knows her screen lovers, said to me about Mike, "He has an air of moving on that makes him seem unattainable and that's attractive to a woman." Most attractive Englishmen seem to have this—and one American, Warren Beatty.

I believe that if Mike lasts as a star for another five years, he will feel secure enough to take on the responsibility of supporting a wife. For a long time his dream has been to be enormously successful, and as John Wheeler, used to cliché to his syndicate salesmen who took their wives along on sales trips, "He travels fastest who travels alone."

Mike has not changed much in the six years I have known him, except that he now is less afraid of spending money on himself. At one time he was going to buy the latest Rolls-Royce model and he had his eye on a beautiful penthouse in Portman Square. The next time I saw him he had canceled both expensive projects. "I don't have to prove anything," he explained in Paris where he was playing one of Shirley Mac-Laine's men in *Woman Times Seven*. "Very sensible," I nodded. Eighteen months ago, with his balance bulging in the bank in Switzerland, Mike believed he could afford to prove he was rich in dollars and pounds. He disgorged a six-figure sum to buy an apartment in Grosvenor Square and he bought a Rolls-Royce, but he hasn't had the time or the nerve to learn to drive it. In talking to him, you get the feeling that he still believes he might wake up one morning and find it all gone. He always goes to the same few restaurants where they know him. "If I go to another place and try to cash a check, they'll say, 'Who's that bum?' and it will embarrass me."

In spite of his success with women, he is still not too confident about them. Talking to me of when he lived with Stamp he said, "I would always flush out the birds. I'd chat them up and they'd go off with Terry." The actors met when they were understudying Peter O'Toole and Robert Shaw in *The Long, the Short, and the Tall*—the play made a star of Peter. Caine and Stamp played the roles on the road. Terry made it on the screen first in *Billy Budd*, and Michael, after twelve years of trying and failing, was delighted with Terry's success. He is not an envious man. He is more concerned with what he is going to do rather than what someone else has done. He is a realist and more intelligent than either Connery or Stamp. He knows that success is a fluke, and he is prepared all the time for failure. But even when he was broke he managed to live elegantly. Where Sean, who sometimes wears a kilt at home, looks casual-to-untidy in public, Michael is always impeccably groomed. And he has excellent taste in all forms of art. The walls of his mews home on the North side of Hyde Park were covered with interesting paintings. His younger brother lives there now. The new apartment is magnificent. The furniture is a fascinating mixture of Persian, Spanish, Louis XV, and Regency. His bed is king-size. "For the birds."

The Giants: "Duke," "Coop," Garbo, "Bogie"

The giants of Hollywood. Stars who will never be forgotten, names that bring a reflective look, a smile of recognition. In the old days Hollywood was full of giants—Valentino, Chaplin, Mary Pickford, Douglas Fairbanks (the first news story I covered in America was their divorce), Charles Laughton (*Ruggles of Red Gap*, Captain Bligh), Muni, Harlow, Monroe, Garbo, Cooper, Bogart—they cannot all be mentioned here, but is there anyone in the '60s who can match the magic of the stars of old?

In my time in Hollywood I have seen them disappear until today there is only one giant on the screen—John Wayne. Garbo preferred to retire rather than destroy the legend. Bette Davis and Joan Crawford dimmed their fame with cheap horror films. Mae West, seventy-five years old and still dating young athletes and muscle men, is trying for a comeback and selling some of her land in Van Nuys, a suburb of Los Angeles which made her a millionaire many times over. (Land. Why didn't I buy it when I came to Hollywood?)

It used to be a cheap town to live in. Now it is only cheap because of the poor quality of its television films and the uninteresting people. But no one would call John Wayne uninteresting. He is still very active and important in today's

Hollywood. When a film reviewer for *The New York Times* described his performance in *The Green Berets* as "dull," Senator Strom Thurmond stormed publicly, "John Wayne can never be dull." I agree. No matter how awful his acting, how stereotyped his role, he has a big-name quality, a sort of dumb lovableness that has kept him in the first ten at the box office for most of his forty years as a star.

He is a king among his colleagues. A working star. All the others are bluffing. He has an image. People are always shaking his hand. They feel he is approachable. Only one man can put him down—John Ford, who gave him his first role in *Hangman's House* in 1928. They have been friends ever since, although Ford, who is sadistic, used to treat him like an illiterate cowboy when he was a young actor. Duke, sixty going on sixty-one, has made more than two hundred films. The best was *Stagecoach,* directed by Ford. Like all great hits in all mediums, it had the feeling of its time.

Four years ago, but for the merest chance, Wayne would have died of lung cancer. "When my picture *In Harm's Way* finished ahead of time," he told me, "I said to myself, you haven't got anything to do in this period, why not take the physical at Scripps Clinic. I hadn't been there for eighteen months, and I usually went every year or so, as you know." I do. In 1955 after finishing a grueling eight and one-half months with a daily television show, I had collapsed in the Clinic at La Jolla, but revived immediately when I learned that Wayne was also a patient. We used to meet in the waiting rooms for the indignities inflicted on us in the name of a check-up—it was rather embarrassing when we had both taken purges for an X ray of the colon. We kept excusing ourselves.

"Before the picture, the insurance doctor as usual had examined me with the rest of the cast and said I was fine. I was X-rayed at Scripps, and they found a lump in my lung as big as my fist. I've coughed all my life and the day after the operation—one lung was removed—I coughed and broke the stitches and had another six-hour operation." I asked him if smoking had caused the cancer. "I don't know, but I smoked a lot." And drank a lot. Not as much now, but when he was younger, he could drink anyone under the table. During a press party in Mexico for *The War Wagon* with Kirk Douglas—the set was a Western bar—Wayne insisted "no beer." After all, he was on the wagon. Like hell he was. Before the reporters arrived he downed one glass of tequila after another. "Let's wait for the party," they begged him. His answer was "Another." When the press came at four-thirty Wayne was singing and bawling at the top of his voice and staggering happily around. He was supposed to do a scene for the benefit of the reporters. "He can't," they said, but when the lights went on, he did, nice and easy. The next day he wailed, "It's a shame I didn't do the TV tape for Merv Griffin yesterday." "You did," he was informed. "You were on for fifteen minutes."

He started chewing tobacco in college—he had a football scholarship to the University of Southern California. "I still chew when I'm working on location or in the desert." He's a neat, fastidious man and I am always startled when I see him spewing out the tobacco juice. When his wife Pilar visited him on location, he stopped chewing. She dislikes the habit. But now with small children, she does not come so much to the locations, usually in difficult terrain. I have seen him through three marriages. All his wives have been small, elegant Latin types. His first, Josephine, was a devout Catholic. John was interested in another woman and Josephine found out. She asked Father McCoy of Los Angeles to come to the house and talk to her husband. Wayne was contrite and promised, "I'll never see the girl again if Josephine will never bring up the subject again." She agreed. No sooner had Father McCoy left, when Josephine, still hurt, brought it up. "That's when I knew the marriage was over," Wayne, nicknamed Duke, told me. The divorce from his second wife, Esperanza Bauer, cost him $500,000 payable at $50,000 a year for ten years, plus the home, a car, and the usual appurtenances that wives of a Hollywood star collect in a divorce.

The one time he was annoyed with me was when I printed

that Esperanza had undergone an operation to become pregnant. He considered it his business, not mine. She was the only one of his wives who did not give him a child. He had four with Josephine, three with Pilar of Peru. Their courtship was amusing to watch—she so tiny, he so tall. Of his seven children, Michael at thirty-two, the oldest, produces some of the films for Duke's Batjac company. Patrick is an actor. His youngest child, Marisa Carmela, was born on Washington's Birthday 1966. When I last talked to him, his grandchildren totaled "fifteen and one in the oven. I've got grandchildren to baby-sit for my kids. We have a get-together one month after Christmas for a combined holiday celebration."

Duke is not always good-tempered. He can look angry when actors are not on time. When he glowers, you must watch out. That is when he is ready to lash out. His language can be pretty strong, but he won't swear when women are around and he won't play a scene if he has to hit a woman (you can't count the spanking he gave Maureen O'Hara in *The Quiet Man*). When Kirk Douglas was late one morning, Wayne said sarcastically, "Well, we're waiting for our star. He's ruining our happy atmosphere." Then he stomped off, talking under his breath. It was the year Ronald Reagan was campaigning for governor against Pat Brown. Kirk is a Democrat, but he never talks politics on the set. Duke is a fierce Republican. He has a profound hatred of Communism; he believes the Communists are dangerous because they never compromise. "We are the ones who give in and we should stop it." He would say to Kirk, "You goddam liberals," then put his arm around him and say, "You know I wasn't mad, I only do this to people I love." The make-up man, also a liberal, couldn't take it, and quit. Nonetheless, Duke insists that in his way he is a liberal himself and that those on the other side of the political fence today are radicals. During *The Hellfighters* he did not talk too much about politics, except when he was asked, "Who is your choice for President?" "Anybody but Rockefeller," he replied. He was for Goldwater, then Reagan and Nixon.

Wayne is the same man I first met in 1936 when he was under contract to RKO, except that now he is more sure of himself. Success has given him authority. He was always battling with his bosses in the late '30s. They were not paying him enough and taxes were rising and he would complain bitterly to me. But he was never a cry-baby, not even when the money he loses is his own. He borrowed $750,000 as his share of *The Alamo,* which he had dreamed of making for eight years. Some of his Texas friends put millions into the disastrous film, and it has taken him ten years to pay back the $750,000. The other backers now have most of their money back. "I had an offer of two million dollars to sell *The Alamo* for television, but I'm holding out for more and that will pay off the interest on the $750,000 and finally give me a profit."

He is bossy on the set. He will tell people who argue with him, "Shut your mouth." During *The Sands of Iwo Jima* he explained to one of the other actors how he should have done the scene. He was interrupted by Robert Dwan, who said, "I'm the director and I like the way he did it." Wayne pouted but did not walk off. He is always early, always knows his lines and everyone else's. He is good to the crew and loyal to the actors who work for him. Paul Fix, his chief production assistant, began as his drama coach in 1929. It's the same crew and often the same actors; the late Ward Bond was in every one. George Coleman, in charge of Batjac transportation, has been with Wayne for twenty-six years. His boss growls at him, swears at him, and loves him. Years ago when Duke was making another film in Mexico, he was in a cheap bar and started dancing with one of the girls. His driver stepped between him and the girl's lover and got it in the ribs. Wayne set him up in business, and every film company on location in this vicinity has to go to him for cars. His secretary for twenty-five years, Mary St. John, was in the secretarial pool at Republic when he poked his head in the door and said, "When I'm a big star, Mary, I'm going to ask you to be my private secretary."

Wayne is a definite man. He is the kind of optimist who would have driven west in a wagon. He feels his presence is necessary on the set as a morale builder whether he is in the scene or not. He was not in the opening action of *The Hell-fighters,* but he stayed until twelve-thirty the first night and the next until 4 A.M. He was on his feet, never resting, chewing tobacco filched from the stuntman. When I asked him, "Why did you want to do this picture?" (about oil-well fighters), he dead-panned, "Oh, about a million dollars."

Wayne, born Marion Michael Morrison in Iowa, came to California with his family when he was five. "I got the title of Duke when I was a little boy going to school. I had a dog named Duke. He chased the fire engines and I chased Duke and the men used to say, 'Here comes little Duke with his dog.'" In the mid-thirties he seemed to be trying to lift the film industry out of the doldrums caused by the Wall Street crash that had culminated in the closing of the banks in 1933 by President Franklin Roosevelt. "I made thirty-four films and then went into a slump until John Ford brought me back in *Stagecoach.* To do it I had to fight Republic Studios [for whom he was forced to make some terrible films with the boss's wife, Vera Hruba Ralston].

Today Wayne is big business. Apart from his Batjac company, named for a Dutchman he admired, he owns three big cattle ranches in Arizona. He was in the shrimp business at one time with Dame Margot Fonteyn's husband, the now paralyzed ex-Ambassador Roberto Arias. He got out without losing too much. The hotel he owns in the Mexican resort of Acapulco has proved profitable, as well as his apartment houses in Los Angeles. He is a big spender, always carries a large wad of notes in his pocket—he never knows how much. Surprisingly he is an art enthusiast, and his new home in Newport Bay, where he keeps his yacht, is full of good paintings—French Impressionists—and antiques. He can recognize a Georgian table across a crowded room and can tell you a block away if it really is a signed Tiffany lamp. He owns a big collection of Charles Russell bronzes. He is a good bridge and chess player, and you'd better not interrupt him on the set when he is deep in the problems of a game. Again surprisingly, he is a shy, emotional man. When his role in a film is over, he leaves quietly without saying good-by. He is afraid of choking up.

The bar-room brawls you see in films were invented by Wayne in his early Westerns—the "pass blow," it is called. It looks as though a fist has slammed into a face but it passes; when it does not, you have a real fight. He insists he has never made a propaganda picture. "What about *The Green Berets*," the film about the special U.S. unit in Vietnam I asked him. "That was a subject that needed my attention," he replied. "We weren't making a message picture. It was an actor's picture—an entertainment vehicle rather than a message vehicle. It was a John Wayne action picture. It was not a Dick Lester antiwar picture. This is the difference between the old films and the new. The old pictures were entertainment. Ours is a business of illusion. You don't have to show a man picking his nose."

He believes the government hurt Hollywood irrevocably when it removed the control of the theaters from the people who made the pictures. "They took away from the United States the prestige of being the world's center for making films, and Hollywood was also damaged when film executives and actors refused to accept television. In 1955, I had to talk Jim Arness into doing *Gunsmoke*. [Actually it was offered first to Wayne.] 'You're ruining my career,' he said. 'What career?' I said. 'This will help you.'" Mr. Arness is now richer than Mr. Wayne, whose old films on television have given him another generation of fans. "It sometimes makes me sad to see how thin I was, such wavy hair." He smiled when he said it. He has matured. He is like an elder statesman. He is a star.

COOP

To be a giant, there can only be one of you—you cannot be another Errol Flynn or another Marilyn Monroe. It is the unique quality you alone possess that sets you apart from the others. There never was anyone in Hollywood like Gary Cooper, not only on the screen but in real life. He was the *parfait gentilhomme*—it seems more knightly in French.

Gary was the first person I interviewed in Hollywood. He was starring in *Desire* at Paramount, and I desired very much to meet him. I was rather shy in those days, and I hesitantly set up a luncheon interview with the handsome man who had taken my girlish heart in *The Winning of Barbara Worth* in 1926. I was in such a hurry to get to Gary, and trying to think of what I would say to him, that near the studio I crashed into another car. Shaken but resolved, I ran the rest of the way. I was too late. He was already married. After a series of love affairs—Clara Bow when he was twenty-five; Lupe Velez, who was to commit suicide; the Countess Di Frasso, who had met him in Rome when he was recuperating from Lupe's death— he had wed an eastern socialite Veronica Balfe (nicknamed Rocky) in 1933. I remember thinking as I watched the crowds elbow Mrs. Cooper out of the way in the scramble to get Gary's autograph, that while it would be marvelous to be married to Gary, it must be hard on a woman's ego. I learned what it was almost like, and it increased my ego when I accompanied Gary to Dallas in 1940 for the premiere of *The Westerner,* directed by Willie Wyler for Sam Goldwyn. There were about fifty of us going to Dallas, and two planes were rented to fly us there. Planes were small then, and the flight which now takes three hours lasted about twelve hours and we went overnight and slept in berths on the plane.

'We slid off the endless desert and over the table-lands, dyed with many colors like the white sands we dyed with colors when I was a child.' Mack Miller, who was Bob Hope's press agent (Bob was to be master of ceremonies at the premieres in Dallas and Fort Worth), had asked me which of the two planes I preferred, Bob's or Gary's. "Gary Cooper's of course," I said. Scott Fitzgerald drove me to the airport, and Mack, not knowing of our relationship, said in a loud voice, "I put you in Gary's plane as you asked me to." I didn't dare look at

Scott. But even though I had bought a cowgirl outfit and a brown cowboy hat made especially for me by Rex at my own expense, I had no real designs on Gary. He was a dream that would become a man if I touched him and I already had my man. But it was nice being in such proximity to this glorious male who became more so as I became more airsick. Those were the days of unpressurized cabins, and I was invariably sick even when it was smooth. We were all talking and enjoying ourselves and Gary was flirting outrageously with me and the champagne was flowing and I was somewhat flushed with excitement when I felt the pink glow turning green. In a few minutes I would throw up. How awful to do this before my idol. "I must lie down," I said weakly. Some of the berths had been made up, and Gary took me in his arms as though I weighed two pounds (I was much thinner then) and placed me on a top berth. He was very solicitous. "Shall I rub your tummy?" "No," I implored in a whisper. It would have been disastrous even with Gary doing the rubbing. His lanky frame reached over me, and he patted my hand until he was sure I was all right.

In Dallas we were met by a cavalcade of new Cadillacs, and Mack had arranged for me to ride with Gary and it was marvelous. There was a horseback parade in the afternoon, but I was still shaky from the trip and not a good enough rider to risk the humid streets of Texas, but Gary rode at the head of the horsemen and the crowds went mad. I was his girl for the film premiere, sitting close to him in the small two-seater sidecar of the motorcycle driven by a policeman. It was a motorbike parade to the theater with the sirens howling on the roads packed with people. After the film the local radio station asked me to say a few words with Bob Hope. He had not prepared anything. Bob has ad libs for every occasion— written by his team of writers. But they had not prepared anything for this interview. Neither had I. It went something like this. Bob: "How do you like Dallas?" Me: "I like it." Long pause. Bob: "Have you been here before?" Me: "No, never." Long pause—me looking desperately at Bob to say something funny, Bob looking at me desperately to say anything. He is faster now.

I was the first to arrive for the party in a big suite at the Adolphus Hotel. I dashed through the bedroom into the bathroom for make-up repairs. When I came out, Gary was in the bedroom. I had obviously overplayed my adoration. Gary, who never made the first move with a woman, took my hands, drew me close (what ecstasy), and stood there looking down at me while I looked up at him. But only for a few seconds, then I felt a giggle coming and I broke away. The other guests started to arrive and we went into the large sitting room. Why does a dream drop into your life at the wrong time? It's a strange thing. In my long time in Hollywood several of the attractive men have intruded into my dreams, but never Gary Cooper.

Gary died in May 1961, as he had lived, quietly and gently. He had known for a long time that he had cancer. As far back as 1959 when he was starring in *They Came to Cordura,* whenever he had to mount a horse, he would grimace with pain, but he never said anything. The world knew he was dying when Jimmy Stewart, one of his close friends, substituted for Gary at the Academy Awards (Gary was watching on television) and in a voice that broke, ended his speech, "The thoughts of all your friends are with you." We knew he was ill, but not how little time he had left—a few weeks. In January of the same year he had been in New York dining at Sardi's with another man and myself. He picked up the cigarette lighter on the table and said, "I kind of like this lighter." "It's yours," said the other man, and Gary put it absent-mindedly into his pocket. We went off to a show, and when the cab hit a couple of bumps, Gary winced. "Anything the matter?" I asked him. "Yes," he replied, "I've got this thing that's going to kill me . . . well . . . er." He changed the subject and gave the lighter back with a wry smile.

The funeral was at the Church of the Good Shepherd in Beverly Hills, which has seen some glamorous film-star weddings and some noisy funerals. But this wasn't the usual shoving and screaming Hollywood funeral. All the stars were there—Fred Astaire, Audrey Hepburn (who had been Gary's girl in *Love in the Afternoon*), Norma Shearer, Joan Crawford, John Wayne, Jimmy Stewart, Bob Hope. But there was not a sound from the crowd—a sign of the tremendous respect for Mr. Cooper. He never did a mean or a small thing in his life. He was a decent man. When Carl Foreman was in trouble with the House Un-American Activities Committee, Gary, a strong Republican, called him and asked, "Is there anything I can do for you?" It was almost as good as destroying your career.

"He was unlike any star I have ever known," Carl was reminiscing in London last year. "Before *High Noon,* in 1952, we had decided to rehearse for two weeks before starting the picture. We had some new people—it was Grace Kelly's first film—and we wanted to break them in. Sometimes you can get the star to rehearse with the lesser players and sometimes you can't. We figured that Gary wouldn't want to rehearse, so we started without him. After four days Gary came to me and said, 'I hear you're rehearsing. How about me?' 'I thought you wouldn't want to.' 'No, I'd like to do it.' " Unlike some other big names in this book who would say, "You were trying to trick me."

Gary was always somewhat embarrassed about being an actor. "Silly way to earn a living," he said to no one in particular when he walked off a set at Warner Brothers. It wasn't easy for him to act. He once told me, "When they say I'm just being me, they don't know how hard it is to act to be a guy like me." He was a purist as far as acting went and with everything else in his life. He never let himself get mixed up, never complicated. He never sat back and analyzed the picture business or himself. He once said to me, "There's too much mysticism and magic, to analyze it." Simplicity was the Cooper trademark. He had a reputation for never talking, just saying "yup," and it was often true, especially if he wanted to sleep in his chair on the set and if anyone interrupted him. But sometimes he would utter several sentences, although he would speak in a low tone as if he were uncomfortable with speech. Randy Scott tells the story of when he called on Gary with his new car and said, "Let's go for a drive." They drove around for an hour without speaking a word. On the way back a bird flew overhead. Coop put his arms and hands into the shape of a rifle, said, "bang," and that was it.

On location—many of his films were Westerns made away from the studio—he would sit by himself under a tree and eat a whole cherry pie and a quart of milk for lunch, then push his cowboy hat over his eyes and sleep. He was the best sleeper I ever knew. He could sleep anywhere and eat anything, sea slugs or Scotch smoked salmon with capers and Pouilly Fuisse; he could adapt himself to any conditions and communities, rich or primitive. When he was on location for a film in Western Samoa, he wore pink pants, white loafers, and a yellow straw hat to the parties. He would dance the native dances with great concentration.

Gary was a romanticist. He could give and was able to receive, without self-consciousness or guilt. He wanted to marry Pat Neal, whom he met in 1949 when they costarred in *The Fountainhead*. She was the only woman apart from his wife that he was ever deeply in love with, but Rocky was a practicing Catholic and even though Gary brought Pat to Cuba to visit Ernest Hemingway and she went to many of his locations, when they realized they could never marry, Gary returned to his wife from whom he had been separated and more or less patched up the rift. He became a Catholic when Maria, the daughter he loved, could not be accepted at a good Catholic school until her parents were married in the church. Previously he had accompanied his wife and daughter to an audience with the Pope—he knew it would please Maria.

After the films were wrapped up, he'd go off somewhere to hunt, often with Hemingway in Idaho or Key West. He was also a fine dry fisherman. His fishing friends have told me, "He'd use a delicate fly rod with the fly he made himself." The pure sportsman would never fish with a big rod. Rocky introduced him to scuba diving and the family spent vacations in the Caribbean, often wearing the skin-tight rubber suits that flatter no one.

Like Wayne, he was an easy man for the public to approach. He was walking in the Central Park Zoo in New York with a friend. A man and his small daughter rushed over. "My little girl would like your autograph," the man said. Afterward Gary laughed. "That little girl doesn't know me from a monkey in this zoo." He broke a cap on his tooth in New York, and in the elevator after leaving his dentist a group of middle-aged women stared and one piped up, "Oh, I know him—it's Randolph Scott." Gary roared. The press agent for his film had scheduled an interview at the *New York Daily Mirror*. They had both forgotten it was Lincoln's Birthday and no one was around. The p.a. was embarrassed, but Gary said, "Forget it. We'll go look at the tits of the pretty girls on Fifth Avenue." He was a great admirer of the female chest. "Look at the knockers on that girl," he would remark.

He loved black ties and yellow shirts and in the last two decades of his life was considered one of the best-dressed men in America. Gary had been a casual dresser—Levis and open-neck shirts when he first came from the mountains of Montana to Hollywood in the mid-twenties, but he was not the illiterate cowboy that some writers of the time made him out to be. His father was a judge, and Gary had been educated at a private school in England. He was working as an illustrator-cartoonist when a friend asked him, "Would you like to pick up a few bucks as an extra in a Western?" He knew how to ride, and that's how it all started.

Gary was always natural and unostentatious. The parties he gave with Rocky were beautifully done. The greats from all over the world came to the Coopers'; the food was exquisite and exquisitely served. It was the elegant time of Hollywood—no longer the noisy parties of early years. Today there aren't any, just the small group that gets together in each other's homes. When a socialite like Mrs. Elsie Woodward comes to California from the East, she is rotated from house to house, seeing the same people she saw at other houses. The Coopers knew many people, and Gary was so popular they had a large list from which to choose their guests. The Jack Bennys, Armand Deutsches, Freddie Brissons (Rosalind Russell), Kirk Douglases, Vincente Minnellis are charming people, but when you see them at dinner night after night, you can't think of anything new to say to them.

Gary was impulsive. He sometimes forgot where he was and would follow a thought. He loved cars—he had the first Dusenberg in Hollywood. He was walking on Park Avenue at Fifty-sixth Street in New York and stopped at the Mercedes-Benz showroom. They had a new car in the window with a special suspension. Gary crawled under the car in the window to inspect it while a crowd collected. He was a bit embarrassed when he came out from under. He was always kind to the ladies, past and present. A girl he had known had a niece of fourteen who liked to paint. Gary sent her a complete painting outfit: easel, brushes, paints. He picked them out himself.

He was one star who never had a retinue. He was never suffocated by the usual army of hangers-on in Hollywood. In death the people come to his grave at the Holy Cross Cemetery in Inglewood. The tourists like to have their photographs taken with Mr. Cooper, the first gentleman of motion pictures.

GARBO

In the early days of my time in Hollywood, Norma Shearer was considered an actress and Greta Garbo a personality. But when you see Garbo's old films on television, you realize she was the best actress of her time. She could still be a star, like an antique commode that is always in fashion. But she prefers to remain a myth and has steadfastly refused the enormous offers to return to her Hollywood career which began when Mauritz Stiller brought his timid protégée with him to America from their native Sweden. When I arrived in Hollywood, she was still functioning as an important star; she had still to do *Queen Christina, Anna Karenina, Camille, Ninotchka,* and *Two Faced Woman.* The last one depressed her so much she vowed, "No more." Her good friend Gaylord Hauser, the nutritionist, believes she might make another film, "If it would help humanity." But a quarter of a century is too long away from the screen and she enjoys her legend.

It started in the publicity department at M-G-M. Garbo never in her life has said, "I want to be alone." It was foisted on her by the studio because she did not understand English, and by the time she did, she had become the biggest star in motion pictures and it was an easy hook to avoid the bother of speaking to the press and the press agents.

During *Queen Christina* she turned to the director, Clarence Brown, and said, "Who is that?" pointing to a man on the sidelines. "The publicity man for the picture," he replied. "Throw him off the set," she said in proficient English. There were all sorts of rumors printed about her at this time, that she was eloping or that she was ill, but when reporters called to check, they were told, "She's not going to deny or confirm it." There was a film affair in Argentina. The head man wanted a message from Garbo to start the festivities. They knew at the studio she would not talk to him so they put on a secretary who could imitate Garbo and all went swimmingly until the man in South America said, "Now I am putting on the Swedish Ambassador who will talk to you in your own language." Much giggling on the Hollywood end and a "Terribly sorry, but I vant to be alone now."

In reality she loves people and has many friends in Hollywood and New York where she strides about freely, haunting the antique shops on Third Avenue wearing her handbag around her neck and chatting to babies in their carriages. She recently lunched at the M-G-M café in Hollywood with her hair stylist. Some of the old-timers came over to talk to her, and she was delighted to see them. In recent years when no one has been writing about her, she has wanted the press to pursue her, but we have been indoctrinated too well to intrude on her privacy.

Jimmy Stewart was reminiscing recently. "In 1937 I was making *Wife Versus Secretary* at Metro and Garbo was making *Camille*. I knew the sound man on the picture and I made a deal with him: 'Call me when you break.' I barrel-assed from my stage, ran into the woman, and almost knocked her down. I met her after that at someone's house, but I was tongue-tied. I just listened."

She is a legend for the legends. Recently Marlene Dietrich and two *Life* magazine staffers were lunching at Maud Chez Elle in New York when Marlene said, "Look who just came in—Garbo." She was alone, as she often is. "Why don't you speak to her?" said one of the staffers, sensing a great photograph for *Life*. "I would not speak to her unless she spoke to me first," said Marlene. Myrna Loy was at a restaurant on the East Side and was rendered speechless after stuttering, "The wraith that went by, that was Garbo." And yet Greta is as excited about celebrities as the next girl. At P. J. Clarke's, on Third Avenue, she was told "Dorothy Kilgallen is over there." She sidled over to peek at the late columnist. Greta and I have the same dentist in New York, and I would willingly have a tooth extracted (well, not really) to get the final interview with her. I keep going to the dentist but so far, no luck.

"You would not find her difficult," I was assured by Mr. Hauser, who has known her since he put her on a diet of fish, meat, and eggs in the '30s—before that she was a vegetarian. "She was so pale and tired." Hauser cooked for her; her first meal from him was wild rice and a nutburger. "When you talk with her she is completely natural if she is not being treated as a legend. Treat her as a human being and she'll respect you. She saw with clear eyes the superficiality of Hollywood, the nothingness, and that's why she left."

Another intimate assured me she is aware that being unavailable to the press results in the attention she secretly loves. In her day Vivien Leigh received almost as much attention without the bore of removing herself. She was chatty, witty, and affectionate. Vivien's world was full of amusing people.

It was alive. She could never, as Garbo did, put herself in a straitjacket of solitude. When women live alone—and men as well, perhaps—it becomes complete self-involvement; they have only to please themselves. And Garbo has lived for herself alone. She might have married John Gilbert, with whom she was madly in love during the filming of *Flesh and the Devil* in 1926. Ten years later she almost eloped with Maestro Leopold Stokowski, but she could not share herself with anyone. Now she sighs, "I would have liked to be married. I'd rather not live alone." She will be sixty-four in September and you don't usually marry for the first time at that age.

There are nieces and nephews in Sweden; she was the third of five children born to a laborer in the City Sanitation Department, living in one room in the Soder District, the poorest part of Stockholm. We know that at fourteen she worked in a barbershop, soaping the faces of the customers, and that she was a shop assistant and a photographer's model and won a scholarship on her eighteenth birthday to the Royal Dramatic Academy in Stockholm. It was a "Beauty and the Beast" saga—like Loren and Ponti—with Stiller, who dominated the Swedish cinema world at that time. She struggled against the name of Garbo which Stiller and Louis B. Mayer (who had been impressed with *The Great Gabbo,* starring Erich von Stroheim) substituted for her real name, Gustafson. "It sounds like garbage," she protested, but Mayer was a dictator and you did it his way or not at all. During the late '30s and early '40s, when Garbo's appeal was waning, Mayer kept her on the payroll, for prestige and because her pictures made money in Europe. She had been earning the unprecedented sum of $300,000 a film and made three a year; with only 10 per cent income tax, she became a rich woman. At one time Greta owned half of Beverly Hills. I was in Long Island years after Greta retired, at the house of the banker who handled her account, and I said, "Is she really all right financially?" He laughed and said, "She's more than all right." Her brother is a banker in Sweden and has helped to multiply her investments.

There were always rumors that she had been killed, but investigation usually found her sun-bathing—in the nude in the garden of her friends, the Carey Wilsons (he produced the first *Ben Hur* with Ramon Navarro). Carey had lived with John Gilbert in their early years. They each rocketed from $200 a week to $15,000 a week within a year. I was with Fred MacMurray when the same magical wand transformed Fred's weekly pay check overnight from $200 to $2,000. This is why Hollywood is the breeding ground for so many ills. You have nothing one day and a fortune the next. It's a perpetual gold-rush city.

Garbo was not only the highest-paid actress of her day, but the most powerful. While Gable and Shearer worked until seven at night, Garbo left promptly at five. Miss Shearer—Mrs. Irving Thalberg in private life—saw every inch of her "rushes." Garbo refused to see the interminable "takes" in the projection room, or previews or premieres. The truth was she did not like herself on the screen. She was making a film with Bill Daniels as her cameraman—he made twenty films with her. "We were one third of the way through," Bill told me, "when she received word of John Gilbert's death. She was too upset to continue and took the day off. That was the only time. She was always ready at nine and we'd be ready because we knew she would leave on the second of five." Her best feature was her eyes. She had a good side—her right profile—and Daniels, without letting the star know, would make sure it was the good side he photographed. (Claudette Colbert insisted on doors being on one side of the set to avoid her worst profile.) I believe the myth of Garbo's big feet has been exploded. According to her closest intimates, she wears a 6 ½, which is not large, especially for a woman as athletic as Greta. She still performs all the Swedish calisthenics and is still a health bug.

"Garbo Talks." I remember the campaign to advertise her first talkie—*Anna Christie* in 1930. In those days they had the sound playback on the set. The first time Garbo heard her voice, she said, "Oh my god, is that me?" Her voice was a low bass, but it did not kill her career as did the high falsetto of John Gilbert (with today's sound equipment they could have brought it down). *Ninotchka* in 1939 was Garbo's last good film. She would fight the front office for better stories, but never with the people in her picture. The crews loved her and her associates protected her. An actor was drunk in one of her films, but she helped him through the picture. In *Romance* a monkey bit her. Instead of throwing a fit she finished the scene, then picked up the monkey, slapped it on the bottom, and said, "Now you stop that." She has a fairly happy life today, not so lonely as people imagine. She lives in a beautifully furnished apartment near the river in Manhattan's East Fifties and has a great collection of French Impressionists. (Do anyone but Hollywood stars own these paintings? Edward G. Robinson's collection is now valued at $3 million even after the community-property split.)

Garbo has been offered a million dollars to write her memoirs but she says she never will. "Why should I do it?" she demands. "I'm a private citizen." But as long as people have memories and her old films are still so excellent on television, she can't. Five years ago my son, who was then eighteen, saw *Grand Hotel* on TV in Hawaii and he could not tear himself away from the small screen. He has made a point of attending all the Garbo film festivals, including the one last July in New York at the Museum of Modern Art—the twenty-seven Garbo films ran four weeks. Today's young generation has discovered her, although they are not interested in Shearer or Harlow or any of the other women of their era, who overplayed for today's taste in films. In a way I am glad I did not get to know her—just "how are you" at some of my early visits at the home of her close friend, the writer Salka Viertel. I prefer to keep her where she belongs, on celluloid, on the screen, to look at and admire.

BOGIE

I knew him at the beginning and the middle and the end, and sometimes I liked him and sometimes I detested him. The man, not the antihero on the screen. There has been so much written about him in recent years—books, articles, television documentaries. But while they have touched on his pranks (he was a cruel prankster), they have, it seems to me, overlooked the keystone of his character. In death he was more courageous than any of the heroic characters of the screen, but in real life he was a timid man. He was afraid of all his wives, at least the three I knew. He loved the last, Lauren Bacall, the most. But he was more intimidated by her than the others.

I met him soon after he came to Hollywood in 1936 to repeat his stage role of Duke Mantee in *The Petrified Forest,* with Bette Davis and Leslie Howard. He was married then to stage actress Mary Phillips. "What's new, kid?" he would ask me in his lisping gravelly voice. And, "When are we going to have that affair? I can't wait forever." I'd laugh and say, "We'll consummate it in heaven."

"But how do I know I'll be me and you'll be you?"

"We will be," I promised him.

It was a game. After his success in *The Maltese Falcon*— George Raft had turned the role down, Bogart wanted more money as they all do after they hit. Jack Warner would not budge and Bogie tormented him in every way he could think of, slandering him all over town, but not to his face—when Jack bawled him out, he apologized—but refusing films and going on suspension. What a strange contradictory character he was. He said to me once, "People are always saying I'm pretending to be tough. The truth is I'm defensive." He was afraid to fight although he would when attacked, but even then he had to ginger up his spleen with liquor. He was no match for his third wife, Mayo Methot. He once showed me his scalp, scarred where she had hit him on the head with a bottle. And once I was entering the Stork Club in New

York, at the moment a taxi stopped to let them out, and the kids with autograph books shouted, "Here he is!" Bogie and Mayo were screaming at each other, and she suddenly hit him over the face with her handbag. One youngster said, "Let's get his autograph." Another said, "To hell with his, let's get hers, she's tougher."

There was something of a scandal when they went to North Africa during World War II where Bogie was supposed to entertain the G.I.'s. The high command decided the Bogart battlefront was more dangerous and booted them back to America. I thought he would never have the courage to leave Mayo, but "love conquers all," and when he fell in love with another strong-minded dame, he risked annihilation and lost his bankroll to marry the young model turned actress who made her debut in his film *To Have and Have Not* at Warners. I would see this determined lady—known as Betty Bacall to her intimates—with Bogie at Robert Benchley's apartment at the Garden of Allah where Bogie was hiding from Mayo with a guard stationed outside the door. It was obvious Lauren and Bogie were deeply in love, but I would not have given odds Mayo would ever let him go. A settlement of $300,000 proved irresistible, plus the realization she was up against a stronger woman. After Bogie's marriage to Miss Bacall at the home of Louis Bromfield, his luck was all good until the terminal cancer. He made a new deal with Jack Warner for $250,000 a picture, with a clause allowing him to make outside pictures on his own. *The African Queen* brought him a million dollars and an Oscar. He was proud of his sharp slender wife who could keep him in check just by saying "Humphrey!" And he was delighted to become a father—a boy and a girl. His wife was so determined they would have children it simply had to happen.

It is hard to know where to begin with all the things that happened in the time I knew Bogie. He was a monster at times but always amusing—if the joke was not on you. In 1953, Alan Ladd was starring in *Hell Below Zero*. He was working on a large rostrum on scaffolding. One of the crew members climbed up to adjust something and fell thirty feet down the tubular steel. He had worked with Bogie in *The African Queen*. Bogie at this time was doing *Beat the Devil*, but to nettle Ladd's producer, he went around saying, "The guy isn't getting the right care." It caused several fights and one free-for-all. "Take it easy," he was told, "everything possible is being done for the man." "What d'ya mean, take it easy?" and he would put up his fists in a threatening manner. It was too much and the producer finally told him, "Aw, go fuck yourself." Everyone waited to see what would happen. Bogey shut up at once.

A couple of months later in the South of France the producer of the Ladd film was at Le Drap D'Or. In came Bogart and Bacall. The star glared at the man who had humiliated him. Again the producer said, "Take it easy, Bogie." Bogie's frown disappeared. He started to laugh. "What are you doing tonight?" he asked. "Gambling at Monte Carlo." "I'd like to come with you, but I don't know anything about gambling." "We can play *chemin de fer* and I'll tell you what to do." The croupiers almost dropped their sticks when they saw their idol. His new close friend told him, "They expect you to gamble big—don't bid unless it's a big pot." Bogart lost every time. Finally he yelled, "Jesus, they're murdering me." The producer rushed him out before he could say anything worse and topple from his pedestal.

Bogie wanted to play the boxer in *The Harder They Fall*, but he detested the producer Jerry Wald and raised hell when Jerry came on the set. He'd bawl him out and throw him off, with words only of course. While he was a great threatener, he would fight only when he was drunk and not always then. It was around Hallowe'en during the location in New York near the East River, and lots of women and children were around. The film's press agent asked Bogie if he would pose with a couple of kids with toy guns who would stick him up and say "Trick or treat." "Sure, kid," he replied. The photographers were ready, the boys pointed their guns, and the press agent motioned to the actor to put up his hands. "Drop dead, you prick," said the man who was often an antihero in real life. A woman screamed and Bogie meekly put his hands up, stood still for the photograph, and then savagely ordered the press agent and the photographers off the set.

He fought with Billy Wilder during *Sabrina*. It was Audrey Hepburn's second picture, and Bogie believed that Wilder was paying her too much attention at his expense. He felt left out. When Billy and Bogie disagreed about some of the dialogue the actor snarled, "Get this city writer off the set and send him to Monogram [a studio for minor films] where he belongs." The writer walked away. "I kept walking," he told me, "and Bogart walked after me, swearing. I couldn't help laughing, he looked and sounded so silly." Bogie went back to the scene and Wilder said, "There will be no further shooting until Mr. Bogart apologizes to my writer." He did immediately, then went back to work and afterward called the writer into his dressing room and apologized again.

I was on the set of *Knock on Any Door,* and Bogie bawled me out for something innocuous I had written about Miss Bacall. Then he came over to me, put his arm around my shoulder, and said, "Now that's over, what's new?" He had been kidding, but I do not understand this kind of joke and walked off the set. "Aw, let her go," he shouted after me. We did not talk for months after that. There was a cocktail party at the Mocambo and I appeared to be alone and he was going to let me have it, when my escort joined me and Bogie's "hell" became "hello."

Bogie wanted to give an impression of leadership, which is why he founded the "Rat Pack of Holmby Hills." His Rats were the stars who lived on the same street, including Judy Garland and, at the beginning, Sinatra. But almost anyone who seemed tough could put him down. During *Beat the Devil*, Bogie espied Truman Capote—who had written the script—on the set and demanded, "Who's that little bastard?" Truman walked over and threw Bogie over his shoulder. He had studied judo. After that they were great friends.

During the filming of *The Desperate Hours* in New York,

I was dining downstairs at "21". Bogie was at the bar with Dewey Martin and Miss Bacall. Dewey, who had a role in the film—whatever happened to him?—was accosted by a friend and he said to Bogart, "I'd like you to meet—" As Bogie turned, his elbow hit the man next to him at the bar. "I'm sorry," he apologized. "Forget it," said the stranger. "I told you I'm sorry," Bogie persisted. "It's all right." Bogie caught the man by the lapels and shook him and said, "Look, I said I'm sorry. I demand you accept my apology." Then up spake Miss Bacall: "HUMPHREY!" The tiger became a pussycat.

I was not there when he tackled the girl at El Morocco for the toy panda. He was barred from the nightclub and from "21" and from the Mocambo in Hollywood. When Mervyn LeRoy, the director, wanted to take him there one evening, he explained "I've been barred for two years." Mervyn went inside to the owner, Charlie Morrison, and said, "Bogie's outside waiting to come in." Charlie shrugged. "O.K., Merv." They went to get him and found him in the gutter wrestling with the cab driver.

On his boat, the *Santana* (he was happiest with the sea breeze on his beaten-up face), two of his guests, Paul Douglas and Jan Sterling, decided to become engaged. Bogie was at the tiller when Jan and Paul told him their good news. Without turning the skipper of the ship gruffed, "Don't come to me with your fucking troubles." He was always trying for the shock effect. At an exclusive party in London he was talking to a gentleman from India who spoke perfect English. Bogie said, "You speak English well for an Indian." "I had an English governess." "Did you fuck her?" End of elegant English conversation.

But there was the other side of Bogart. During the New York location for *The Harder They Fall* the company was working near Stillman's Gym. The punchy fighters of old were still charging around with bent noses and cauliflower ears, and hanging around were boys who wanted to be champions one day. "Hey, kids, bounce out of here," Bogie admonished. "What do you want to do, wind up like them?"

He could be funny sometimes without realizing it. When his business manager said he was spending too much and put him on a small allowance, Bogie was furious. The next day at Romanoff's he told his cronies, "Boy, did I fuck my business manager today." "How?" "The son of a bitch put me on $25 a week, so I went to Saks, Robinson's, and Bullock's— every department store I could think of—and charged thousands of dollars' worth of stuff. Wait till he gets those bills!"

He always pretended not to care about Hollywood or his work, but he did. When he was up for an Oscar for *The African Queen* he secretly hired a press agent, and every day he would call him to ask, "How's it going? What are the chances?"

In the bleak mid-fifties Darryl Zanuck made a statement that what Hollywood needed to survive was new blood and new faces. A friend teased Bogart, "Yeah, where will you be when they get rid of all the tired old faces? Your hair's gone, you're run down. No one will want you." "That's a lot of baloney," Bogart retorted. "What they want is Clark Gable, Gary Cooper, and Cary Grant, at $75 a week." This was the era of Brando, Rock Hudson and Tony Curtis. Bogie took an advertisement in the trade papers with some of the famous pugs and rechristened them Rock Bogart, Tony Baer, and Humphrey Walcott.

When he was dying, 5:30 every afternoon was Bogart time. He would sit in the den in his beautiful home and his close friends would come. John Huston, Sam Spiegel, Capote, Mike Romanoff, Joe Hyams—and they would talk about what was going on in the outside world. The latest play on Broadway, the next political maneuver in Washington, the news from London, Paris, and Rome, the latest films and the latest gossip of Hollywood. Bogie would do his share of the talking and no one mentioned the grim topic. As Charles Laughton (who was to die the same way) said, "It's only a question of death." Only the doctor and Bogart knew he knew. He was a giant in death as he was on the screen.

21)

Good-bye, Hollywood

So many have died or left. The successful and the defeated alike have moved on. With films now made all over the world, many of the important stars of today do not live in Hollywood. Perhaps this is a good thing. Migration has thinned the destroying sickness of Hollywood success. The new stars stay for a film and return home. Vanessa Redgrave came for *Camelot*. She liked the yellowing warmth of the late afternoon sun and the easy living, but she prefers London. She will continue her campaign against war. She will still praise Fidel Castro, although the story she gave me about him almost canceled her visa to work in Communist-hating America. Jimmy Stewart has bought land in Hawaii and will live there one day. Frank Sinatra said the smog was killing him and sold the home he had shared with Mia in Bel Air. Bing Crosby moved away years ago to raise his new family in a suburb of San Francisco.

His partner on the *Road*, Bob Hope, is building his Xanadu on the highest mountain peak in Palm Springs. It has already cost one million dollars and it won't be ready until October. He will commute to Hollywood in his private jet for films and television, but his doctor has warned the sixty-five-year-old star to take it easy. He came to Hollywood in 1937 for *The Big Broadcast of 1938,* for which he was paid $25,000. At lunch in Lucy's restaurant near Paramount he told me his option had not been picked up and he was worried. When I reminded him of this recently he said wryly, "Thanks for the memory." He told me he first came to Hollywood in 1930 and made a test. "They did not like it and I left on the next train for St. Louis. I had a hate campaign against Hollywood and when they asked me to come back seven years later, I told my agent, 'Who needs it? I have $100,000 in the bank.'" Now he admits to $150 million (*Time* magazine puts the figure closer to half a billion dollars). And now he is leaving. "The pace today is hysterical. The kids have taken over. They are doing things on the screen I wouldn't do in bed . . . if I could. All you see on the screen and television today is murder, drugs, violence, robberies, and rape."

Joan Crawford lives in New York where, in her last apartment, her white carpets and plastic covers on the upholstery and the Billy Haines decor were a copy of the house in Brentwood she shared with three or four husbands. She has reverted in recent years to the person she was in *Dancing Daughters.* Living it up. Spiking her Pepsi. Telling bawdy stories. On the set of her last blood-and-screamer she told me she needed a vitamin shot during one of her tours. "The doctor came to the airport. There was nowhere to go except the men's room, which was empty. I bent over. Can you imagine if a man had come in and seen my bare ass!"

Bette Davis now lives in Westport, Connecticut, to be near her married daughter, nicknamed B.D. Bette's marriage to masseur William Sherry cost her some money, but there is enough left for her to live comfortably with an occasional film job. A decade ago, when the pictures were slow in coming, she advertised for work in the Hollywood trade papers. Before that she told her friends, "Imagine, they want me to play Burt Lancaster's mother!" (in *The Unforgiven*). I think she would play his grandmother today.

Judy Garland has gone. They blame her mother for forcing

her to be an actress, but when I first met her at the family home in Beverly Hills when she was fifteen years old, she seemed happy and well adjusted. She read me the poem she had written to Oscar Levant, with whom she was madly in love. Now, thirty years later, she is a lost lady. Judy never learned to cope with success and fame. She needs reassurance all the time and looks for it in sleeping pills—she has suffered from insomnia since she was three, she says, working in vaudeville. As an adolescent star in Hollywood she started with one seconal, now handfuls. She brings her own brand of whiskey to parties. She has attempted suicide countless times—they were almost too late reaching her one time in London (she had miscalculated the slow telephone system) and went into a coma waiting for rescue. She owes the government between $200,000 and $300,000 in back taxes. She is the victim of anyone she leans on. She has a sense of humor, mostly self-deprecation, but no confidence until she starts singing, and lately not even then. Bing Crosby told me, "You have to tell her over and over before she goes on that she's very good. Good? She's the best." But that was twenty years ago. Now her career is a history of broken dates and not being able to pay her bills.

She was delighted to land the role of the bitchy actress in *Valley of the Dolls*. She was on the set every day and then did not show. "Give us a week," her advisers begged. "We'll have nurses looking after her around the clock." But Richard Zanuck, who runs 20th Century-Fox in Hollywood for his father, Darryl, is of this realistic generation, and he said "No!" They paid for the week and the nurses. She had wanted it so badly and was heartsick. Isn't there someone who can take her over the rainbow, 'way up high, to start again with the knowledge of what she is and what she can do?

Monty Clift was beautiful when I met him in Hollywood on the set of *Red River*. The last time I saw him was during his last picture in Vienna, where he was pathetically attempting the title role in *Freud*. John Huston had directed him in *The Misfits*, and there had been no trouble with liquor. "I can handle him," said John. On the way from London to Vienna, Monty got stoned. The stewardess, not knowing of his phobia against any kind of restraint, insisted that he fasten his seat belt. When he refused, she leaned over and yanked it tight. He was like a madman trying to get out and calling her everything under the sun.

He was only forty-five when he died. It would have been better for this sensitive man had he never come to Hollywood, never heard the shrill trumpet of success and the canned laughter of this desperate insecure society.

Rita Hayworth, the great glamorous star of the forties, rarely works in Hollywood or anywhere today. The last time around she played Claudia Cardinale's mother. She was never happy as a star or as a wife. Orson Welles sawed her in half and she married him because she thought she could lean on him. The joke—and the weight—was on her. When I asked her, "When were you and Jim Hill married?" she couldn't remember. Then, "Oh, yes, it was Ground Hog Day." I attended her marriage to Dick Haymes in Las Vegas, with the click-clack of the dice for a wedding march. She has enough money left to live in Beverly Hills, next door to Glenn Ford, her old costar (*Gilda* and *The Loves of Carmen*).

She is luckier than Hedy Lamarr, who has not made a film since 1957, *Love of Three Queens,* and when last heard from was living in New York. Hedy was the most beautiful girl in the world when she came to Hollywood in 1937 to costar with Charles Boyer in *Algiers.* After she was cleared of a shoplifting charge she told me, "I am living in one room in Westwood. I have no money." In the next sentence she wanted to rent my beach house. She made quite a bit from her memoirs, *Ecstasy and Me.* I hope for her sake it was enough to give her an income for life.

William Powell was eighty years old last birthday. He moved to Palm Springs decades ago following his colostomy. His *Thin Man* wife, Myrna Loy, owns a terraced apartment in New York, tours on the road, and is now hopefully on Broadway.

All the Barrymores are dead, and John, Jr., was unable to wear his father's famous shoes. Clark Gable's widow still lives on the ranch he loved in the San Fernando Valley, and the son he did not live to see, John Clark Gable, is eight going on nine, and at boarding school.

Jean Harlow was caricatured in two terrible movies and one outrageous biography. "She was not like that at all," Bill Powell told me furiously.

Thrifty Claudette Colbert saved her money and lives in Barbados and New York. Her elopement with the late Dr. Joel Pressman was my first news story when I arrived in Hollywood on Christmas Day, 1935 . . . Mickey Rooney, the beloved Andy Hardy, is broke after six marriages and six divorces . . . Hopper is dead . . . Louella, Hollywood's Boswell, is forgotten in a sanitarium. They say she glimmered to life when told she had outlived her rival . . . Merle Oberon, rich and desperately bored, brings society and cinema stars to her lavish homes in Mexico.

"We had the best of it," Van Johnson sighed recently, adding "I wouldn't give up one day, but I wouldn't want to repeat it. I'm fifty-two [I expressed shock]. Yeah, I'll look like this to the day I die, and may that day come soon. Yeah, it will be better up there. Frig everyone down here." Unlike Jennifer Jones, he thought everyone loved him. That's the fastest route to disaster. Only Ingrid Bergman perhaps was a bigger star of the forties than Jennifer. As Mrs. David Selznick she ruled the roosters of the big major studios as Norma Shearer had as Mrs. Irving Thalberg. The film offers died with their husbands; Jennifer's offers died before. I watched while she was pushed aside at the glittering premiere of *Camelot,* and soon after they found her awash in the tide at the foot of a Malibu cliff. When she cried piteously, "Let me die," her friend Van Johnson said, "Why did you do it? Don't you know we all love you?" "But nobody told me," she wept.

Hollywood is not the same, but neither is the world, which seems as hell-bent on extinction as Hollywood is. Bogart,

Cooper, Tracy, Hepburn, and Wayne were winners because they did not believe the publicity. They knew they were drifting in a deceptive lush dream where you were an overnight success or just as swift a failure. You could have everything, but it was nothing. They were not taken in by the Faustian nightmare. They knew it was an illusion as *we* must know that giants exist only in anxieties and bad dreams, that film actors are ordinary people, some pleasant, some nasty, even as you and I, and that because of our neurotic need to identify with something more glittering than ourselves, we have permitted dwarfs to cast a long shadow.